L. LAWRENCE EMBLEY

DOING WELL

*The
Marketing
Link
Between Business
& Nonprofit
Causes*

while DOING GOOD

PRENTICE HALL
Englewood Cliffs, New Jersey 07632

Prentice-Hall International (UK) Limited, *London*
Prentice-Hall of Australia Pty. Limited, *Sydney*
Prentice-Hall Canada, Inc., *Toronto*
Prentice-Hall Hispanoamericana, S.A., *Mexico*
Prentice-Hall of India Private Limited, *New Delhi*
Prentice-Hall of Japan, Inc., *Tokyo*
Simon & Schuster Asia Pte. Ltd., *Singapore*
Editora Prentice-Hall do Brasil, Ltda., *Rio de Janeiro*

© 1993 *by*

PRENTICE HALL

Englewood Cliffs, NJ

10 9 8 7 6 5 4 3 2 1

Library of Congress Cataloging-in-Publication Data

Embley, L. Lawrence.
  Doing well while doing good / L. Lawrence Embley. -- 1st ed.
     p. cm.
  Includes index.
  ISBN 0-13-219874-6
  1. Social responsibility of business--United States.
  2. Corporations--United States--Charitable contributions.
  3. Marketing--United States. 4. Corporations, Nonprofit--United
  States--Marketing.   I. Title.
  HD60.5.U5E43 1992
  658.4'08--dc20   92-30234
                                                           CIP

ISBN 0-13-219874-6

PRENTICE HALL
Professional Publishing
Englewood Cliffs, NJ 07632
Simon & Schuster, A Paramount Communications Company

Printed in the United States of America

Dedication

This book is dedicated to the people in my life that mean the most:

To my grandsons, Devin and Matthew—the future belongs to you—we love you.

To my daughter Jacque, "Cricket"—your spark ignites my flame.

To my son-in-law Chip—your character is a blessing to all.

To my son Larry—your silent determination will bring your personal quest into a reality.

To my life partner, the motivator's motivator, Jackie my wife—who didn't sleep when I didn't, who worked on this book when I worked, who encouraged, loved, counseled, and pushed—without you darling, there is no story.

Acknowledgments

The list of friends and supporters to this first-time writer's effort was enormous, and for that I am most thankful. Special thanks need to be expressed to the following people:

To staff editorial assistant, Julie Ferweda—you made this monumental task easier through your organization and follow-through

To Gretchen Rowe of the Arizona State University—your early organizational support was vital

To Sheila Martin, my Public Relations Director—your spiritual and emotional support was invaluable

To my staff: Jim Poneta, Carolyn Johnson, Maurie Helle, Patti Piccoli, and Mike Royal—your tolerance was greatly appreciated

To my business partners, especially Jack Felice—your belief in our efforts and your motivating support helped to keep this project on course

A special thanks to the USA Print pioneers and their belief in a better world. This initial core group provided the basis for a dynamic cause-aligned model to be developed:

Adam Avrick
Deer Park, New York

Joe Combee
Duluth, Georgia

Dennis Disman
Alexandria, Louisiana

Matt Edwards
Knoxville, Tennessee

Frank Eichman
Broomall, Pennsylvania

James Finger
St. Louis, Missouri

Jim Glenn
Birmingham, Alabama

Tom Graves
Little Rock, Arkansas

Mike Held
Columbus, Ohio

Roland Hernandez
San Antonio, Texas

John Keys

Miami, Florida

Howard Lake
Manassas, Virginia

Mike Long
Los Angeles, California

Jim Lower
Norwich, Connecticut

Willard Neufeld
Fresno, California

Ed Nowokunski
Charlotte, North Carolina

Jeff Relth
Phoenix, Arizona

Jim Smith
Goleta, California

Ned Smith
Honolulu, Hawaii

Chuck Viverette
Tampa, Florida

Buzz Warren
Overland Park, Kansas

THANK YOU FOR OUR RESEARCH SUPPORT TO THE FOLLOWING INDIVIDUALS:

National Basketball Association
Ms. Mary Nergory

McDonald Corporation
Ms. Linda Fontana

International Business Machines
Ms. Kathleen Ryan

Entrepreneur Group
Mr. Jim FitzPatrick

The Body Shop
Ms. Leslie Corge

Ben & Jerry's Homemade, Inc.
Mr. Lee Holden

Nike
Mr. Bob Fletcher

Coors
Mr. Dave Taylor
Mr. John Goldman
Ms. Mary Burch
Ms. Janet Rowe
Mr. Joe Fuentes
Ms. Becky Winning

Social Venture Network
Andrea Werlin

Proctor & Gamble
Ms. Linda Ulrey

Stonyfield Farms
Ms. Nancy Hirshburg and Mr. Greg Hirshburg

3M
Mr. John Schroder

Pepsico
Ms. Jackie Millian

Coca Cola
Ms. Andre Owens

Miller Brewing Co.
Ms. Yvonne Lumden Dill

Home Box Office
Mr. Allen Levy

American Express
Ms. Maureen Baily & Mr. Barney Vavrock

Time Warner
Ms. Tory Fay

Turner Broadcasting
Ms. Adrian Puller

Apple Computer
Ms. Yolard Davis & Mr. Bill Kegan

Life Magazine
Ms. Margaret Boyer

Kellogg Co.
Mr. Dick Lovell

AG Edwards
Mr. Ben Edwards, III and Gregory G. Carr

Covenant Investment Management
Ms. Jill Selgrad

Inserts
Mr. Robert Shand

Network Earth
Ms. Dee Spiro

Nike
Mr. Dusty Kidd

Patagonia
Ms. Megan Montgomery

American Airlines
Ms. Bill Harless

American Re Insurance
Ms. Carol Griffin

A.T. Cross Co.
Ms. Claire M. Carlino

Aveda Corp.
Ms. Nan Upin

Back 2 Back
Ms. Suzanne Gross

Brown Forman (Jack Daniels)
Mr. Richard J. Cahill

Best Western International, Inc.
Ms. Vicki Cabianca

Centel Corporation
Mr. Tom Ray

Continental Insurance
Mr. Martin L. Frimet

Children's Organ Transplant Association
Mr. Dave Speicher

Council on Econ. Priorities
Ms. Emily Swaab

Diane Freis International
Ms. Holly Takahashi

Esprit de Corp
Ms. Cassie Hughes

Make-A-Wish-Foundation
Ms. Judith K. Lewis

MasterCard International
Ms. Lisa Piteris

Matsushita-Panasonic
Ms. Ann Ballas

Moschino Jeans
Ms. Michelle Stein

Mutual of America
Ms. Rita Conyers

Phillips Petroleum Company
Mr. Tim Taft from Tracy-Locke

Rolex Watch U.S.A., Inc.
Ms. Barbara Howell

Selected Financial Services
Ms. Merrillyn Kosier

Shearson Lehman Brothers
Ms. Barbara Glasser

State Farm Insurance Companies
Mr. Thomas R. Nelson

Toyota Motor Sales
Mr. David B. Doyle

Xerox Corporation
Ms. Nancy Wiese

Matrix Essentials, Inc.
Ms. Karin Elliott and Kimberly Chapman

1928
Ms. Lynn Plafker

Massachusetts Mutual Life Insurance Company
Mr. Joseph Mondy

Preface

It will be my intention in this book to demonstrate to you that, in fact, we as a society are changing, and, may I note, improving. Although the book was originally intended primarily for a defined business audience, I have found through research and discussions that the topic of American business joining directly with non-profit organizations to address the country's social needs was of great interest to all. The American public finds the concept of doing well while doing good a very effective way of dealing with many of our societal problems. No matter what their political bias or agenda, they all believed that nothing good can happen in our society without a sound economic environment. Pro-business or anti-business factions recognize that our inner city problems can be improved with the hope of jobs, that the future is really in the hands of our children, and that education and opportunity must stand as a motivator. The concepts *helplessness* and *hopelessness* cannot be by-products of our future generations.

As I spoke to people throughout this country on these issues, each had a very defined concept of our social problems. Much of the time it had been brought home by their personal experiences and their motivation was self-directed to their specific area of concern. The single unifying factor with which each agreed, was the core concept—when a business gives back to the community's problems, they should be rewarded with buyer loyalty or consumer support. Just as important, those businesses that don't support in this manner, shouldn't benefit. I found consumers very willing to share their opinions, feelings, and thoughts on the subject. They are much more aware than one would think. A flood of socially responsible messages is pouring from the great information machine—news media, entertainment media, and the sports media. It seems that the entire magazine publishing industry from *Redbook* to *Rolling Stone* is capturing the topics of social responsibility on their pages.

In my travels, it became clear to me that we still approach the subject of social responsibility along the same stereotypical divisions as we do with most highly charged issues. I originally intended to define the issues as they have been defined before, liberal vs. conservative, pro-business vs. anti-business, and so on. However, if I chose those definitions, I would be reinforcing stereotypical think-ing myself, and in fact accepting or rejecting ideas from various groups with their own built-in agendas. I chose instead to define the issues with a model that is hopefully less political or biased.

Since motivation is at the center of a company's action, fueling a decision to engage the strategy, I defined my business model of social responsibility with two primary motivators—the *heart* and the *head*, two non-offensive or-gans shared by each of us. The full description of the model is in Chapter 1. I wanted to keep my agenda focused down the middle of the road. I am not naive. I do realize how the various camps view each other. My purpose was to seek out the areas of commonality and unity. The reality of one planet is a fact. How we go about caring for it can be debated, as one group's perceptions will differ greatly from another's. I wanted to focus on the area of agreement first. We have one planet, and if we continue to destroy it, it won't fix itself.

The American public should beware of the companies that project a social responsibility message in their television and print ads to pull in viewer sentiment and increase sales, but are either doing nothing to help, or worse yet, are hurting. These companies use the trend conditions of consumers supporting corporations that are doing well while doing good, but their emphasis is only on doing well. Companies that use this public image concept are "spin masters." They are motivated simply from their bottom line—profits.

Companies that use sentimental advertisements are effectively endearing themselves to the customer. According to the Ad Council, $100 million will be spent by corporations claiming an environmental protection mission statement. "Green marketing," as it has come to be known, is a result of consumer awareness associated with environmental consciousness. Not all green marketers are spin masters, some are for real. The challenge for the consumer is to discover which is which.

I personally find positive signs even with the spin master who claims to be socially responsible. First, it tells us they are thinking about such issues—a large step in itself. Next, they are on the hook, so to speak, with a socially responsible campaign. This sword cuts both ways. The message attracts consumers to companies and opens them up to follow through on their programs or images, or forces them out of the hype business altogether. The critics simply call the spin masters frauds. I call them classically naive. By setting up a false facade, they are now more deeply captured by their own hand, more so than by all the federal compliance orders they would ever fail. On the other hand, I found that good companies recognize the importance of doing it right to begin with.

Our research brought us into hundreds of companies. Some I write about in this book. I tried to show a representative sample, but unfortunately, I could not include many of the companies to whom I spoke. And for that

I do apologize. I have even placed some companies in the book who have tarnished reputations from mistakes made in previous policies and decisions. My decision to include them was based on their attitudes and their desire to turn themselves around. They received a strong share of negative press, and I wanted to see if we could provide them with some positive press. Hopefully they will continue to do good.

I also wrote about the economic realities enjoyed by good companies in Chapter 6, "The Heart of the Deal." Social investing is hot! So is social venture capital. Although some companies featured in the chapter are far from household names, I wish to acquaint the reader with what's happening in all facets of the business community.

Also included in my research, and subsequently placed in Chapter 4, "Icons and Images," is the role that is being played consciously or subconsciously by celebrities, athletes, entertainers, and news personalities. I chose to include this information because of the impact they have on us and our children as it pertains to our *values*, and how American business is deploying them into our relationship with products and services.

A 1991 Massachusetts Mutual research report conducted by Meilman & Lazarus focused on how America obtains family values, keeps values, and how values translate into better citizens. One area that I found particularly interesting was who has the most influence on you and your values. As the research indicated, the most influence by far comes from television, entertainment programs, and movies. This is significant, because it is in these media that our young people find their role models. "Icons and Images" points out how the message spreads, and in this case, who the messengers are.

Today it's more a matter of right versus wrong.

No matter what label we choose to put on this new aspect of our society (*enlightenment* is how I see it) my purpose is to acknowledge those who are making a difference, and are building strong companies at the same time. Anita Roddick, founder of The Body Shop, has stated that principles and profits are not mutually exclusive.

This method of doing business can benefit almost every company, and we as individuals would benefit from businesses that are doing well while doing good.

Businesses need long term strategies to build beyond good service and quality products. The consumer doesn't see quality and service as elective or optional—they are now expectations. If businesses intend to attract and keep customers, they are going to have to draw the relationship between company and customer closer together. It appears that businesses that have recognized that fact are enjoying tremendous consumer support. The formula of price, service, quality and social responsibility will become the foundation for continued success.

Introduction

The landscape of American business is changing and redefining itself as we speak. There is a growing philosophy within business that is promoting the concept of doing well while doing good.

It manifests itself in the business community as:

- Corporations that recognize the economic importance of defining themselves as being socially responsible.

- Entrepreneurs/capitalists who define their business mission around the socially relevant purpose.

- Investors who choose to invest in companies that are making a contribution to a better world.

- Companies that develop marketing tactics that promote products and also promote causes simultaneously (cause-related marketing).

- Entrepreneurs who create companies to benefit social causes directly while benefiting themselves as well.

- Businesspeople who invest their time and talent in causes and issues that are important to our society.

Each definition carries with it a strong economic reality. This entire movement toward social responsibility can be called *philanthropic economics.*

■ RESETTING PRIORITIES

There have been literally hundreds of forceful issues that have collided with us as a society. Some are of a political nature; others are brought about by the shrinking global society. All the issues have brought a new level of awareness, not that we now have answers, but more likely, we now know how to ask the questions. Surely the collapse of communism resets priorities. The vagaries of our world have not only positioned us to define our priorities as a culture but have given us the means to act on them. Increased social conscience is a phenomenon that is 40 years in the making. The trend movement had been adopted by earlier generations but continues to mature and evolve positively in the most recent generation. No one group or faction can claim credit or, for that matter, decline the accolades.

We have become aware of social relevance and its importance in our lives. Consider the scenarios:

- Environmental abuse goes unchecked.

- No one is willing to help the functionally illiterate find their way into self-maintenance and mainstream society.

- The cost to society of providing basic health care to a growing population of disenfranchised poor is unmanageable.

- The disadvantaged, the homeless, and the unemployable will fall farther away to the fringe, putting more financial pressure on towns, cities, and neighborhoods and, in some cases, causing total economic collapse under the weight of total cost.

- AIDS research now has application in the heterosexual community.

- There is no future for our children if we don't invest in their lives, education, and safety.
- All is lost if we fail to recognize minorities and their economic development.
- We lose a valued treasure if we destroy our wildlife and their habitats.
- We don't care for the elderly and abandon our aged.

The list of real social issues seems endless. The fact is: we have *no options!* Solving today's social problems is not someone else's, even government's, role. Each and every one of us has to respond to today's social problems.

What are some possible solutions? The role of the news and entertainment media in today's information society is important. A research report commissioned by Massachusetts Mutual Life Insurance survey results indicate that television, entertainment programs, movies, celebrities, athletes, famous people in the news, musicians, and music videos have the most influence on young people's values. This indicates the various media are powerful and persuasive tools in educating and influencing the general public.

In recent years, the media are beginning to reflect more on specific social issues. With their greater attention now on internal, domestic concerns, the nightly news on television and the morning newspapers are filled with coverage on socially relevant topics. The entertainment and sports media are also beginning to project a greater sensitivity in the areas of youth and family values.

Newsrooms are becoming information clearing houses for local charities. New in-depth specials and investigative reports are now being developed on a full range of social topics. This brings social issues, for many of us, right into our homes and offices each day. The newsroom has also impacted the stations' programming departments as well. Television programming is beginning to deal with social issues directly, subjects ranging from child abuse to the plight of the homeless.

The focus of this book is to explore how American business is responding to the challenge of social relevance.

The confidence being projected by business is based on how consumers will respond. Without the evolution of the intelligent consumer, the task of corporate social responsibility would be insurmountable. Businesses need to do more than strike an emotional chord with the consumer; they need to deliver. At stake are our life-style and even our lives. As consumers, we need to discover who the socially responsible companies are and support them. Included in this book are some of the companies that you should know about, and there are others, and every day more are joining the list of the social conscience. When you buy a product, make it a point to know where a company stands on what you feel are redeeming social issues.

The companies illustrated in the book represent only a handful of the growing number of companies that are subscribing to the ideologies and principles that define them as socially responsible companies. These companies have gone beyond public perception and developed socially responsible missions within their corporate culture.

Contents

	PREFACE	ix
	INTRODUCTION	xv
CHAPTER 1	A NEW WAVE	1
CHAPTER 2	A DAY AT THE BEACH	17
CHAPTER 3	BACK TO THE FUTURE	31
CHAPTER 4	ICONS AND IMAGES	57
CHAPTER 5	PRINCIPLES AND PROFITS	81
CHAPTER 6	HEART OF THE DEAL	111
CHAPTER 7	AMERICA'S ADMIRED	143
CHAPTER 8	PHILANTHROPIC ECONOMICS IN MOTION	199
CHAPTER 9	INITIATING A PHILANTHROPIC ECONOMIC BUSINESS STRATEGY	217
	INDEX	245

1

■

A New Wave

A new business phenomenon is underway. Businesses of all sizes are entering into partnerships with consumers by supporting dozens of socially relevant issues that affect all of us in direct and indirect ways—issues such as the environment, education, the homeless, children and the elderly. The list of social issues being addressed by American business/consumer partnerships is increasing every day.

This new thrust of business activism has developed into a strategy that I call doing well while doing good, an outgrowth of a concept we have dubbed *philanthropic economics*. Firms large and small are embracing this strategy. In the following chapters, we examine who these firms are and, just as important, what motivates their managements to undertake philanthropic economics. In profiling the results of these corporate strategies, the motivation of the American consumer will also be examined.

How is it that as consumers we have recently developed deep and broadening social concerns, ones about issues that in many cases may seem as if they don't affect our lives today, but they do? The great myth of the uniformly passive consumer will soon be exposed. In 1988, then-presidential candidate George Bush spoke of a kinder, gentler nation and a vision of the "thousand points of light."

Little did I realize that four years later I would write on the very same topic, nor did I realize that this topic would alter the way I conduct my business. In fact, social activism led me to move my business into a direct partnership with child-related initiatives. I have experienced a form of enlightenment over the past several years, and sharing this experience is the purpose of this book. My understanding and motivation came through study and research into the entire phenomenon.

Some of the personal profiles of innovators who link their business mission with a social mission are very telling. These innovators are self-described as enlightened capitalists. They have turned around their business strategy by placing equal emphasis on social relevance first as well as company profits. This extremely inventive strategy is providing them with exciting ways of managing their business, ways that allow them the oportunity to make a contribution to society as well as to the shareholders.

What kind of person can place values and personal commitments to do good alongside of conventional business logic? What happened to those businesses and their owners—did they fail? There is controversy surrounding this business strategy. Many believe that businesses bent on providing social characteristics would do less well economically than companies that chose a strict profitability profile. Quite the opposite is true. The following profiled companies are not your mainstream corporations, but they are some of the most passionate of the models of socially sensitive companies in the country. For many executives in the country, these enlightened companies will become the models of the future.

The following are some of these smaller enlightened companies:

- The Body Shop, founded by Anita Roddick, is an $800 million company that is helping thousands of people around the world through her environmental stance and her human rights activism.

- Ben & Jerry's Homemade, Inc., was founded by Ben Cohen and Jerry Greenfield. This dynamic duo has built an $80 million business in the town of Waterbury, Vermont, based on a business mission of helping local farmers by buying their milk/cream.

- Patagonia was founded by Yvon Chouinard and prospers as a privately held $117 million company creating clothes for a range of adventures such as climbing, skiing, sailing, fly-fishing, and kayaking. Adventure is a byword of Patagonia, which gives substantially to, and strongly supports, more than 300 environmental organizations.

- Matrix Essentials, Inc. was founded in 1980 by husband and wife team Arnold and Sydell Miller. Their haircare products are naturally effective and environmentally sound. Matrix joined Dick Clark productions to produce "What About Me? I'm Only Three," an environmental television special targeted towards the misuses that continue to deplete our world of its natural resources.

- Esprit de Corp, giants in the trendy clothes industry has a department called the "Eco Desk," which coordinates environmental and community affairs encouraging individual volunteerism in a wide range of environmental activities.

- Aveda Corporation was founded by Horst Rechelbacher in Minneapolis, Minnesota. Aveda's number one concern is manufacturing green. They produce perfume, skincare, haircare, and household cleansers. Aveda compounds endeavor to naturally ensure personal and planetary preservation and rejuvenation.

- Stonyfield Farms was founded in 1983 with two goals: (1) to produce the purest, most natural and nutritious yogurts available, and (2) to encourage consumers' support of family farmers and local agriculture in the northeastern United States—objectives include "serving as a model that environmentally and socially responsible businesses can also be profitable."

These companies, and many others, are doing well while doing good. Larger companies are also responding to the growing awareness of community and world social issues. They are modifying corporate culture to incorporate social responsibility initiatives and philanthropic economics into their everyday business. Some of these companies are Colgate-Palmolive, Hershey Foods, Johnson SC & Sons, Kellogg Company, Procter & Gamble, Polaroid Corporation, and Quaker Oats. The programs of several of these companies, and others, will be profiled in later chapters.

The motivation or the motivator, which comes first? Why is it that as consumers we are moved by this way of doing business? In this book, we will examine how and why we as consumers have evolved into a socially sensitive society. We may be living in the most socially relevant time in U.S. history. This book will prove beyond a shadow of a doubt that there is life beyond profit for the truly enlightened capitalist. As a marketing strategist for major corporations and an entrepreneur, I see and hear about numerous business problems and, just as important, the steps taken toward proposed solutions. The problems these firms face are twofold:

1. Building their businesses with a strong belief in product, service, and quality

2. At the same time facing the social problems in their local communities—feeding the hungry; sheltering the homeless; educating and protecting the children; defending and safeguarding the environment; dealing with substance abuse; providing health care for the elderly; and preserving the history, arts, and culture of the community.

The list of social needs can be overwhelming. The answer may lie in the new alliance of social activism and business involvement called *philanthropic economics*. By taking a highly visible and active position of social support, firms have altered forever the ways in which they will conduct business. To date, consumers have responded favorably.

■ THE ENLIGHTENED CONSUMER

The enlightened consumer is acutely aware and educated as to the current state of our society. They make their buying decisions more astutely as a result of that information. They will not support companies that are not socially responsible. They will know the difference between a company's socially relevant public relations campaign and its real business practice. They will favor companies that demonstrate principles and values in their workplace and in the products they develop, and will look at how the company behaves as a community citizen. The new consumer will influence and dictate the financial well being of many companies.

In all fairness, the enlightened consumer is a paradigm that has of yet not fully emerged. At the rate in which they are growing, I believe it will be fair to say that in ten years the enlightened will outnumber the unaware.

Economic Realignment Results in Consumer Realignment [1]

Consumers have been motivated essentially by two determinants:

1. Wants
2. Needs

Needs are basic, the definition of "basic" being relative: what is basic to one person may seem a fantasy to another. Business has played a role in finding ways to make *basic needs* fulfillment become basic *wants* fulfillment. *Want*, however, is beyond basic need and fulfills some other desire that the buyer may have. The conflicts between *needs* and *wants* are the battles that American businesses wage every day to fit their product or service into the ap-

---

[1] For purposes of the explanation of the trend dynamics around business and social issues, I'll refer to the interest in the environmental issue as a model.

propriate target audience, to develop selling strategy, merchandising, distribution, packaging, advertising and promotional tactics that move their business into the *minds of the consumer.*

A result of the last 25 years of various cultural, social, and world changes has developed a trend that clearly defines the emergence of the *sensible* or *intelligent* consumer. The sensible or intelligent consumer is much harder for business to define clearly outside of the pure wants versus needs methods of prior years. This growing number of intelligent consumers is the trend of the future; as a result, we will become more informed and therefore buy smarter. American businesses need to redefine themselves on how to appeal to the new consumer.

A society of our magnitude has hundreds, if not thousands, of different factions, groups within groups, communities within communities, families within families, and values. Some issues are defined only within the limits of a specific area or ethnic group, and of those, the general public unfortunately remains unaware or unconcerned. Then there are issues that affect a majority of us. Issues such as children, the environment, or the spread of AIDS are widely ranging core social issues.

The growth of the intelligent consumer, will send a clear message to business. That message states: "If you want to sell products or services to us, you must be *responsible.*" The growth of nonprofit organizations over the trend period has acted in many ways as a barometer. For American business, it clearly points out what the new consumer feels strongly about. This very basic fact is the reason some American businesses are beginning to take a socially responsible stance.

Consider, if you will, the basic fact that to some greater or lesser degree, every American citizen recognizes that we have an environmental and ecological problem—some 240 or so million people. If you are intending to conduct business with any of these 240 million people and you are environmentally irresponsible, you may have a real problem!

The tremendous growth of environmental and ecological groups, such as the Sierra Club, the World Wildlife
Fund, the National Conservatory and the National Parks,
Foundation, over the last ten years is a clear signal that
the American public is concerned. These organizations
represent just a few of the better known groups, and
their members and subscribers total tens of millions of
people. The numbers are very impressive—so much so
that the numbers are now beginning to take on a dynamic
of their own as they generate even greater numbers.

Development Beyond Critical Mass

When environmental and conservation issues begin to es-
calate, they do so at all ends of the socioeconomic scale.
They infiltrate our basic educational settings and recreational time, including news media and entertainment media.
They then begin to impact our buying decisions, which
will ultimately alter our life-styles and culture.

Awareness is the first step in a progressive chain
toward the ultimate goal of *elective* or *selective change*.
Change is what is required for ecological survival and
environmental salvation, but awareness may be sufficient
for another less volatile issue or cause. Awareness itself
does not require change, but *getting the message out* is
critically important.

Consumers are either driven by their own original
concerns about the environment, or now that business
has either joined or initiated the awareness campaign, it
is a moot point. The fact is, environmental issues are
important for the intelligent consumer. Businesses that
want to attract the informed consumer will need to be
more responsible to this group. Green marketing done
with a slick public relations campaign will not match
their buying criteria. These issues are now just as important
to business that wants to attract intelligent consumers.

As the connection begins to emerge between social
issues and business issues, the lines begin to blur. The
messages are sometimes left to the consumers' interpre-
tation. Today, more and more companies recognize that

environmentally or socially conscious reflections in their advertisements and public relations campaigns are having a positive effect on sales and company image. The informed consumer can discriminate between fact and fiction. Unfortunately, the majority of consumers still can't. The questions that all consumers should be asking about a company are:

1. Is the company using environmentally unsound components to manufacture its products?
2. Does the company require animal testing in its research and development?
3. Is the company's packing and merchandise material environmentally sound?
4. Is the company promoting positive awareness internally to its employees as well as promoting it outside through its advertising and promotions?

Motivations vary. Certainly, some managements are more sincere than others. In each and every case, the environmental issue is further enhanced. It is not for me to be a watchdog on a businesses level of sincerity. It is my purpose to show how the two dynamics now interrelate. It is important to understand how the consumer is alerted to or made aware of certain social issues when attempting to create linkage between the company and the social issues.

■ METHODS OF AWARENESS

There are two basic motivational models that increase awareness: 1) the heart motivator model, which relies on sentiment, empathy, compassion, emotion, and alignment of personal values with issues; and 2) the head motivator model which relies more on facts, data, logic, and statistical findings. These two models are the means by which American business is attempting to reach the consumer. This thinking model applies both to the motivation of the business responding to the enlightened consumer, and to the consumer. Consumers become aware of their social responsibility based on the two primary models — heart motivator and head motivator. See Figure 1-1.

Figure 1.1
THE BUSINESS MANAGER'S THINKING MODEL OF SOCIAL RESPONSIBILITY

POSITIVE		NEGATIVE
Heart Motivated Model (Proactive)	**Head Motivated Model (Reactive)**	**Profit Motivated Model (Exploitative)**
• Driven	• Moved • Substance	• Sentiment
• In Time • Economic Soundness	• Timely	• Short Term
• Philosophical Ideals • Morals	• Major Trend Condition	• Hype
• Required • Intelligent	• Necessary	• Topical • Gaining
	• Leadership Positioning	• Promotional
• Enlightened	• Educated • Rational	
• Passionate	• Strategic • Purpose	• Tactical
• Mission • Principles/Profits	• Economically Sound • Effective	• Crises Plan
• Focused	• Targeted	
• Remorseful	• Aware	• Narrowly Defined
• Proactive • Reactive		• Unaware/Uninformed
• Guilty • Ethical • Risky		
• Feelings • Outraged	• Concern • Common Sense	• Bottom Line
• Education	• Information • Manageable	• Concept
• Compassionate	• Logical	
• Sensible	• Reasonable • Conservative	• Facade

9

With growing frequency, businesses are showing up in areas that were once reserved strictly for nonprofit groups or governmental concerns. In many cases they are reacting to issues that are affecting what the company would call *their customers*. If their customers are concerned, the company must be concerned. Just as important to attracting customers is keeping the ones you have, and should the new enlightened customer discover that your company is behaving in nonresponsible terms, the customer will have an impact on your market share. Whether consumers are responding to their feelings or their thinking, their actions will begin to have an effect on businesses. Business therefore must move beyond price, service, and quality commitments, and move towards a socially responsible commitment. The informed consumer will be concerned with the company's packaging, manufacturing processes, research methods, and its impact on human rights, the environment, health, safety, and well-being, to name a few.

Is social responsibility offensive strategy or defensive strategy for American business?

Advertising messages and statements seem far removed from the conventional communications about product or service coming from corporate America. Today, "promotional" statements are being made when, in fact, there is no product affiliation or endorsement at all other than what the corporation is bringing forth in its message. The content of their very expensive television and print advertisements will more often reflect a more dramatic social concern than a product endorsement. Advertisers will position their product behind social concerns such as the environment, teenage drinking, drug abuse, literacy, the plight of the homeless, and so on. This method of advertising is being deployed by companies in an effort to attract the consumer from a values position versus the conventional wants and needs method.

This highly effective method of reaching the consumer will be a sincere and responsible statement by some, but for others it will be only a method of hype.

Companies throughout the country are now sending this kind of message; a message of change. It is fascinating to think that this strategic tool of combining business with social responsibility may be the beginning of a new way of conducting business.

This new philosophy is spreading throughout advertising agencies and public relations firms in the United States. These enterprises can see how their clients can benefit from cause-aligned initiatives because consumers feel better about companies with a "soul" and are more likely to buy from them.

It may not be acceptable in the future for any business to sit on the sidelines of this social trend shift. Early entry companies have been rewarded with great financial success and increased prestige in the mind of the consumer. One such company, Ben & Jerry's Ice Cream, of Waterbury, Vermont, appealed directly to the enlightened consumer with their policies and philosophies of creating a direct relationship between their company's profits and their principles. This concept is a reflection of their 1960s culture of peace, love, sharing, and ideology that has unique appeal to a large group of consumers who identify with these same principles. The economic result of Ben & Jerry's principles and policies was to make them the darlings of the ice cream world, and distanced them from their competition. In addition, they just happen to make great ice cream. The news media thought well of Ben & Jerry's and provided them a unique and powerful public relations machine to spread the word. This is a classic example of the power of the information society. Businesses should be encouraged to adopt approaches like Ben & Jerry's. Without some socially redeeming value, some companies may find it hard to compete.

For the purposes of fully exploring the whole universe of social responsibility, it is important to note that there are extremes. The enlightened capitalist may be seen by some as extremist. I expect to demonstrate that these companies are the mainstream of the future. Their business philosophies and the model they provide are highly effective in pure economic terms.

How did we get to this place in time? What influences shaped us? These questions should be directed back to us as a society. Let's recognize that established long-term American big business is falling into the socially responsible ranks as well. Ben & Jerry's story makes for great reading, and the company has grown in such a way that it stands for something beyond its profit statement. Its story will be told in greater detail later.

H. J. Heinz's Starkist Tuna is another of those early entries into the arena of social consciousness. Its animal rights approach to safe netting fishing practices has saved the lives of thousands of dolphins. This extremely sensitive issue touched a nerve in the American public. Consumers wanted wasteful killing of dolphins to stop. Starkist had only one valid option—take a stand with the people to save the dolphins. Millions of dollars were spent to ensure that the least possible number of dolphins would be affected. Consumers responded by increasing market share for Starkist over its competitors. Starkist's commitment can never be reversed; the effect would be devastating to the company. Starkist truly deserves the consumer and brand loyalty it has gained, and it is only one of many firms using philanthropic economics.

The findings and specifics of actual market share increase have not been made available by Starkist, but one can safely assume that very positive public relations benefited the company's revenue position. Starkist is a division of H. J. Heinz Company, a leader among socially responsible companies as defined by the Council on Economic Priorities.

■ COUNCIL ON ECONOMIC PRIORITIES

Alice Tepper Marlin, a 46-year-old mother of two, is the driving force behind the Council on Economy Priorities (CEP). In 1968, working as a security analyst, Ms. Tepper Marlin was asked by a synagogue to help it invest in companies that had no business interest in the Vietnam war. This request, along with others, showed her the need to create a source of information for other alternative investing managers. In response, she developed the Council on Economic Priorities. Today, her research on corporate behavior is far reaching, covering the entire area of social responsibilities.

She researches and grades corporations based on the following criteria:

- Charitable giving
- Women's advancements
- Minority advancement
- Animal testing
- Disclosure of information
- Community outreach
- South Africa
- The environment
- Family benefits
- Workplace issues

Figure 1.2 is a reference guide that points out which companies are or are not doing the right things. The CEP also provides an annual awards program to recognize those companies that are making a major impact in the area of social responsibilities.

Source: Shopping for a Better World 1992: A Quick Guide to Socially Responsible Supermarket Shopping, pages 108-109

The Council on Economic Priorities
By: Alice Tepper Marlin
Jonathan Schorsch
Emily Swabb
Rosalyn Will

The CEP is both a consumer advocate and watchdog organization. Its focus is on mailing available information to the consumer and also recognizing and awarding companies that do the right things. Of basic importance here is the fact that there are now real measurable criteria

Figure 1.2

RATING CRITERIA FOR SOCIALLY RESPONSIBLE CONSUMER GOODS COMPANIES

Company or Product	Abbr.	$	☺	👐	⋙	🕊	🌐	⚛	🐾	‖	ALERT
ConAgra	CAG	?	✗	✓°	?	✗	✗	No	?	?	✗	safe meat controversy; D.C.C.A.; factory farming
Coors Company, Adolph	ACC	✓+	✓°	✓°	✓	✓	✓°	No	✓°	✓	✓°	Fair Share
Curtice-Burns	CBI	✓+	✓°	✗	?	✓	✓	No	?	✓	✓°	
Dep Corp.	DEPC	?	✓	✓°	✓	✓°	✓	No	?	✓°	✓°	
Dial Corp	G	?	✓	✓°	✓	✗	?	No	?	?	?	
Dole Food Company	DOL	✓	✓°	✓	✓°	✓°	✗	No	✗	✓°	✗	pesticide sterilization suit
Dow Chemical Company	DOW	✓°	✓	✓	✓✱	✓	✓	Yes	✓°	✓	✓°	pesticide steril. suit; nuclear weapons; on-site daycare; makes pesticides
Eastman Kodak	EK	✓°	✓	✗	✓✱	✓	✓	No	✓°	✓	✓	🏹; C.C.A.
First Brands	FB	✓+	?	✓°	✓*	✓°	✓°	Yes	✓°	✗	✓°	
Flowers Industries, Inc.	FLO	?	✗	✗	?	?	?	No	?	?	?	
GTE Corporation	GTE	✓°	✓°	✓	✓	✓	✓	No	✓°	✓	✓°	
General Electric Company	GE	✗	?	✗○	✗	✗	✗	No	✗	?	✗	nuclear weapons; 🏹🏹; INFACT boycott
General Mills	GIS	✓+	✓	✓	✓	✓	✓	No	✓°	✓	✓	C.C.A.

14

Product or Company	Abbr.											ALERT
Georgia-Pacific	GP	✘	✔	✔	?	◡	✔	No	✘	?	?	clearcutting; on-site day care
Gerber Products	GEB	◡	✔	✔	?	?	?	Yes	?	?	?	D.C.C.A.; infant formula
Gillette	GS	◡	◡	◡	✔(*)	✔	✔	YesIN	◡	✔	✔	
Goya Foods Inc.	GOYA	?	?	?	?	?	✘	No	?	?	?	
Grand Metropolitan PLC	GMP	◡	✔	✔	✔	✔	✔	YesIN	◡	◡	◡	⊕; U.K.
Heinz Company, H.J.	HNZ	✔	✔	◡	✔	✔	◡	No	✔	✔	◡	C.C.A.
Hershey Foods Corp.	HSY	◡	✔	✔	✔*	✔	✔	No	✔	✔	✔	on-site day care
Hormel & Co., George A.	HRL	?	?	✔	✔	✘	✘	No	?	?	?	
Int'l Res. & Dev. Corp.	IRDV	?	✘	✘	✘◯	✘	✘	No	?	?	?	
James River Corporation	JR	◡	✘	◡	✔	✔	◡	✘	◡	◡	◡	on-site day care
John B. Sanfilippo, Inc.	JSAN	?	?	?	✔	?	?	No	?	?	?	

✔ = Top Rating	◡ = Middle Rating	✘ = Bottom Rating	? = Insufficient Information	Page 109

o Manufactures surgical/medical supplies and/or prescription drugs

* Company tests on animals but has reduced the number used in testing by 40% or more over the last 5 years and/or has given $250,000 or more annually to alternative research through in-house or independent labs

** Same as * but the company manufactures surgical/medical supplies and/or prescription drugs

15

that are easily understood by all. These measurement criteria
will become the benchmark of the future and the indication
that the consumer will continue to become more intelligent
and socially aware.

2

■

A Day at the Beach
A Personal Journey to Social Activism

Today, I live in the Arizona mountains. Not long ago, I was a committed Easterner, driving against the big, impersonal machine. My personal odyssey is relevant only as a model of how social activism sometimes takes root. Many recent influences have shaped my life, and in doing so have dramatically changed the way I think about business. To some it may appear as a mid-life crisis or a quest for new age revitalization, but hopefully it will appear to be exactly what it is, a higher level of information and education that has brought about a realignment in the way I choose to conduct business, i.e, enlightened mission.

■ THE ROAD TO THE BEACH

For the most part, I was typical of most young people who grew up in the 1960s. I wanted the good life which consisted of finding a job and a wife and developing my own American dream. I grew up in a working-class family with a strong belief in labor unions and the Democratic party. Although my roots appear to be liberal, our family values tended to be narrowly conservative. There was never a time when political activism would come before patriotism. We were poor, but everyone we knew was poor, so we never felt poor. Like most young men at the time, I had two choices after high school—college, if your family could afford it, or the enter the military if they could not. My direction was the latter. The year was 1962, and Vietnam was not a place I had ever heard of. My Irish Catholic values required that I was to be a responsible person, work hard, be honest, and love your family and country in just that order. When I arrived home from overseas, it seemed the world had completely changed. My old friends were either fighting the war or fighting war! I felt that those who had not gone to war had no right to condemn those who did. Those returning from Vietnam found themselves outside of the home that they had left. They just wanted to fit in.

I wasn't going to be a *hypocrite* and I certainly had no plans for being a *hippie*, our definition at that time for the young men and women who chose to stay home and fight the establishment on the principles of war. I needed to further my education and land a job. My concern was self-preservation and finding a place within the world. Within a few years I was on a reasonable tract towards success. By the time I was 27-years-old, I had become a general agent for a leading insurance company. By the time I was 35, I had developed into a recognized business consultant and strategist, and I was definitely affecting the way some companies were conducting business.

■ CONSULTING FOR CORPORATE CHANGE— A DEAD END

When I began my independent consulting practice in 1976, my focus was on how companies brought their products and services to market. I recognized early on that large corporations were for the most part extremely reactive. The bigger they were, the less likely they were to be innovative or creative. An indication of this was that the original business formula brought to the company by its founders was still dominant even if the founder had retired or died. Major corporations will tinker with new concepts, but mostly they were intrenched in proven conventional methods that had been established with the founders.

As my practice grew, my approach to clients was modified to a more strategic dimension. My focus was to define and challenge pre-existing corporate culture and to measure how effective or ineffective that culture had become. The popular craze of many consultants in the mid 1970s was preaching corporate change. The Japanese consensus model of participating management was the hot topic. Quality circles, problem-solving models, interpersonal methods, and how to move toward quality issues or to become service driven or customer driven were also hot topics.

The business community was attempting to find better ways to compete. My practice grew rapidly with a program that I developed known as the "corporate purge." This "take-no-prisoners" program was directed at the staff level, division level, management level, and supervision level. It was a simple program—place managers into a preplanned failure scenario, a program through which their problem identification/solving and interactive skills were assessed. People were forced to deal with real and immediate failure, failure crafted to be a personal failure. The concept behind the program was to measure reaction and behavior associated with failure versus reaction under success. My belief was that failure for major corporate managers was not personalized. Their rationalization was most important to see. In reality, many large corporations had set themselves up so they could not fail. How? Simply take no risks—managers were not motivated to take risks nor were they necessarily rewarded for risk taking.

Before a far-reaching business plan designed to leapfrog the competition could be developed, the executive level managers needed to know the company and its various managers' ability to manage risk and change. I believed then that all corporate cultures could be unlocked if they got beyond the fear of risk.

Hundreds of companies began to immerse themselves in quality improving programs that incorporated concepts of service and responsiveness to customers. Trust is the underlying factor in the concept of working empowerment. Without it, the programs are doomed to failure. In addition to trust, it is the goal of the company to have the workers be invested directly with the values of the company. In other words, the workers take ownership to the problems facing the company and commit themselves to solving them. We will discuss later how social responsibility becomes the extension of the quality improvement initiatives begun by corporations.

■ CONSULTING FOR ENTREPRENEURS— AN OPEN HIGHWAY

My years of major corporate involvement had provided a sound foundation to enter the dynamic, yet unpredictable world of the entrepreneur. I was being asked more often to provide the same strategic consulting that I had provided major corporations, only this time it was to smaller, uncontaminated companies who recognized the need to develop a sound corporate culture.

This was an exciting opportunity for me. I found this group of small businesses to be creative and dynamic in their thinking and behavior. To the entrepreneur, change is constant and creativity is an art-form necessary to survive.

The spirit of the entrepreneur is what this country is all about. It should not be surprising that cause-aligned thinking was initiated from an entrepreneurial setting. Being an entrepreneur means having no superimposed limitations. Trial and failure is a way of life. Risk is the only game in town.

It is a group within a group that has begun the revolution of change by tying social relevance into their business plans. They are defined as the enlightened capitalists. They are the ones who will fully develop principles of philanthropic economics. Through creativity, innovation, and necessity, they are finding ways of improving products, services, packaging, and distribution of their products and services, while incorporating a social sensitivity and understanding to their business. The largest opportunity for American business to respond to the need of social consciousness on behalf of business can be found in the entrepreneurial setting. They outnumber big business a thousand to one and make up 93 percent of all the jobs in America. This group can find creative business development opportunities within the area of social responsibility, while in turn creating for themselves a unique value-added differentiation. Small business can alter and modify marketing practices, sales practices, and product development practices more easily than can big business.

Entrepreneurs hold the key to the recovery of the American economy. Although small business makes up the majority of our gross national product, they still are handicapped in the areas of financial support, information mediums, and educational support that are readily available to major corporations. Risk is inherent for the entrepreneur. They are the true American pioneers. Someone once told me that a pioneer can be recognized by the arrows in their back. Today's entrepreneurs are survivalists, oftentimes charismatic individuals with a dream in their hearts. There's a growing number of enlightened consumers who are leaving big business to pursue their own brand of social consciousness and business opportunity.

This group, their products, and their services are evident throughout our changing society. Some of them will be discussed in other chapters. We will also help to define some strategic and tactical concepts and models that can be applied to literally thousands of small business owners and entrepreneurs throughout the country. It's exciting to begin to see how this phenomena is manifesting itself. An initiative that we have created in our company is the American Business Coalition for a Better World. This association is designed to provide business owners with information, education, motivation, and strategic support to companies choosing to follow the social responsibility format. Other such efforts are also underway.

Entrepreneur magazine and its publisher James Fitzpatrick along with MasterCard introduced the Leadership in Entrepreneurial Achievement and Philanthropy (LEAP) award program. The first annual awards program was announced in the magazine's October 1991 issue. The program encourages companies throughout the United States to demonstrate the LEAP characteristics, the focus being President Bush's Thousand Points of Light program. The LEAP award program provides two key elements. First is recognition. It helps people to know they are being appreciated for their efforts. People the entrepreneurs are reaching may not be able to express their thanks; the magazine and award program thanks the business owner. Entrepreneurs also learn about other business owners like themselves who are doing more. The second element, a prize of a $25,000 Gold MasterCard credit line, may be just the means to help these entrepreneurs reach their next step in achieving more.

Fitzpatrick, publisher of *Entrepreneur,* should also be recognized for taking the initiative over other business publications that are still, for the most part, reporting the facts and figures of stories, but not much more. The concept is to demonstrate the values of social responsibility by applying the entrepreneurial spirit of creative solutions to social problems.

Entrepreneur publishes profiles of businesspeople whose work exemplifies the ideals the LEAP award encourages. One example is a 22-year-old Phoenix man who founded Hotels/Motels in Partnership with Phoenix. The program matches people in need of emergency shelters with properties willing to donate empty rooms. Hotels/Motels in Partnership with Phoenix has more than 700 properties nationwide, and more than 13,000 homeless families, victims of abuse and others in need, have obtained free lodging. Day's Inn of Atlanta has taken the idea one step farther by training homeless people as reservation agents, giving them a job, then housing them in low-rent hotel rooms until they can earn enough to live on their own. The recipients gain self-esteem and confidence to begin rebuilding their lives.

■ A DAY AT THE BEACH—A FORK IN THE ROAD

Corporate social responsibility entered my life in a strange way and unusual place—during summer at our home on the New Jersey shore. The community for the most part was made up of families like ours. Dad and Mom were businesspeople pushing against the tide, trying to get and keep an edge. Most of us were typical of the early 1980s up and comers—the *super achievers*.

The word *competitive* always comes to mind. The beach itself was a kind of a demilitarized zone, a safe place where lawyers talked with corporate managers, entrepreneurs were polite to bankers, and everyone tried to get along—even if in the real world, just over the causeway, we would never have acknowledged one another. We co-existed peacefully with one common denominator among us, the ocean.

Over the years, the shore had remained basically the same, a comfortable and stable place—until this particular day. My indoctrination, or baptism, into cause awareness started on a normal day. Our Sundays were fairly predictable. I would be in my beach chair alongside the jetty by 11:30 A.M., the place where the waves just reached my feet, keeping me cool yet dry. A day of reading and relaxing would be in store. This Sunday was better than most for me; my entire family was there. Devin, our first grandson, was the pride and joy of the family, and, in real Embley tradition, it was time to get him indoctrinated as a real beach mouse. This particular Sunday, I thought I would introduce my grandson to my special place, my spot alongside the jetty, just slightly in the waves. Devin sat between my legs and as the water came in, he kicked his feet and played, not caring at all about the greater meaning of life. In no time he crawled into my arms and, exhausted from his workout, fell asleep on my chest. I tipped back my beach chair and closed my eyes.

Little did I know that my life was about to change forever. When I least expected it, I was about to be initiated into a new phase of my life. As I lay back in my beach chair with my young grandson fast asleep on my chest, I was savoring the moment, totally relaxed, in my private spot. The lapping waves were a friendly reminder that my ocean was nearby. The only danger this spot may have had for anyone was an occasional crab. I became aware of something around my feet and ankles. Not too bothered or even concerned, and not wanting to disturb the baby, I decided not to change my position. Then I felt a stinging prick on my ankle, strong enough to get my attention. I shot out of the chair, clinging to Devin, not wanting to wake him. Before me, turning over and over in the surf, were several medical syringes, used syringes, some with blood still visible in the chambers. My beach was being attacked by a foreign terrorist. I felt a rush of emotions—first disgust, then fear, and soon out-and-out rage. How did this happen, why did it happen, and most important, who the hell was responsible? The problem first affected me, then my family, and soon the entire beach was up in arms. What had been a refuge for the harried weekly warriors was wiped out in one tidal surge that brought this plight on shore, placing the entire area in jeopardy. This was the low point of our time on the New Jersey shore. It was a devastating blow, one that even years later, the New Jersey shore never fully recovered from.

■ BIG BUSINESS' EYES WERE ALREADY OPEN

I had heard of illegal ocean dumping before, but it was something I just accepted until it reached me. In one instant I had gone from being passive, compliant, and disinterested to being a direct participating activist. I had joined the rally movement; I became one of them. Something had to be done! I wanted answers and results. I was now a conservationist, an environmental advocate, and I wanted information. I learned of an initiative underway by the state, area businesses, and a group known as the New Jersey Shore Foundation, whose mission was the preservation and protection of the state's beaches. I called for information. I discovered, much to my surprise, that the concept had been initiated by a large pharmaceutical company, Schering Plough, headquartered in New Jersey. The firm's visionary chair, Bob Luciano, was the initiator, and the company backed it with substantial dollars. Terrific, but why Schering Plough? The answer was simple. One of Schering Plough's many successful products is Coppertone suntan lotion. That made all the sense in the world to me. The company, as did I, had a vested interest in preserving the beaches. No one on the beach, no need for suntan lotion. Clean up the beaches, bring back the people, they'll need suntan lotion—smart! Who better than a successful, large New Jersey business to assume leadership. Quite honestly, if it were left to local or state politicians to solve the problem, I would have felt little or no confidence. Not because of the politicians, but because of all political arenas in general. I felt relieved that private business was leading the way. This was a truly worthy cause.

The brilliance of the strategy became apparent only after I contemplated the situation. Schering Plough did not sponsor it directly, but set up a private foundation and funded it. As a marketer, I saw substantial public relations benefits for Schering Plough if it would only let the consumers know. At the time, the firm had chosen a low-profile role; perhaps it was concerned with being seen as exploiting the situation. I saw nothing wrong with business helping to solve civic or community problems. That is my perspective of businesses' role in community affairs, and they should benefit from that involvement. This would encourage them to get involved more often. However, this strategy was not typical of big business. What was going on here? Was this a fluke or was big business in the business of social responsibility? The event was a turning point in my awareness about business taking an active role in community or national issues. I was getting excited. The question I asked myself was, "Is the climate right for acceptance for that kind of marketing, or was it already happening and I just wasn't aware?" I had hundreds of questions but very few answers.

By now I had learned more about this emerging business concept of cause alignment. It had its roots close to home; in fact, it even had a name—*corporate social responsibility*. It was a relative new term, but it showed common sense and was easy to understand. Another aspect of this method of thinking was getting a test; this one, however, dealt directly with a product of sorts with a promotional slant, and a new name for this type of crossover promotion. "Cause-related marketing" was coined by American Express for a program it had initiated with the Ellis Island/Statue of Liberty Restoration Fund in 1982. The concept was simple yet elegant. Every time a cardholder used his or her American Express card, a percentage of each card use transaction was donated to the restoration fund. What would be a more powerful symbol for America and its melting pot of citizens than the symbol of hope and freedom? What an emotional chord to strike. However, this program was an isolated occurrence that year. I could not see how that emotional response could be duplicated. Once it was refurbished, it was done—period! I had found the roots in American Express' program. That company gave cause-related marketing its title, but somewhere an entrepreneur had to be at the center.

■ THE TIME IS RIGHT

The question that kept coming to mind was, "Had our culture changed?" If so, why and how? I was skeptical about the warm side of our human nature. The horror stories heard in large cities kept people constantly on the defensive—keep up a guard or lose big. In such an environment it was difficult to believe in a kinder, gentler people. My impression, however, would change one day when I was not even considering the situation.

Strangely enough, the occasion of this enlightening again occurred at the New Jersey shore, where just ten months earlier I had been incensed at the destruction of my beach. But this time, the beach was filled with hope and promise. The event was called "Hands Across America," on May 25, 1986, a national initiative to help the hungry and the homeless. I was on the beach that day when people just seemed to begin to gather. Lacking any instruction or commands, they simply and quietly began to congregate along the shoreline. Families found friends, and friends found strangers, and for a brief moment in time, they became connected and friends. I was amazed that the line stretching the beach represented nearly every demographic category in society. The old, young, black, white, rich and not so rich gathered quietly along the beach. Thousands of people spread along the ocean in a silent and quiet gathering. This event inspired all who took part. It was a strange and wonderful feeling being connected this way. I felt as if I was part of the circle, that my place in line mattered. To hold hands with thousands of strangers was a very personal moment, one that I would reflect on long after it was over. A powerful feeling was shared, brought about by individual action and individual need.

So that day began the odyssey that would change my life. This book is really one of hope. A hope that my finding is not just one more small sign that we as a people had nothing better to do that day than stand peacefully on the beach. That quiet and very peaceful demonstration that took not more than 15 minutes made a statement that simply said, It's time!

I had begun the long road towards awareness, and my business would soon reflect my new and growing understanding. Now I wish to share with you what this journey has taught me so far. This book will serve as a narrative for those who find the subject matter interesting or intriguing. At the conclusion of this book, you will feel like the rest of us. You will find a way of doing well while doing good!

■ GETTING STARTED TOWARD SOCIAL ACTIVISM

After leaving the beach the day of "Hands Across America," I was ready to get started in defining my role and finding out who else was involved. The first step was to look back in time for some answers to see how and why corporate social activism was happening. People do not change overnight, but yesterday everyone had seemed cynical and hard edged. Now they seemed like warm, sensitive, caring souls. Was I just ignorant, or had they just changed mysteriously overnight? The 1980s had been the decadent decade, the time to grab it all based on the motto "Greed Is Good." I was in the thick of it with both children in private schools, a beachfront house, and a couple of exotic European cars—I was under 40 and out there winning in real economic terms. This was an unlikely time for a self-examination. Certainly, a bull run to find mainstream social consciousness was more than a shock. Yet social consciousness was breaking out everywhere. This was going to be a journey, not a destination.

Awareness grew slowly at first out of my visceral vision. Since that day on the beach, I have viewed and reviewed hundreds of companies that have embarked on this new socially conscious marketing phenomenon, each with a common characteristic, yet each different based on its application of the strategy.

■ WHO IS IN CHARGE HERE?

Is the consumer changing the way corporations market, or are corporations educating the consumer? The oldest business principle of getting closer to the customer is one approach that seems to build consumer confidence and develop brand loyalty. Social responsibility realignment goes even further in saying that what is important to customers is also important to business, and customers feel strongly about social issues. This movement could create a greater linkage between customers and companies, a connection of *shared values*. The psychology of this relationship touches at the center of our structure. When I was consulting in the Midwest, I heard a story about John Deere and Company—a firm that had earned almost blind loyalty from its customers. To hear John Deere's competitors tell it, if John Deere equipment was visible in the yard, they simply headed back to the main road and didn't bother to make a sales pitch for their product.

What had John Deere done to earn that kind of loyalty? How could Deere stand up to the rebate wars of the late 1970s when every farmer needed help? This was loyalty above and beyond. The story is a great one, one that has been passed down from father to son like a cherished family heirloom.

When the Great Depression hit this country in the early 1930s, the farmers were not spared. They fell behind on payments for their equipment, and every manufacturer but one raced to confiscate or repossess their goods. John Deere and Company stood behind its customers with a simple but powerful message: "Fellahs, you'll be back, and when you are, you'll need your tractor." Socially responsible philosophy moved ahead of pure economic logic. The short-term financial risk was rewarded with long-term loyalty—a predictable by-product of a company's social responsibility statement.

The 1980s investment banker would have collapsed over such a foolhardy move and probably would have cleaned house. I am not saying I would disagree with the banker, but the result in pure economic terms to John Deere was overwhelmingly positive. Deere's high-risk move displayed the theme/philosophy of doing well while doing good, an innovation which I believe, and so do Deere's customers, was motivated from the heart. The benefit to the farmers was vital, and they never forgot.

Not many companies can rise to greatness in this way. Had more done it sooner or more often, it might not have taken America so long to react to the threat of foreign competition. Industries might have survived, and companies and families might have been saved.

When I examined the Deere story, part of the answer to the question of who was leading the charge, the consumer or the corporation, was apparent. Corporations are made up of consumers: "We have met the enemy and he is us." The simple fact is always the hardest to prove. Perhaps the people who worked at John Deere then were from farm families who knew firsthand of the impending doom and how they would feel if they were losing the farm.

In any case, I was obviously not alone in developing an awareness of the events that were occurring. For whatever reasons, social activism was becoming strong, and I determined to find out why.

To begin the research I had to find the model, and to find the model, I would have to create one. There was only one way to go forward, and that required a look to our past.

3

■

Back to the Future
Analyzing the Trends of Social Activism—The Move Toward the Enlightened Consumer

A strategist's primary tool in determining trend development is a simple model known as *force field analysis*. The concept is to determine the power of two forces (see Figure 3.1):

1. *The driving force:* This force is the positive influence factors moving forward.

2. *The opposite force:* This force is the negative influence factors moving in opposition to the driving force.

The World War I military strategist Lyndall Hart was a brilliant tactician and a master at determining the forces and influences of the military development of troops. It was Hart who developed and refined the science of this strategy and the understanding of the success of frontal assaults, bypassing tactics, encircling tactics, and guerrilla warfare (sniping). In marketing, the stake is market share. Competitors are the opposition. The matching of various strengths and weaknesses is the tool of competitive analysis, and the method determines how and when to position a product or service against the opposition. The analysis brings both real and perceived forces to light, that is,

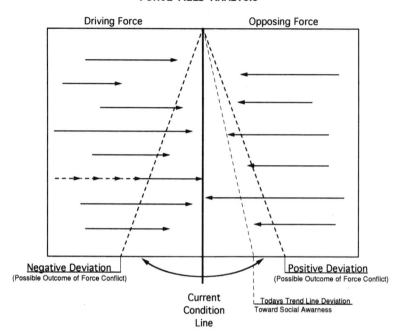

Figure 3.1
FORCE FIELD ANALYSIS

territory, coverage, sales strength, average unit price versus competitors, consumer studies, advertising, and so on. The role of the strategist is to determine the value or weight of a company's driving forces against the value and weight of its competition. This will determine whether to take competitors head on or snipe at their flanks. For example, an all-out price war, or direct frontal assault, comes down to a company's staying power. The company with the deepest checkbook usually wins.

The force field analysis for this model of corporate social conscience is a bit more abstract. The trends had begun to take shape some time back. The task was to determine what forces had been brought to bear in recent history that would shape this new society. The forces all have a variable value or weight from 1 to 10. Force 1 can be defined in terms of a passing fad or fancy. A similar model was developed to determine the forces affecting our society and culture. This model would be concentrated primarily over a period of the last fifty years. The object of the model was to determine what factors had shaped the American consumer into socially conscious and responsible people.

The determination of a force condition is an event, invention, activity, or specific knowledge of information that has an impact on the actions or attitudes of the general society. These forces have long term or short term implications. Short term implications have less staying power than do long term, therefore, an event, although powerful at the time, will fade from memory or be replaced with another event either more current or of greater magnitude. A short term force would receive, for my purposes, a low rating on a scale of 1 to 10. Level 10 is an earth shattering, long term, society-altering force, changing forever the way we think or react. (See Figure 3.2.)

The model of force drivers is necessary to develop prior to applying the force field analysis model to create an effective trend forecast.

Force 10 Drivers

The forces that have shaped this new phenomenon are not likely to relent; therefore, they can be described as *a level 10 driving force*. A force level of 10 is earth shattering. A force with level 10 characteristics has no equal opposing counterforces to alter its direction, allowing it to become a reshaping and culture-altering force. In the past four years my consulting firm has tracked and monitored these forces, and incorporated them into a development model.

This chapter is designed to relate the existence and effect of these force fields. Each is easily recognizable on its own, but when they impact society in a cumulative fashion, their cause and effect are multiplied in rapid succession. An individual force coupled with other forces moving in the same direction builds to an overpowering speed with which it hits society and alters the culture structure.

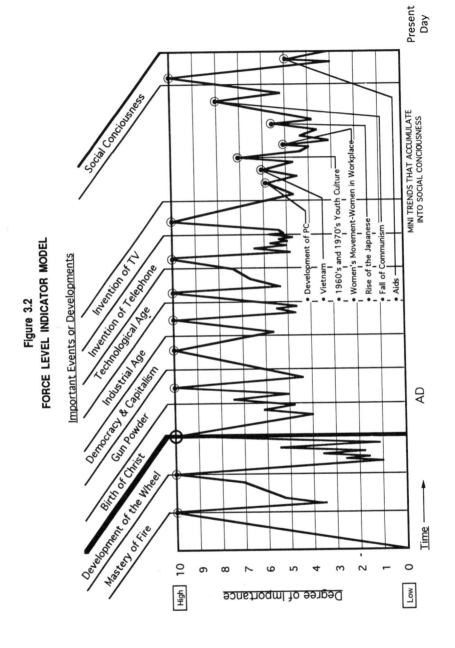

Figure 3.2
FORCE LEVEL INDICATOR MODEL

Important Events or Developments

Social Conciousness
Invention of TV
Invention of Telephone
Technological Age
Industrial Age
Democracy & Capitalism
Gun Powder
Birth of Christ
Development of the Wheel
Mastery of Fire

Development of PC
Vietnam
1960's and 1970's Youth Culture
Women's Movement-Women in Workplace
Rise of the Japanese
Fall of Communism
Aids

MINI TRENDS THAT ACCUMULATE
INTO SOCIAL CONCIOUSNESS

Present
Day

AD

Time

Degree of Importance
High
10
9
8
7
6
5
4
3
2
1
0
Low

34

The approach is the commonsense model—if it looks like a duck, if it walks like a duck, if it quacks like a duck, then it must be a duck. A process of trend forecasting, looking forward, begins by looking back. The important question is how far back. U.S. culture and society have been evolving for little more than 200 years, but humankind has been evolving for a couple of millennia.

In the evolution of mankind, one can only imagine how early man reacted once fire was contained and civilized as a device for survival. Fire may have simply extended the life cycle of early man, or it may have been the single event that allowed the species of man to survive. As an event, controlling fire had a force level 10 impact on society. In recent time, we are still experiencing force level 10 events that impact the human race in very direct terms. Breakthroughs, inventions, and events will continue to alter the way we live and behave.

We will examine the forces that are currently impacting us. Forces fall into two areas: driving forces (positive) and opposing forces (negative). Imagine, if you will, the impact of a cure for cancer on society. The positive side is that life expectancy would go up and the national annual death rate of 2.5% would lower. The opposing forces would also be placed into effect. With the death rate going down and people living longer, society might suffer with over-population, thereby overtaking the economic infrastructure of many governments and cultures. In trend forecasting, the process of cause and effect is always taken into consideration.

The level 10 forces previously mentioned prevailed through generations as the *great equalizers*. Equalizer theory is important in that it creates at least a level playing field. In the Old West the Colt .45 and the windmill—peace and water—were equalizers. Marketers constantly look for equalizers when working with clients. Parameters were set in the first research phase to isolate the trend forces. It is significant to speak to each of the forces in the individual and how in unison with other forces they create a cumulative effect. The weight associated with a force is ultimately evaluated using the cumulative tactic when appropriate.

Having seen past cause and effect patterns, the creative person has the courage to make some intuitive leaps. These rational and logical assumptions are relatively safe. The goal is to get ahead of the reactive curve in most cases and develop a process called horizontal thinking, right-brain thinking. Creative thinking is defined also as horizontal thinking that is opposite to left-brain thinking, logical thinking, or vertical thinking. The proactive approach in all cases is desirable.

Good trend marketing is not mysterious, but it is also not an exact science. As each of the forces that creates the cause-aligned trend is discussed in this chapter, recognize that the effect has already had significant impact on how businesses market their products. One issue is as follows: to forecast how companies are already using social consciousness in their marketing plan and how they will continue to deploy the strategy. If IBM has in place a socially responsible strategy today, what will its strategy look like in ten years? IBM will mature its involvement. Another issue is how businesses that would not normally be considered candidates for social realignment will begin to become involved. Also of significance is the way in which the entire issue of social consciousness will unfold in the coming years.

In reading this book, keep positioning your company, product, or service against the information. This entire subject is full of creative and entrepreneurial features and opportunities. The goal of this book is to show you that you can do well while doing good, that running a profitable business and being socially conscious are not mutually exclusive.

Once the driving and opposing forces have been identified, the strategist develops a tactical plan to deploy forces to address the opposing forces. The methods associated with acquiring and maintaining market share are a constant issue for all businesses. Only one thing is certain in business—change.

■ THE CONTEXT: THE BABY BOOMER ERA

In setting about the force analysis of corporate social responsibility, I chose the starting focus—the great birth
burst of the 1940s and 1950s—the baby boomers. My goal
was to discover how this group was moved through time
and what changes to U.S. culture they encouraged, clung
to, or abandoned. The parents of baby boomers were an-
alyzed as well, from the point of view of their inherent
values and traditions, deeply implanted by their heritage
and ethnicity brought into focus.

■ DRIVING FORCES

Freedom

One defining reality of our society is freedom—freedom to be allowed to experiment with various philosophies
and ideals.

The major forces that shaped this generation are numerous. A significant change to this group was and still
is the attitude projected by the parents to their children.
The children themselves were looked upon differently from
children of earlier groups. Children were encouraged more
openly to achieve more, which translated into more freedom
of expression, thought, and action. That radically altered
the concept that children should be *seen* and not *heard*,
with greater freedom given to this generation. (This group
would become the conscience for the nation in the coming
years.)

A shift of power became more apparent. Success became a driving issue in the minds of America, and this
free enterprise society was waiting. More times than not,
parents vested their hopes and dreams in their children,
which tipped the scales even more. Freedom also allowed
greater flexibility as it pertained to older, more traditional
structure and discipline that our grandparents were raised
on. This flexibility, once exercised, was difficult to harness.
Progressive parenting was seen as chic while typical par-

enting was seen as "old fashioned," and the groups and
values clashed. Peer pressure and class involvement became
operative. Being "in" was better than being "out." Popularity took on a whole other dimension. In looking for
clues to the future, it was important to see this factor
clearly. To go back in time personally and reflect on those
forces affecting one as a young person, reliving those
formative years, and examining the type of parenting received as a child, versus the type of parent one is now,
was thought provoking.

Motivation and Enlightenment

With the focus of attention on the development and
maturation of the baby boomers, it was extremely interesting to recap the events that shaped this group and
their values. Motivation and enlightenment seem to be
at the center of this awakening to social consciousness.
The concept of motivation is nothing new to those of us
who choose to compete. Enlightenment is something one
heard of, but hardly ever practiced. Without motivation,
nothing happens; instead, there is cosmic inertia (energy
at rest). Motivation for the enlightened seems to be a
two-sided issue—positive and negative. This great mass
of baby boomers is now coming to grips with its own
mortality versus the state of unconscious immortality. Mortality and immortality are two extremely powerful shaping
influences in people's lives. Immortality allows people to
risk all, shun fear, boast of courage against insurmountable
odds. Mortality, however, is "conservative." An interesting
dynamic, reality, occurs when mortality and immortality
become one. As youths and young adults, people believe
they will live forever; that is, they believe in immortality.
As people age, the reality of life beings to take hold,
and they begin to modify their risk in direct proportion
with gain—they engage in risk-reward thinking. Baby
boomers, the privileged generation, never really gave up
on the concept of immortality, so they invented ways to
prolong life, for example, exercise, diet, plastic surgery,
all in an effort to retain life or existence. This generation

is absorbed with immortality and may represent as much as 50 percent of the gross national product in services designed to keep people forever young or at least alive a very long time.

The motivation behind socially conscious marketing is a basic human need to be *significant*, meaning in this example, sustaining, enduring, lasting—in a way a bit immortal—to leave something that will matter and that will have long-term effects. People may be subconsciously looking for their own immortality, and some find it in philanthropic efforts. To have made a valuable contribution to society as a whole, this core motivation is a powerful driving force in our culture, and it is more apparent as the baby boomers reach their fifties.

Television—The Advent of the Information Age

In 1950, the baby boomers were beginning to associate with the world much as their parents had done before them at the same age. One of the differences with the baby boomers was the invention of television—a force level 10. Television was to become to this generation what *fire* was to the caveman. It would revolutionize the way they would think and react and live forever! In the early days, it was used primarily as entertainment. There was little graphic violence, just mindless comedy acts, Edward R. Murrow visiting Jack Benny presented in a type of format that could have come straight out of the Kremlin. The main fear of the mothers and fathers in those days was the myth of dangerous invisible rays coming from the television, so viewers had to sit at least 10 feet away— from a little 10-inch screen! However, television had a greater role to play than entertainment in the lives of this group: it was to become media, blasting thousands of messages and slogans, and it would not and could not be stopped. Many baby boomers' perceptions of values came from early television programs and experiences, for example, "Father Knows Best," "Leave It to Beaver," "The Nelson's," "Sky King," "Howdy Doody," "The Mickey Mouse Club," "Dick Clark and American Band Stand,"

"Good guys always wear white hats," "The Honeymoon-
ers," "Toast of the Town," and "I Remember Mama."
Television would entertain this group, and children
found it to be their most trusted friend. Turning off the
television was the hardest thing to do. It was no work
or effort to maintain a relationship with this box full of
joy. Just pull the "on" knob and set the rabbit ears. It
would also become businesses' greatest tool in bringing
their product pitches right into the home.

In addition, television had an effect on shaping personalities. It was seen by many parents as the great brain
killer, and in many respects, they were right. Education
often took a back seat. Television was also a new and
powerful reward and punishment tool that could motivate
many members of the household. It competed with various
family values and structures, but above all, it was here
to stay. (The baby boomers emulated the characters they
saw before them.) Television itself became a magical looking
glass that allowed one to go and do what no others before
could have imagined. When baby boomers look back to
their early years in front of the set, they know that television
played a large part in their growing up. The 1950s' and
1960s' children experienced freedom of expression to a
greater degree than any earlier generations of young people,
which allowed them the courage to move beyond the
stereotypes of their mothers and fathers. They pushed
the limits of new lifestyles. This group would directly
challenge the concepts of the family and the government
in the years ahead. They were also a bit naive regarding
the rest of the world. Many were from poor immigrant
parents who had come to this country with a dream and
the ability to work hard. Now these children didn't need
to earn money with their hands; they could do it with
their heads instead. The baby boomers were released for
the most part from hard labor; to some they were just
spoiled children, yet the innocence of this generation was
a wonderful thing. Sex then was more openly discussed
than practiced. Women still wanted to retain their virginity
or at least the perception of their virginity! European tra-

ditions demanded it. Young men were locked in the struggle between boyhood and manhood, never quite sure they wanted either to start or end.

The images of this group in the 1960s are powerful. They changed the way people lived and made their antiestablishment voices heard. Baby boomers did not want to be identified as mainstreamers. Their revolt developed the subcultures, some relating more toward nature than to man. Environmentalist roots go back to those of the 1960s and 1970s who chose to live by nature's rules. They clung to and developed their philosophy of the new world order. They had no respect for the existing system. Spiritualism and reality-altering methods were developed, from inner peace meditation to LSD and everything in between, all in a mixed statement of protest and personal escape. This generation was split, one went to war in the jungle, the other went to war on the streets. Both groups prepared to make sacrifices, each group was misunderstood by the other. More distrust and more confusion. Casualties rose on both sides. Some suffered flesh wounds and amputations of body parts, others lost their lives to drugs, alcohol, and street violence, all losses due to the conflict. Was it more noble to die in Vietnam or at Kent State? The boomers now know they were all saying the same thing, only their tactics were different.

In retracing the roots of social change, I learned more than I ever believed I would. I learned that principles come only with commitment to what is right. What is right is basic, fair, and just. If this generation did one thing, it repeatedly asked the question, "What is right?" Is civil rights right, is protecting our planet and environment right, is seeing a peaceful co-existence with the world right? Is providing education, health care, and safety for children right? What is right today is the common sense taught to by a group of youths in the 1960s and 1970s.

Vietnam would soon become the galvanizing force that would trigger a shift in society and become a focal point that would give voice to the youth of this generation. A voice that would develop into a roar, a voice that would forge new ideals, standards, ethics, and practices. It would not happen easily. This *was* a domestic war, a war hard fought on the streets of Chicago, Kent State, and Birmingham and on the Capitol steps. Their voices came from various sectors: street poets, song writers, artists, self-made student leaders, black and white, more poor than rich. From Bangor, Maine, to the Iowa cornfields to the concrete corridors of every big city. This generation of boomers was on the move. The passion developed out of fear initially, then moved quickly beyond self-preservation to a generation preservation. "Why have thousands been killed for an unjust war? Is this right?" they asked. Peace and love, nature, fairness, equal rights, civil rights, pollution, and human rights all were germinated in the 1960s and 1970s. Distrust of everything and everybody in the establishment became the focus, from government leaders to political leaders to big business, the war machine was using 18-year-olds as cannon fodder. The youth, and a few adult supporters, were struggling between the old world and the new undefined world. They were placed into a time and space that was moving at a terrible pace. The time of innocence was running out. There was trouble at home—the clash of the traditions and values and trouble across the seas in a place called Vietnam. The breakdown was about to take place, if this group shunned the old values of their parents and grandparents, and the new values were not yet defined. As a generation caught without a direction, this mass of the misunderstood, some would find comfort in following the path that their parents had, some would seek blindly for a divine intervention, some would choose revolt and opposition to anything that closely resembled the past, and some just followed. Others planted the seeds that would become the voice of our conscience, asking one unnerving question—What's right?

Vietnam and the generation came together, and the result is a driving force. The generation of hippies and "hooligans," the ones who broke their parents hearts, the ones that government tried to stop, the disrespectful ones— changed forever how society would look at the world.

As time passed and the war ended, they slowly began to drift away from the communes. They got married, put away their pipes, found themselves in car pools and the morning commute to offices, plants, farms or shops. They turned off Jimmy Hendrix's music; they slowed down their pace. They kept in touch with some but lost the images of others, they took their place quietly in the world. However, they never, ever, gave up or away the values or principles of what is right!

The Women's Movement

The next major force began with the women's movement of the early 1970s. This force would also join the ideology being forged in our society as a result of the Vietnam conflict. The two movements of cultural forces were redefining the world. The women's movement began our contemporary stage for the examination of cause-consciousness. The entrance of women into the work force made the largest impact of any on the way we will think and behave in the future. Exploring women's impact on business is a most exciting dynamic. To frame the impact, let's state that the age variance for women entering the work force was between 18 and 32 beginning in 1970.

To do justice to the analysis of the results of women in the work force, we must attempt to describe the differences between men and women, both in fact and in perception. Clearly a difference exists, one that is not just *anatomical*. The following statements are not meant as stereotypical sexist remarks, rather a reflection of the facts of the perception of women in our society prior to the advance of the women's movement. That perception propose that women have been the keepers of our traditions and values. It was safeguarded with them. Women were perceived as the nurturers. Their sensitivity and emotions in their thoughts and actions were tolerated. Women raised the young and shaped their values. The only control women were perceived to have had was through sex. The role that women would eventually play in business would alter significantly the Great All American Boys' Club.

The radical feminists of the early 1970s were playing right into the hands of the boys. When women chose to be dominant and aggressive, they were easy to dismiss and disregard, and would ultimately became sacrificial lambs of the early women's rights struggles. Through perseverance and commitment, with the support of affirmative action and demonstrations, they would eventually gain entry. Equality was another issue. After the initial assault phase, the balance of women found the beachhead, if not totally cleared of mine fields, at least traversable. Women who entered the work force in the 1960s and 1970s went into areas that seemed suitable for them in the eyes of their male counterparts—administration, sales support, customer service, public relations, community affairs, advertising, and so on. The hard science areas were fairly well closed. However, by entering the side of business most often seen by the customer, it will eventually allow them to be the architects of their own fate. This is where their role as society's value keepers will shine. It has been said that the role of a woman is to *civilize* a man. For women to civilize corporate America, they had to pull it away from its savage state. Did business in the 1940s, 1950s, and 1960s fit the image of a savage state? *Webster's* has several adjectives that seem apt: "cruel," "barbarian," "primitive." Would that describe business in this society? Ask the labor unions and their early organizers about work and safety conditions, fair play, medical benefits, and treatment. They might have an opinion or two.

What impact women have had to business during the past 30 years is worth noting. For purposes of the model, women's impact on business is examined by looking at how business was conducted without the female influence, post-World War II. The mind-set of management in the 1930s, 1940s and 1950s was management by results (MBR)—tonnage, piecework units sold, versus units shipped, were the basics. Heavy emphasis was placed on results, little emphasis on people. One management theory is Douglas McGregor's theory of X and Y—X defined people as needing to be constantly supervised, pushed, and driven to perform work tasks, whereas theory Y subscribed to the concept that people wanted to work to accomplish, to achieve. The 1950s style of management was most clearly theory X. Management thinking did not change much over the next ten years until motivation and competition were introduced into the practice of management. This carrot-and-stick approach was not much better because management could not sustain motivation over long enough periods of time.

The next behavioral model that was introduced was the combination of grid theory and Peter Drucker's management by objectives (MBO). Nowhere did this evolution of management thinking include a subscription to individual leadership quality models. Again, management thinking was on specific results. Labor issues and human rights were slow to draw much attention from business. The philosophy of participation management brought a new and expansive aspect to the older McGregor management models of Theory X and Y. A hypothesis by William Ouchi combined X and Y theories to include trust, yet retaining aspects of paternalism and authoritarianism. Ouchi's Theory Z was defined in his book *Theory Z: How American Business Can Meet the Japanese Challenge.*[1] The oriental concept of theory Z arrived on the scene about the same time as did women. These two factors combined to change the business world. This was hard on the boys; business had been built around sports, sex, and war games. This is how they had been taught to communicate.

When men are around women, they can be categorized into three groups—the persecutor, the victim, or the rescuer—all in the name of sex. Sex is power, the boys have power, but they do not have sexual power. Power is the operative issue in business. This brings up the next force in the analysis, the force of power. Who has it and how does one get it? The power force is varied in this model. Forces in themselves generate power; therefore, power

---

[1] Reading, MA: Addison-Wesley Publishing Co., 1981.

must be a force. It will be helpful to understand how power is gained and how it is used. All power bases must be achieved, with one exception, sexual power. The female receives it as a birthright. The forms of power and power structures usually fall into the following categories:

- *Information source*: The ability to withhold or make information available.

- *Personal power*: The ability to influence or inspire, the subtle power that moves the masses.

- *Reward or punishment power*: The ability to give or withhold prizes.

- *Specific knowledge power*: The special skills or talents that are held in high esteem.

- *Legitimate power*: The ability to lead that is obtained through respect, belief, character, and personal history.

The variation on power is a strange dance that is played out every day in every facet of American business. Women brought with them to the dance their birthright—sexual power. Men react differently to power and power brokers. Women were seen as power brokers.

When women began to be recognized for other power forms, did they begin to impact corporate America? Women had the ability to civilize America's business, and they needed to get to work right away.

What women wanted to do to business was to remove the bully image, to make business more approachable by the customer. They needed to show that business cared and was *concerned* rather than blatantly indifferent. Their previous business skills were old-fashioned common sense: "You catch more bees with honey than you do with vinegar." Women knew the problems of the consumer, since they had been consumers for years. They knew what was important. First, get in step with customers; second, give them what they want; and third, be there when it is not right, and fix it. If that is done, they'll be back, period. Unfortunately, American business was slow to learn and still slower to implement. Some women are shaping company images and campaigns today, very effectively. And their male counterparts have begun to think in these terms too.

The cultural influences and social programs have been impacted most positively by the advent of the American working woman. Her intellect is enhanced by her ability to perceive two sides of an issue. The effective balance of intellect (head motivation) and empathic humanistic responses (heart motivation) provides a unique management dimension that is effective in today's socially responsible times. Today, more and more business headquarters are the centerpiece for the art community. Women also encouraged and led the way with many community-based programs that addressed health, education, and the environment. In partnership with corporate America, women have transformed the corporate culture. Many of them are accurately aligning themselves with the needs and feelings of the consumer. Women have proven themselves to be a vital element in the business world, and as they begin to establish their entrepreneurial instincts, they will innovate and create a new dimension of cause-conscience business. Women's issues are long from resolved in corporate America. Women still have not been provided the opportunity they have earned, and to say that they single-handedly changed corporate America into a socially responsible system would be an overstatement. My statement is that in the shaping and formative years, they will continue to be a powerful influence.

The Rise of the Japanese

The next link in the driving forces analysis chain was a classic. In this force, timing was highly effective. The impact that the Japanese would soon have on American business would redefine and redistribute the world's wealth. The oriental culture would soon be felt directly by American business. The Japanese surprised America's business world with their ability to improve upon the most basic economic concepts.

For years after World War II, Japan's goods were known basically as cheap and shoddy. How does a country that was destroyed by war and bankruptcy become a world economic leader in just 30 short years? The Japanese success in the U.S. automobile market was good timing. After World War II, Japanese production facilities were weak, their labor unions troubled, and their basic industrial infrastructure was in ruins. What was intact was their proud culture and their strong work ethic, which together developed into a business ideology that would redefine quality, with more affordability. They introduced into the U.S. market the first Honda car. Their marketing positioned it as a reliable and affordable means of transportation. Now this was not a great marketing conclusion on their part; it was a defensive strategy because, basically, that was all that the Japanese could produce during this time.

Americans in the 1950s and 1960s had a love affair with their cars; they loved the wings and fins. They might not have relished the 8 miles to a gallon they got from gas-guzzling cars, but America was infatuated with the cars themselves. There was not a single red-blooded American male who wanted to be defined by a Honda in 1970. Muscle cars were in at the time. So what were the dynamics or forces that would alter the American ego in just a few decades? The Japanese arrived with their box car just about the time Mom took a day job. She was not going to earn much, so she needed cheap transportation. Dad was not going to give up the wings and fins—Mom bought the Honda. For the Japanese to catch this fresh market, they simply were available to provide the affordable alternative. Their product hit the U.S. shores when women went off to work.

The emerging American domestic youth market would become the next viable market for the Japanese. The definition of the American youth market in the early 1970s showed a strong economic market. Young people were buying fashions, music, cosmetics, and electronics at a much higher rate than had any previous generation of youth. The youth of the 1960s and 1970s enjoyed the benefit developed by their parents and grandparents.

The Japanese would innovate and repackage the basic transistor radio and this single product known as the Sony Walkman would captivate the American public's favor. The transistor broke ground for the great electronics industry that would sweep across America, catching the entire electronic industry sound asleep. The Sony Walkman was a clever bit of repackaging an old technology to position it for the youth market and the emerging fitness trend. Brilliant or lucky, who is to say? The result, however, will change forever the way U.S. industry behaves, and so we gave the Japanese success a powerful force rating.

The Japanese, on the heels of their marketing success, also exported their management style to American business. The Great Industrial Giant of American business would be redefined. The one leading motivator for American business is not the gain of market share, but rather the loss of it. The Japanese had hit American business where it hurt. If American business was going to defend its market share, the logical determination would be to emulate the very different, yet effective, method of management that the Japanese subscribed to.

The Japanese methods of participative management and quality circles, of developing and encouraging employee involvement, were brought to the U.S. business community. The business concepts of the Japanese hit U.S. industry about the same time the female worker entered the marketplace. They too wanted a voice in the business climate. The cultural influences being now shaped by the information age explosion, the seeds of ideology planted during the Vietnam war, the advent of women entering the workplace, and the Japanese management style of employee empowerment, were clearly influencing not only our largest American businesses, but the very lifestyles of the American public. The Japanese and U.S. women became unconscious allies. They roused U.S. industry in the 1970s. Many companies started dealing with new issues.

The concept of corporate culture was first recognized as a result of the growing awareness of American business. Companies were developing mission statements, quality improvement programs, employee recognition activities, and their promise of quality and service to their American consumers. Companies spent millions of dollars to create an image of corporate culture participated management and quality. Many of those companies would fail in their attempt to alter their corporate cultures from the rigid Theory X mentality. It was during the late 1970s that the impact of the intelligent consumer was beginning to be felt by American business.

In business, women fit the Japanese style more often than did men. They appeared to be more patient, accepting, and consensus seeking. They did not demonstrate confidence in team building activities as they tended to be passive. However, more often than not, they did possess superior information that earned them more team legitimacy. These two forces of women and Japanese methods of management reinforced each other. The timing was perfect. Both groups benefited and brought the issue of corporate America's trustworthiness into the public's awareness. To be trustworthy, one must *act* in a trustworthy manner. Wholesale reorganizations were occurring in U.S. industry, from centralizing to decentralizing work units, to employee-driven quality control groups.

American business had entered a new era where culture, lifestyle, attitude, and behavior were redefining the American family, the American consumer. In order to secure their economic survival, they would have to behave in a responsible manner—responsible not only to the consumer, but the workers, communities, and the environment. American business was experiencing the first wave of corporate social responsibility.

The Decadent Decade

During the early 1980s the radicals were quiet and the bulls were running. The great communicator had arrived with a message—"Supply Side Economics." The trickle-down concept. The *decade of greed* had begun! The issue of values was translated into new economic power, the operative word being *power*. The society was experiencing what some believed to be the American dream. The increase in pure economic gains was influencing the lifestyle of Americans. The concepts of image, glitz, power, and influence significantly alerted our concept of values. What began in the mid-1970s, was now a full-blown epidemic— the American family value structure was under siege. The growing drug culture and decay of the traditional family structure placed more emphasis on feeling good than being good. The effects of the 1980s would leave us empty and barren, and lead us to question the concept of instant gratification.

The 1980s would springboard many to question their own psychology in matters of esteem and self-worth. The questioning would open up an area of spiritual rediscovery. An entire industry was crafted from this search. Self-help and personal development programs, information, and publications were prolific at the time, and a certain segment of the population sought a 1960s version of spiritual enlightenment known as New Age thinking. The devotees to this new ideology came from all facets of our population. Intellectuals and academics seemed to lead the way, followed by conservationists, human rights activists, and those of the population who were left unfulfilled by the glitz and the glamour of the decadent decade.

The baby boomers had rushed through life at breakneck speed, thinking they were immortal. They did not have much of which to be truly proud. The high-risk, high-reward life-style means reward only if it has real value. Self-discovery allows one to remove the blinders; filling one's pockets with gold is allright as long as the soul is as full as well. Baby boomers had deep pockets, but they were emotionally broke. The human spirit feels healthy and well only when doing for others, not out of duty, but out of self-dignity and self-worth—the impact will last forever.

The Microprocessor

The next driving force we identified was the advent of the microprocessor—the second major advance in the Information Age. Techno-based speak is in, the world of instant gratification is taking hold with speed, ease, and access. The spin is on the generation in the fast lane, and 1970s and 1980s are filled with one image, time—how to get it, how to control it, how to enjoy it. The compression of time is a symptom of technothink.

Time became a diminishing resource in the high speed world of the fast tracker of the 1980s. The personal computer added a positive information delivery system, while at the same time creating anxiety and pressure on the time-sensitive population. Time became the defining rationale that would become the destructive force that would control relationships, disrupt families, and reset priorities. Time was something that no one had in the 1980s. The personal computer became an irritant to those who had not yet harnessed its power. Instant gratification and instant information seemed to go hand in hand.

AIDS

The next major driving force, an opposition force, impacting this group was the infectious human immunodeficiency virus (HIV) that leads to AIDS. This little-known and highly feared disease was viewed differently by all various sectors of the community. Each group had its opinions. The long-term effect of this virus may be a force level 10. No one knows absolutely how it will affect society, but some forecasts are possible. In mature adult groups, it is bringing back monogamy. Monogamy will reinforce family ties and values, requiring lifetime commitments by the partners. Sex education is reaching younger people, which can only help to deal with unwanted pregnancies, child neglect, child welfare, and so on. Regarding the affected groups of gays, our society has grown in compassion and understanding as it begins to recognize the valuable contribution this group has made to our culture and society. Society can hope to effect change in society to slow down drug use, but drug use is tied to self-worth. This group may be helpless and lost. AIDS will change the world—for better or worse. It's a fact.

The trend movement gathered great speed during the 1980s. The great Wall Street crash of 1987 put a painful end to the decade of greed, to be followed by the decade of decency. The time had come, the enlightenment had begun. The past few years have cast in stone the realities for this generation to explore fully the human spirit.

■ OPPOSING FORCES

Much has been discussed about driving forces. The other side is opposing forces. What counterforce would be significant enough to alter this developing, driving trend line? The most powerful force imaginable is *war or environmental collapse*. With the fall of communism in the Soviet Union and the tearing down of the Berlin Wall, one major opposing, predictable force is likely avoided. The victory in the Persian Gulf was a display of the strength of the free world. Other potential opposing forces include the environment and its survival and the impact of the AIDS epidemic, two forces that have yet to manifest themselves fully. Short of a complete meltdown brought on by the greenhouse effect, or AIDS reaching such a plague proportion as to affect directly 50 percent or more of every household, the future trends are aligned and predictable. It is important to note how these trends impact our daily life with images that are projected on people's minds every day.

The Evolution Toward Enlightenment

The same people who were questioning their own concepts of values were deeply immersed in American business. They would soon begin to influence even further how American business should behave. Some found their voice from within their existing corporate walls, others chose to leave and define their own corporate walls. As the 1980s unfolded, they began to impact their workplace. They clung to their ideals, principles, and morals, and voiced their concerns in unison, creating a foundation for the first socially conscientious consumer-driven programs. They translated their concerns and values through their purchasing decisions, and through their workplace. They began to organize again, this time in special interest groups, associations, alliances, initiatives, and programs both locally and nationally. They begin to influence again. This time they have the economic power to sustain the education they started 30 years ago. The new intelligent consumer was the political protester—the heart-motivated questioner, or the new ager of the 1970s and 1980s.

It is amazing how this took place. As trend analysis shapes and flows, it is important for all to recognize the passion and the commitment of this group known statistically as the baby boomers. As they enter middle age, and mellow with time, their principles of *what is right* will endure.

Social consciousness and social responsibility is the flower of the planet. It is growing in cities, towns, and states. It is growing in boardrooms, plants, factories, schools, and shops. The boomers brought to closure the Vietnam war. When their power and influence manifested in love and support of the Gulf War troops, that warm welcome home was an enlightened welcome for *all* U.S. men and women who served in the war.

The dropout, do-your-own-thing generation now has new battle cries: don't do drugs, stay in school, save the seals, and so on. Their names are the same, their faces have aged, their approach is more common sense solutions and less threatening. They still dress for themselves. But gone are the long hair and the tie-died T-shirts, sandals, and beards. Behind the modern look, however, lies the same heart of a still restless spirit finding and making a way home. Only now, the once rebuked capitalist is *them*.

They converted the parts of capitalism they did not like and retained the parts they did. Somewhere along the way, they realized that change came with a price tag. To afford change, they needed a device that could pay the price. Business became their answer.

Today, as I reflect back on the time when this new business phenomenon was beginning, I see images of health food shops, head shops, natural products, and early energy alternatives. I cannot help but feel sad that so many of these dreamers with their visions were pushed aside, put down, or even legislated against.

In the next chapter, we discuss icons and images, and the shaping of our minds. The contributors to growing enlightenment are many. The cast of contributors runs into the hundreds. Gone are the days of the street meetings and sit-ins for this group. The hawks are sleeping, the doves are in full flight.

The principles, values, and traditions of goodness and wellness are truly the answers of tomorrow—making the world aware that this group of now mellowing, stabilized, change agents has found a place in history. Maybe in a few hundred years, when other researchers attempt to find the seed that helped the world grow into a safe, sensible, and responsible planet, they will discover this group as originating those values and traditions.

In conclusion, I think it's safe to say that as a society we have experienced significant events in our lifetime. The result of the chaos, destruction, war, glitz, glamour and our personal search for fulfillment are all realities of our lifetime on this planet. Perhaps these forces have shaped us and allowed us to evolve to a more civilized state. Wars have proved one thing over the years—no one wins. The move beyond barbarianism is the quest of our future generations. The seeds of enlightenment are taking root and as a people we will benefit from their fruits. In the following chapters, we will demonstrate how this new enlightenment is being cultivated, nurtured, and influenced by literally thousands of soundbites, visual messages, influential role models, and we the American consumer who have chosen the path back towards a more meaningful co-existence with our world and the people in it. The American family lies at the center of our future. We are each responsible for our values, principles and behavior. Much is to be gained by integrating those same values and principles, once spoken of only in lofty terms, into our direct relationship with the businesses we run, manage or influence.

4

■

Icons and Images

■ INFLUENCING THE MASSES

The concept of demonstrating responsible actions and values is becoming very popular. The American public, who once had a love affair with the underdog, is now more inclined to support leaders. Those leaders have a powerful influence on how we think and behave. Today's leaders who demonstrate heightened social concern and awareness clearly draw more favor from the American public—good guys are in. Good guys that go beyond their occupational roles.

Many American icons and celebrities are acting as the messengers for peaceful political and social change and awareness. As pointed out in the 1991 Mass Mutual family values research study, much of our concept of values is reinforced by the celebrities and role models of our society. The American consumer is more inclined to believe a corporate message delivered by a celebrity spokesperson who they believe shares their common values. The measurement that is used in determining successful public relations programming is oftentimes defined by the popularity of the spokesperson and his or her known values. Therefore, the combination of social consciousness and corporate social responsibility go hand in hand. It seems that there is an increasing rise of social responsibility on the part of the sports, entertainment, and news media. Actors, athletes, and news anchors are showing up and involved in many socially relevant camps. As a result of their celebrity status, they attract the news media to those camps, thereby allowing the social message to be heard. Our celebrities are an intricate component to the success and popularity of many socially relevant matters. For celebrities, there is a valuable by-product for their interest—the cause oftentimes allows them to retain their presence (popularity) with the American public. One should not care whether the celebrities have a personal agenda. They are an effective means of building awareness for social commentary. The American business and the socially responsible celebrity can send a compelling message to the American public. The various media groups have also recognized that it would be the appropriate time for them to show responsibility. The news, sports, and entertainment media all are playing a vital role in disseminating information to the public concerning social matters. This tactic is resulting in support from the American viewing public.

In this chapter, we will look at just some of the many hundreds of celebrities who are speaking out and standing up for a better world. Many have direct initiatives and programs that the public may never be aware of.

■ CELEBRITY CHAMPIONS

Celebrities like this small group listed below are impacting society in very powerful ways:

- *Don Henley*, member of the 1970s rock group the Eagles, writes about the environment in his songs, and additionally, all profits from his book *Heaven Is Under Our Feet* (co-written with Dave Marsh) go to the conservation of Walden Pond, an historic property in New England.

■ *Paul Newman* took a simple salad dressing recipe to create Newman's Own, whose primary business mission was to set aside all profits to build a camp for children suffering from cancer. With his wife Joanne Woodward, he also established the Scott Newman Foundation, which developed the "All Babies Count" program.

■ *Robert Redford*, actor, director and producer, is the president of the Institute for Resource Management, which sponsored a conference on global warming with the Soviet Academy of Sciences in Sundance, Utah in 1989. He serves as a board member for both the Environmental Defense Fund and Natural Resources Defense Council. For his support of environmental issues, in 1987 he received the United Nations Global 500 award, and in 1989 the Audubon medal.

■ *Tom Cruise* developed a deep commitment to the environment when in 1989 he witnessed the uncontrolled destruction of the Amazon rain forests firsthand. He has served as master of ceremonies for Earth Day in Washington, D.C., keynote speaker for the entertainment industry's environmental conference and as a contributor to "Cry Out," an environmental booklet for children.

■ *Whoopie Goldberg* is known for her tireless humanitarian efforts on behalf of children, the homeless, human rights, substance abuse, and the battle against AIDS.

■ *Elizabeth Taylor*, who is devoted to AIDS-related issues and charities, developed with Elizabeth Arden a line of perfume called "Passion," with all of the profits going to support AIDS research.

■ *Richard Dreyfuss* initiated a community service clearinghouse in Los Angeles.

- *Willie Nelson* has been a champion for the small farmer in our society for over a decade. His Farm Aid program continues to be an effective voice for the dying breed of the American family farmer.

- *Ted Danson* and his wife Casey founded American Oceans Campaign after a 1987 trip to the beach where they found the water so polluted they could not swim. He is a member of the Walden Woods Project Advisory Board.

- *Kirstie Alley* is an actress as well as activist and environmentalist. After recovering from a pesticide poisoning, she led public protests against misuse and overuse of pesticides. She produced "Cry Out," a children's environmental booklet used across the country, and a national public service announcement radio campaign for the environment. She is founder of the Alley Foundation, dedicated to environmental education.

- *Michael Jordan* has created the Michael Jordan Foundation for children.

- *Bo Jackson* is in his second year as the honorary chair of The Children's Miracle Network.

- *Chi Chi Rodriguez* has a higher calling in life than his tremendous golf skills. He has created the Chi Chi Rodriguez Foundation for Children. This charismatic Peter-Pan splinter of a man has demonstrated an understanding and sensitivity for the disadvantaged children in our society.

- *Arnold Palmer* has quietly over the years been a driving force in the development of the Arnold Palmer's Hospital for Women and Children located at the Orlando Regional Medical Center in Orlando, Florida. He and many other touring golf professionals have come to the aid and support of charities throughout the country. The PGA tour alone has contributed over $200,000 million to worthwhile local and national charities in the last 20 years.

■ *Howie Long,* founder and director for the nonprofit group Athletes and Entertainers for Kids, spends a considerable amount of time in coordinating events and fundraising to support dozens of children's charities. Howie is representative of an ever increasing list of socially responsible athletes our young people can look up to.

■ *Kenny Loggins,* a tireless entertainer, gives freely of his time and efforts to support numerous children's charities and environmental education programs. Kenny, who may have written the anthem for this time of enlightenment in his song "Commitment of the Heart," continues to became a influential spokesperson of our time.

■ *Spike Lee,* writer and film producer of topical social issues, is also committed when the cameras aren't rolling. Spike, who works passionately with high-risk youths, has become a positive spokesperson on racial harmony.

■ *Phil Collins* is a dedicated and committed spokesperson for the homeless of our society. Phil has made not only significant financial contributions by using the proceeds of an album to benefit the homeless, but also tirelessly champions the cause through personal commitments.

■ *Magic Johnson* may be one of the most important spokespersons of our time. Magic's misfortune in being infected with the HIV virus may prove to be a single event that ultimately will save the lives of thousands of youths. In the light of Magic's tragedy, his courage and conviction go far beyond one's expectations. One of Magic's many activities since his diagnosis was the Nickelodeon Special Edition: "A Conversation with MAGIC," which was a conversation between Magic Johnson and a group of youngsters, ages 8 to 14, on AIDS-related issues and concerns.

- *Marie Osmond* founded The Children's Miracle Network with the assistance of John Schneider and honorary chairman Bob Hope. The concept was a national event that would join together children's hospitals and local television stations, and host a telethon. Children's Miracle Network raised over $100 million in 1992 alone.

- *Dave Winfield* for several years has had the Winfield Foundation for inner city youths.

- *Leonard Marshall*, a New York Giant, created a foundation for children with Leukemia.

- *Bob Lanier*, former NBA player, is the national chair of the NBA "Stay in School" program. Lanier, who has a life-long commitment to young people, delivers an inspiring and personal message of pride and self-esteem in visits with students across the country. To date, he has visited more than 300 schools in conjunction with the program.

Our fascination with our celebrities is a by-product of our American society. It is deeply gratifying to see that these highly successful and motivated individuals have moved beyond the perception of self, and developed a better understanding of their role in society and their effectiveness as positive spokespersons. From a strategist's perspective, awareness is the operative word for each social problem. Without it, no solutions can be forthcoming. American businesses understand the good guy image as well, and incorporate this into their advertising campaigns and promotions. Celebrities, whose talents and social enlightenment we have grown to respect, become highly prized spokespersons for American business's products and services. The affiliation of a product or services with a spokesperson that American consumers trust has a powerful and influential support to a product. The roles of our celebrities are important to our society as role models. We want to believe that they share in our principles and values. More and more celebrities are being very selective with their promotional support of companies who behave in a less than responsible manner. The role of the influential spokespersons is extremely important in building recognition for an issue. Our society in general will benefit from their voices and deeds. American business should find a valuable partnership with the icons of our society and collectively begin to focus on solutions. Each side of the partnership can benefit directly by incorporating the concept of philanthropic economics.

The following section is on America's love affair with television, the platform and medium primarily utilized by our icons and celebrities. Television and celebrities are an extension of one another. Each is seeking to demonstrate a higher degree of responsibility in current times.

■ TELEVISION—AMERICA'S PRIMARY INFORMATION SOURCE

Television and cable executives all over the country are beginning to recognize the powerful growing sentiment for values and socially relevant matters in our society. Their various divisions, including news, sports and programming, are beginning to make significant changes to their ideology. Television, whose primary role has been entertainment, is now expanding into the serious side of education and awareness.

The news departments and their various news media magazine formats, such as 60 Minutes, 48 Hours, 20/20, and Dateline, are allocating the majority of their broadcasting time in and around the concept of socially relevant subject matter. More often than not, the investigative nature of this style of reporting is less focused on corrupt business and practices or the criminal element in our society, and more focused on issues relevant to the homeless, the disadvantaged, the environment, education, and inner-city problems. The news departments have found a higher national rating with this subject matter, and as a result will obviously continue to provide socially relevant programming through their television magazine formats. Local news departments and personnel are also incorporating socially oriented themes and messages into their 30-minute time slots. Much of the news format is dedicated by current events with regional or local impacts. News departments are moving beyond the hard-edged news format of world events into world social issues.

Television shows continue to expand upon the popularity of socially relevant concerns in their programming as well. Many made-for-television movies are now developed around socially important issues such as child abuse, battered women, homelessness, AIDS education, racism, class barriers, and drug and alcohol abuse. Corporations that advertise with television commercials find favor with being identified as a sponsor when the programming segment contains socially relevant messages.

Cable television has also been a leader in the development of responsible programming. Turner Broadcasting in Atlanta has developed a format aired Sunday evening known as *Network Earth*. This environmentally driven programming attempts to address problems and solutions to the growing environmental concerns. Home Box Office (HBO) and its annual *Comic Relief* program special for the homeless is another example of effective cable television programming. The Discovery Channel is also directing its programming toward the enlightened consumer with documentary segments primarily dealing with the topics nature, conservation, and the environment. The Family Channel is programming exclusively to the general audience. Public Broadcasting System (PBS) continues to be a stalwart in the television media for engaging topics covering all aspects of social and cultural issues.

Television and its sponsors can prove to be a highly effective information source for the American public, and they should be acknowledged for their responsiveness. Negative television programming that exploits violence, racism, and sexism ultimately will not be popular with the sentiment growing in the American culture.

An opposing view of television would be the hypocrisy of its double-standard. Sex still strongly sells to the American public, and television programming and commercial advertisements have become an open forum for sexually explicit material. Unfortunately, the television industry still doesn't get it. There needs to be a responsible step taken that allows commercials that promote safe sex and condom use to be incorporated into their socially responsible formats. The American public deserves the right to promote and develop consciousness through this medium.

■ AMERICAN VALUES TRANSFERRED TO THE MOVIE SCREEN

The movie industry has also recognized the change in our ideology over the last several years. Much of their efforts are being directed towards socially relevant movies, as well as value and sentiment statement movies.

The success at the box office is being measured quite positively by our new appetite for old things. Nostalgia, values, traditions, and patriotism dominate the movie industry. An example of the new ideology follows: Imagine, if you will, standing in long lines to see a 3-hour movie with subtitles, where the Native Americans defeat the United States Cavalry. *Dances With Wolves*, directed by and starring Kevin Costner, with its huge box office success, is a reflection of our times. Producers and directors are perpetuating and continuing that theme in their selections to develop product.

We the consumers have also shown our love for the past in our response to the 1940s super hour characters. The recent box office success of movies such as *Batman*, *Dick Tracy*, *The Rocketeer*, *Indiana Jones*, and *Hook* (the Peter Pan movie) indicates a trend movement back to basic values. We are attempting to recapture our youth, when life seemed less complex and frustrating. Movies reflect our mindset.

Other subject matter dealing with social content is finding popularity. The blockbuster movies *Boyz in the Hood* by John Singleton, and *Do the Right Thing* by Spike Lee, are accurate portrayals of segments of our society under siege. Health-related movies like *Awakenings* and *Rainman* have drawn national attention to subject matter that was once pushed aside. The development of the General Audience ("G") rating is a positive response towards the issue of responsibility.

The impact of AIDS on the creative movie-making industry has awakened many new voices. The Academy Awards presentation of 1992 took on an aura of an AIDS benefit. This powerful and influential industry can do much to support social awareness through its development efforts. It should be noted that this too is an extension of the philanthropic economics concept. The popularity of these types of movies returns economic rewards to the industry stake holders. Again, my personal sentiment comes forth in an affirmative response that says these companies are doing well while doing good.

Independent film makers such as Oliver Stone have presented other subject matter important to our time. His movies reflect clearly on moral and ethical questions that to this day are disturbing. A biased, yet correct, assessment is reflected clearly in his efforts. Movies such as *Platoon* and *Born on the 4th of July* deal harshly with the realities of war and the society that engages in them. The movie *JFK* does more than simply create suppositions. It challenges each of us in a direct way about our role in society—to simply become more than sheep.

■ **CORPORATE MESSAGES REFLECT CONSUMER VALUES**

America's business has had an image overhaul by the nation's advertising and public relations community. It's been determined that if you want your message to at least be seen, if not heard and understood, you need to present it to the American public in a manner that they will respond to. Companies throughout the country have developed a format based exclusively around our values and sentiments. Product and service pitches now directly incorporate themes such as the environment, individuals with handicapped conditions, illiteracy, education, and pure emotional sentiment. Many companies are in fact behind those very images they project with company-driven initiatives to support the subject matter they portray in their advertisements. Other companies, however, are simply exploiting the opportunity to raise consumer confidence associated with the product and services through sugary imagery, when in fact their corporate initiatives stop with the advertising campaign. Public relations firms are the spin masters of this strategy. They create an artificial persona exclusively to create corporate gain. A good reputation is harder to come by than simply creating an illusion. American consumers and their growing intelligence will eventually discern fact from fiction. The end result for corporations that simply spin a message could be economic chaos.

Today, there are literally dozens of watchdog organizations whose primary purpose is to inform the American public of corporate hypocrisy. The Council of Economic Priorities (CEP) in New York City is one of those watchdog organizations, and if CEP places an "X" rating on a company, the company will lose much more than it gained financially from its misleading advertising.

Let's change the focus of this discussion back to the evolution in advertising towards values and sentiments. For purposes of this discussion we will look at the evolution of this method of advertising and replay for you some familiar themes.

This trend in advertising began with a highly successful Coca-Cola commercial featuring football legend Mean Joe Green. The commercial shows a young boy timidly handing a Coke to this huge, dirty, tired and battle-worn football player coming off the football field. Green takes the Coke, turns and begins to walk away, then calls the kid and throws him his game jersey. Clearly, the commercial's intent was to show a kinder and gentler side to this brute of a man, and the tenderness and sensitivity he experienced as a result of the gesture of the child. AT&T quickly followed suit with their very effective "reach out and touch someone" commercials, which usually highlighted a family or a relationship being re-ignited due to the power of the phone. Some commercials were so touching and effective they literally became 30-second melodramas.

Dupont shows firefighters saving a baby's life from a house fire. Slimfast is now using disabled athletes in television commercials. Budweiser Beer and its alcohol initiative commercial ("friends know when to say when") has a social responsibility message. FTD Florist has a global warming commercial. Even Bartles and James wine coolers successfully capitalize on a down-home value image.

Goodness and wholesomeness sells. The good guys get the greatest consumer support. American business was finding out that they could communicate with the American consumer directly through the consumer's heart and values.

■ CORPORATE PRINT ADVERTISEMENTS HAVE GREATER MESSAGES THAN PRICE, SERVICE AND QUALITY

American business has also brought its public image statements into its print advertising. Some messages are a direct statement, while others are wrapped in a subliminal sentiment or emotional image. These advertisements also reflect what the corporations who developed them want you to think about when you think of them. The following pages contain advertisements, reproduced with permission, illustrating the socially relevant messages incorporated into their product endorsements.

■ THE NBA "STAY IN SCHOOL" PROGRAM

An example of the sports media and marketing initiative is a league-sponsored effort on behalf of the National Basketball Association (NBA) and their program entitled Stay In School, which incorporates three significant components: 1) the use of athletes as icons; 2) the medium of sports; and 3) corporate sponsorship, to direct effective awareness campaigns to at-risk youths.

69

MATRIX ESSENTIALS, INC.—An environmentally oriented advertisement supporting national parks and conservation

70

XEROX CORPORATION IN AFFILIATION WITH POINTS OF LIGHT
FOUNDATION—Support for abused children's issues

The people at Xerox are experts at enlarging and reducing things. Just look what they've done for the child abuse problem in Kansas City.

Every hug, each bit of praise, every minute of one-to-one attention Xerox employees give the children at the Niles Home helps lessen the pain these abused children must suffer. But, more impor-

The Foundation is a non-profit, non-partisan organization founded in 1990 in hopes of encouraging community service. And like Xerox we are committed to solving serious social problems on a local level — with innovative solutions.

And although employees often donate time to these social programs during business hours, companies have reported only positive effects on their businesses, such as enhanced employee self-esteem and morale, and improved leadership and teamwork. Of course, without the support and par-

tant perhaps, is the impact their time and effort has on the battered children problem as a whole.

That's what Xerox Chief Executive Officer and President Paul Allaire had in mind when he helped pioneer Xerox's Community Involvement Program (XCIP) in 1974. XCIP provides a means to channel funds to employees for community projects.

Some of the social problems on which Xerox employees have already had meaningful impact are youth at risk, environmental problems, illiteracy, AIDS, and the disabled.

This is the kind of corporate activism that the Points of Light Foundation is hoping to promote.

ticipation of people such as Xerox's President and CEO, Paul Allaire, programs like these would never be possible. It takes the power only our nation's business leaders can provide to solve their communities' problems.

For more information on corporate involvement in community service, contact the Points of Light Foundation at 1-800-888-7700.

But please call us soon. Because although a program like Xerox's may be very difficult to duplicate, we would really like to help you try.

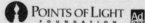

71

They are woven of simple cloth and common thread. Yet they have the power to turn struggle into courage.

Self-doubt into self-esteem. Indecision into leadership. But we're proud to support the Boy Scouts of America

for their enduring ability to perform the most magical metamorphosis of all. Transforming a boy into a man.

PHILLIPS PETROLEUM COMPANY

There are more than 120 merit badges in the Boy Scouts program, each marking an individual Scout's achievement. For more information about the Boy Scouts of America, please contact your local Boy Scouts council office.

BACK 2 BACK—Display advertisement supporting the
Make-A-Wish Foundation

Miles for Kids in Need Has New Partners

Over the past year, through the Miles for Kids in Need program, AAdvantage members have generously provided more than 1,500 airline tickets for needy children and their families. These tickets have provided them with the opportunity to make the trip necessary to receive life-saving medical treatment or make the wish of a lifetime come true.

Now, American Airlines is proud to announce that Variety Clubs International Children's Lifeline program and The Starlight Foundation have joined the Miles for Kids in Need program as participating charities. American and these two outstanding organizations will work together to ensure that miles donated by AAdvantage members continue to brighten the lives of seriously ill children and their families.

Variety Clubs International, established in 1927, supports hundreds of children and children's projects worldwide. Its Lifeline program provides medical treatment for children in countries where required medical treatment is not available.

The Starlight Foundation, founded in 1983 by actress Emma Samms and film executive Peter Samuelson, grants wishes for children who are chronically or critically ill. Many of these children are able to do things like meet their favorite entertainment or sports celebrities – whatever will bring happiness to a child who needs some.

When asked what this new alliance means to American Airlines, Michael W. Gunn, Senior Vice President-Marketing, explained that with AAdvantage members and the charitable organizations working as a team, we can improve the lives of even more children around the world.

Next month, you'll find an expanded AAdvantage Awards Claim Form on the back page of your Mileage Summary. This form will allow you to designate a donation of miles to the Starlight account, the Variety account or the Miles for Kids in Need general fund, which supports many children's charities.

You may donate in increments of 5,000 miles. For every three miles you donate, American Airlines will add another mile, making your gift go further toward helping make a difference in a child's life.

For more information about the Miles for Kids in Need program, call American Airlines at **1-800-882-8880**.

74

CENTEL CORPORATION—Children's oriented charities advertisment
(Copyright 1991, Centel Corporation, ad created by BBDO-Chicago)

Why a leading force in communications supports the driving forces in sports charity.

Our business is making people-to-people connections, with local telephone and cellular service. So what's our connection with golf? It's simply this: the future.

You see, the golfers who represent us, like Cindy Rarick, and the tournaments we sponsor are strongly behind many fine children's charities, including the Evans Scholars, Children's Miracle Network and the United Way. And we feel that putting young people in touch with a brighter future is the most important connection we can make.

CENTEL
WHERE PEOPLE CONNECT

© 1991 Centel Corporation

CONTINENTAL INSURANCE—Environmental advertisement
(Photo: Don Klumpp/Image Bank and John Pemberton.)

Oil spills are everybody's enemy. That's why a global oil giant has engaged Hull and Cargo Surveyors, Inc., a Continental subsidiary, to inspect its chartered tank barges and help avoid spills.

"We'll inspect some 2,000 vessels a year," says principal surveyor Stan Smith. *"We're the only nationwide marine service organization with that kind of expertise."*

Offering a wealth of marine inspection experience to Continental insureds and others, experts like Stan carefully check potential leak points such as cargo piping, valves and machinery. They pay special attention to pollution-control equipment such as containment booms, absorbent material and on-deck containment provisions. Because preventing spills on vessels is much better than cleaning them up on the beach.

Continental has a lot of dedicated people like Stan. People who are there when it counts. People who have helped make us a leading property/casualty insurer and a strong, solid company. They're why, for over 135 years, we've met our obligations to our insureds, our employees, our distributors and shareholders.

STAN SMITH HELPS KEEP OIL IN ITS PLACE.

Mrs. Morse's Students Learn That Math Really Is For The Birds.

With Sallie Morse as their guide, these seventh graders at Cool Springs Middle School in Forest City, North Carolina are exploring the wonders of nature through the lessons of math.

"The first thing my students learn is that the word 'math' is a verb," Sallie explains. "They *participate* in math."

Part of that participation centers around the study of birds. With a bird feeder hanging outside her classroom window, Sallie has devised a range of activities that teach and reinforce the students' math skills.

Using scales, the students experiment with ratios and proportions to formulate different seed mixes. They record information on the number of visitors to the feeder and their food preferences, using graphs to chart results. Finally, they compare temperature, humidity, and activity variables to make observations about the birds' feeding behavior.

"My students enjoy math," Sally says. "They speak it, calculate it and use it to expand their knowledge of the world. They participate in it and understand it. And thus, they love it."

State Farm is honored to present Sallie Morse with our Good Neighbor Award. We are also delighted to make a contribution of $5,000 to Cool Springs Middle School in her name.

Sallie Morse. Through innovative math techniques, she opens up new worlds for her students.

STATE FARM INSURANCE COMPANIES
Home Office: Bloomington, Illinois

Good Neighbor Award

The Good Neighbor Award was developed in cooperation with the National Council of Teachers of Mathematics (NCTM).

77

The "Stay in School" program was created in 1989 to address the critical issue of high school dropouts. Begun as a pilot program in conjunction with the NBA All-Star Weekend in Miami, the program utilizes NBA players—who are among the most recognized and respected heroes in sports—to urge young people to stay in school and complete their high school education. The NBA "Stay in School" program includes several national and local elements designed to deliver the "Stay in School" message to students, particularly those in middle school. The national program is sponsored by IBM, Nestle, and the Upper Deck Company.

The program's national elements include a series of televised public service announcements in which NBA stars encourage students to stay in school and a national tour by former NBA player Bob Lanier, the national chair of the program. Lanier, who has a lifelong commitment to young people, delivers an inspiring and personal message of pride and self-esteem in visits with students across the country. To date, he has visited more than 300 schools in conjunction with the NBA program.

On the local level, the program is focused on the host city of the NBA All-Star Game. The 1992 game was in Orlando, Florida. Middle school students in Orange and Seminole counties who maintained perfect attendance during the first semester were eligible to attend the national televised NBA All-Star Stay in School JAM at the Orlando arena. This third annual JAM featured top NBA players, celebrities, and musical guests who entertained while delivering the stay in school message. The JAM was telecast simultaneously by NBC, TNT, Nickelodeon, and Black Entertainment Television to an audience of 28 million households, including 13 million young people.

In addition, all NBA teams are involved in the "Stay in School" program or similar educational programs of their own. Many of the league's top players regularly contribute to delivering the message to their young fans. All 27 teams participated in the leaguewide NBA National "Stay in School" Awareness Day, October 30, 1991, by visiting a local middle school to urge students to finish their education. The NBA's efforts were recognized in a joint resolution of the United States' Congress, declaring October 30, "National Stay in School Day."

■ CONCLUSION

It should become clear to you that the advent of social consciousness is not likely to relent. When advertising media and high profile celebrities are positioned around the various social topics, a likelihood is that the American consumer will continue to receive information. As you choose your business strategy and examine your corporate ideology and culture, reflect back on the information source provided here. It should be obvious that if your business is directly supported by the American consumer, it would be in your best interest to learn more about this significant trend shift. If your business is directed towards businesses that ultimately affect the consumer, you as well need to learn. In market research and market analysis for target marketing, the emerging characteristics surrounding social matters will play an ever-increasing role in determining your market and sales strategy. The once definable stereotypical class categorization of the enlightened consumer has greatly broadened its perimeters to incorporate large and ever growing segments of the mainstream characteristics. Social responsibility is no longer an exclusive issue with what was once defined as the bleeding heart liberal. Americans throughout the country, in every segment, are stakeholders to the ultimate solutions.

5

■

Principles and Profits
The Path of the Enlightened Capitalist

As noted earlier, there is a clear distinction between the enlightened capitalist who is doing well while doing good and most other factions. He is more motivated by the heart than the head.

Enlightened capitalists are the extremists or purists of the philosophy. Their approach to their business is that it needs to do more than just make money—it needs to contribute to a better world. Their business also provides an economic/political platform from which they can expand on their personal philosophy of what's right.

They are entrepreneurs, which in itself defines them as typically passionate people with visions and dreams—all things are possible. Add to the typical entrepreneur a higher social calling, and this individual becomes the enlightened capitalist. Their motivations are twofold: build a business and change the world for better, or at least influence it. Be heard. Stand up. Put your money where your value is.

Ideals, principles, and ethics are the passwords when speaking to the enlightened capitalist. These individuals think in terms of cause and effect. Better than most, they see a direct correlation between their business and the community or world at large. They typically possess all the strength and all the shortcomings of the typical entrepreneur, but they also possess something else—the ability to inspire, to motivate, and to influence, all for the cause.

■ PASSION WITH PRINCIPLES

The enlightened capitalist is a unique categorization of a business person with a conscience. The following business profiles and the entrepreneurs themselves are different in a sense that conventional business wisdom would restrict adding a personal political agenda into a mainstream business. What enlightened capitalists once perceived as narrowly defined niche markets (targeting their product to specific markets with similar values of consumers who see the world the same way they do) have now received mainstream acceptance. I am sure that when their initial business strategies were developed, the perception of their business models would have been modest by today's standards. The acceptance by the mainstream of their business formulas allowed their companies to grow at unprecedented rates.

The enclosed success stories can teach American businesspeople that there is in fact room for political principles in business, while still providing price, service, and quality. This once perceived high-risk business strategy may very well become the business model of the future. The entrepreneurs themselves conjure up images of the 1960s and 1970s youth culture. They stand more on their principles and ideology than they do on a formal business policy. They are very much perceived as anti-conventional businesses. They proclaim their political concepts more often than their product. They behave as champions of their causes. This concept of business is foreign to the American public. The strategy, however, has helped the enlightened capitalists to position their businesses in a responsible way and at the same time to draw huge support from the American public. The typical American business would find their methods and practices totally unacceptable. The enlightened capitalist creates policies and practices that compensate work fairly in relationship to senior management. One such company has a policy whereby the president or senior managers can only earn as much as ten times the amount of the lowest paid worker. Enlightened capitalists greatly empower their people. They encourage cause-driven sabbaticals and volunteerism where the employee leaves the company for several weeks at full pay to work with various socially relevant nonprofit groups.

Enlightened capitalists incorporate conservation and environmental consciousness into the development of their products, even if the result is more costly to develop. All of the high-risk, politically sensitive conduct has been rewarded by the American public's acceptance of their principles and ideals. A short 20 years ago, such a company with attitudes and behaviors illustrated by today's enlightened capitalist would not have garnered such public support.

Therefore, as you read the profiles of the few companies we choose to highlight, clearly recognize that these companies have manifested their principles in a way that ultimately increased their financial performance. This emerging trend in American business is at the center of our concepts of philanthropic economics and doing well while doing good. This group has served as the inspiration within my company to alter our concepts of the American business owner. It has been our goal to emulate the effectiveness of this business approach. In Chapter 9 we will discuss how one begins the process of enlightened capitalism.

■ BEN AND JERRY: TURNING VALUES INTO VALUE

It all began in a junior high gym class in Merrick, Long Island. Two boys running around the athletic field had found a common bond. Ben Cohen and Jerry Greenfield hated running, but they loved food. In 1978, they decided to go into business together. With diplomas from a $5 correspondence course and their life savings ($8,000), they converted an abandoned gas station into the first Ben & Jerry's stand and started making Vermont's finest all natural ice cream. They used only fresh Vermont cream and milk and the best and biggest chunks of nuts, fruits, candies, and cookies. Before long, the lines for ice cream stretched out the door, and that was only the beginning. Ben and Jerry wanted to run a business that would share its rewards with its employees and with the community. To meet these goals, they set up the Ben & Jerry Foundation, which gives 7.5 percent of the company's pretax profits to nonprofit grass-roots organizations working for progressive social change. Its community services department is responsible for the tons of ice cream donations Ben & Jerry's makes every year. It's all part of Ben & Jerry's commitment to achieve goals outlined in the company mission statement which gives equal importance to the quest for excellence in product quality, economic success and active social responsibility to both local and global communities.

The company has grown to over $96.9 million in sales in 1991, with 90 franchises around the country. The company is known as much for its social conscience as its chunky, funky ice cream flavors. Ben & Jerry's was awarded the 1988 Corporate Giving Award from the Council on Economic Priorities. In 1989 it received the Columbia University Lawrence A. Wien Prize For Corporate Social Responsibility, made to corporations which make contributions of outstanding social significance and value on the national or local level.

Ben & Jerry's philosophy is described in general terms through its mission statement. Specific initiatives will be explored in some detail. First, the mission statement:

Ben & Jerry's is dedicated to the creation and demonstration of a new corporate concept of linked prosperity. Our mission consists of three interrelated parts:

1. *Product mission:* To make, distribute, and sell the finest quality, all-natural ice cream and related products in a wide variety of innovative flavors made from Vermont dairy products.

2. *Social mission:* To operate the company in a way that actively recognizes the central role that business plays in the structure of society by initiating innovative ways to improve the quality of life of a broad community—local, national, and international.

3. *Economic mission:* To operate the company on a sound financial basis of profitable growth, increasing value for our shareholders and creating career opportunities and financial rewards for our employees.

Underlying the mission of Ben & Jerry's is the determination to seek new and creative ways of addressing all three parts, while holding a deep respect for the individuals, inside and outside the company, and for the communities of which they are a part.

The various initiatives underway at Ben & Jerry's illustrate how this mission is being carried out.

Environment Program

Ben & Jerry's has three "Green Teams" coordinated by the company's environmental program development manager. The Green Teams are responsible for assessing the company's impact on the environment in all areas of operation. They develop and implement projects and programs to compensate for any environmental impact. The company's goal is to be 100 percent involved in responsibly managing our solid waste stream, conserving energy and resources, exploring sustainable renewable energy sources, and developing environmentally beneficial community outreach programs. The following is a summary of what Ben & Jerry's is currently doing when it comes to being an environmentally responsible business.

Products and Packaging

- Rainforest Crunch ice cream indirectly benefits rainforest preservation.

- Peace Pop boxes have been switched from virgin to recycled paperboard.

- Research is ongoing to move to recycled and recyclable materials for other packaging.

The Company Waste Stream

- A pilot solar aquatics waste water treatment program was established.

- The company recycles and reuses 100,000 pounds of plastic egg yolk pails annually.

- Liquid nitrogen is being considered as an alternative to freon (a noted greenhouse gas) for use on ice cream trucks.

- High-density polyethylene water and flavoring jugs are recycled.

- The company reuses or bales and recycles corrugated cardboard.

- Company-owned scoop shops, manufacturing facilities, and offices recycle ingredient containers and plastic cutlery.

- The company recycles white office ledger, mixed color, and bonded paper, magazines, newspapers, and plastic film.

- Some shredded newspapers and office paper are reused as animal bedding and packing materials.

- Company stationery and copier, computer, and laser printer paper are unbleached, 100 percent recycled.

- Double-side copies are made whenever possible.

- Laser printer toner cartridges are recycled.

- Printer ribbons are reinked.

■ Promotion posters, brochures, annual reports, and book covers are printed on recycled paper with water-based inks.

■ Soybean-based inks are used where possible, and research is being done on ways to increase their application.

■ Office pens are refillable.

■ Art Department stat chemicals are recycled and silver is recovered from the process.

■ The company encourages the use of reusable dishes and flatware in the lunchroom.

■ All paper towels and bathroom tissue have recycled content, and continuous roll hand towels are used where possible.

■ Sanitary production uniforms are delivered without the customary plastic covering.

■ Holiday greeting cards are recycled.

■ The viability of a companywide composting program is being investigated.

Energy Conservation Issues

■ The company has established a goal of reducing electrical consumption per unit of production by 25 percent over the next five years.

■ Ongoing energy audits are conducted at the Waterbury and Springfield, Massachusetts, manufacturing plants.

■ A newly implemented energy conservation program at the Waterbury plant could save as much as $250,000 per year.

■ Lighting has been improved by using compact fluorescent lights. Motion detectors are used in some areas to turn off lights automatically in unoccupied rooms.

■ Numerous control devices on plant equipment (such as high-efficiency motors) have been installed to help conserve energy.

■ The company is researching higher-efficiency refrigeration systems and the use of outdoor air in wintertime for refrigeration.

■ The company is working on a co-generation project to increase energy efficiency.

■ The company is working on converting mobile ice cream sampling trucks to ˈphotovoltaic-powered refrigeration; they already have one unit on the road.

■ The company has funded a solar energy demonstration vehicle.

■ The company has taken a stand against completion of the James Bay II project and further development of Hydro Quebec.

Community Outreach

■ The company sponsors and supports Vermont's Merry Mulching program to recycle Christmas trees into mulch.

■ The company participates in a paint drop and swap program (reusing paints and solvents).

■ The company will be holding a similar used-tire drop and swap.

■ The Employee Community Fund Committee distributes grants to local environmental efforts.

■ The proceeds from Ben & Jerry's annual "Green Flea Market" go to the Environmental Federation of America.

■ In conjunction with 17 other companies, Ben & Jerry's is participating in a campaign to encourage customers to support a congressional bill calling for an increase in auto fuel efficiency standards to 40 miles per gallon by the year 2000. To date, 60,000 cards have been sent to Congress in support of this bill.

■ Ben & Jerry's New Vaudeville Light Circus Bus, which criss-crossed the United States throughout 1991 with age-old variety entertainment, was topped with 180 square feet of solar photovoltaic cells. This natural energy source powers the bus's freezers, sound system, and lights. While entertaining crowds, the New Vaudevillians also distributed literature to educate people about solar energy.

Corporate Mandates

Support of the Children's Defense Fund's 1992 Leave No Child Behind Agenda

Ben & Jerry's believes that unless Congress uses military savings to make significant new investments in programs that have proven to be effective for children, government budgets will pit children's basic needs against other domestic programs, once again leaving children on the margins of American domestic policy. American children will continue to fall behind their peers at home and abroad, further undermining the nation's ability to compete and lead in an increasingly competitive world economy.

To help get this message to members of Congress, the administration, candidates for public office, and the American people, the Children's Defense Fund and Ben & Jerry's Homemade, Inc., will cooperate in a nationwide public education campaign to put children's needs at the top of the national agenda.

The "Leave No Child Behind" public education effort, begun in February 1992, features store and packaging promotions, community festivals in several major cities, and a traveling circus bus. By increasing public awareness of the crisis faced by America's children and families, the campaign also reminds the public that there is a solution.

As a first step, Ben & Jerry's ice cream stores in 18 states and the District of Columbia provided valentines which franchise stores mail from customers to individual members of Congress. The valentines ask congressional representatives to "Have a Heart" and support policies "that redirect Pentagon spending toward the well-being of our children and ensure that we Leave No Child Behind."

The Children's Defense Fund's Leave No Child Behind seeks a guarantee by Congress and political leaders—of every party and at every level of government—of a Healthy Start, a Head Start, and a Fair Start for every child. Specifically:

- *A Healthy Start for every child:* Every child and pregnant woman must have health coverage now. Congress must also assure that health insurance is not meaningless and that access is real by increasing funding for community and migrant health centers and the National Health Services Corps and assuring that all children are fully immunized.

- *A Head Start for every child:* Assure that funding for Head Start is guaranteed so that every eligible child—not just 4-year-olds—can participate.

- *A Fair Start for every child:* Assure that every child's family has the resources to provide for his or her basic needs, including incomes from jobs at decent wages, a refundable children's tax credit, and child support payments.

"We want to make sure that peacetime is a happy time for kids," said Ben Cohen, Ben & Jerry's chair and chief executive officer. "We have a great opportunity and responsibility to redirect spending from the military to human needs, especially the needs of children."

Said company co-founder Jerry Greenfield, "We firmly believe that business has a responsibility to give back to the community and that children are the future of the community."

"Children cannot vote, lobby, or send campaign contributions to members of Congress, but children can send a valentine, and what they ask in return is a little courage," said Marian Wright Edelman, president of the Children's Defense Fund. "It doesn't take courage for a member of

Congress to tell his own child he loves her, but apparently it takes courage for a member of Congress to love other people's children. These desperate times for children and their families require courageous, bold solutions. Tinkering at the margins will have no effect and will cost America its competitiveness, productivity, and safety. None of us can afford to have our nation's children and future neglected once again in this budget cycle."

New Feature Flavor and Profitable Partnership for Urban Disadvantaged

Ben & Jerry's ice cream and Greyston Bakery of Yonkers, New York, are combining business resources and commitments to social change to produce Ben & Jerry's new feature flavor, Chocolate Fudge Brownie, and establish a profitable way for business to help empower people without homes.

Greyston Bakery is part of the larger Greyston Community Network which reinvests profits into programs designed to provide people without homes, and people close to that situation, with housing, job training, child care, and counseling. "We've been able to employ, full-time, fifteen people, who were previously unemployed or underskilled, to produce the brownies that Ben & Jerry's needs for Chocolate Fudge Brownie," says Bernie Glassman, founder of Greyston Bakery. "Our relationship with Ben & Jerry's supports our holistic approach to making a change in the homeless situation." The Greyston Bakery will be supplying Ben & Jerry's with 30,000 pounds of brownies a month for the flavor. Glassman says that will increase Greyston's annual income by $750,000.

"We're always looking for opportunities to integrate positive social change into our day-to-day business activities," says Fred "Chico" Lager, president of Ben & Jerry's. "We want to show people that you can do well at business while doing good in the community. Our relationship with Greyston and the work they're doing with the homeless is a good example of that." Ben Cohen and

Greyston founder Bernie Glassman met at a Social Venture Conference in 1986. Subsequent discussions between them resulted in the two putting ice cream, brownies, and social philosophies together.

An Alternative to Razing the Rainforest

Showing that tropical rainforests are more profitable when harvested than when devastated by logging and ranching, Ben & Jerry's introduces Rainforest Crunch ice cream, flavored with a buttercrunch that uses nuts harvested in the rainforest.

Ben & Jerry's is buying Rainforest Crunch candy from Community Products, Incorporated (CPI), of Montpelier, Vermont. CPI is buying the Brazil nuts and cashews used in the buttercrunch through Boston-based Cultural Survival, a nonprofit organization working as an advocate for the world's native peoples. In addition, CPI distributes 40 percent of the profits from Rainforest Crunch to rainforest preservation groups and international environmental projects. Another 20 percent of the profits goes to 1 Percent For Peace, a nonprofit organization advocating legislation to reallocate 1 percent of the U.S. Defense budget to fund programs promoting peace through understanding.

"Business and economics have been the root cause of destroying the rainforests," says Ben Cohen. "What we're doing here with Rainforest Crunch is using business and the marketplace to turn things around and help preserve the rainforests."

Ben & Jerry's has adopted a three-point mission statement of product, economic, and social goals. "This is a great example of putting our mission of caring capitalism to work," says Fred "Chico" Lager. "We're buying 20,000 pounds of Rainforest Crunch candy a month from CPI, which means they're buying 12,000 pounds of rainforest nuts a month to supply our demand. It's a great flavor, and it makes rainforest preservation profitable for everyone."

CPI co-manager Martha Broad is pleased with the way the buttercrunch candy is selling. "Rainforest Crunch has really taken off, and Ben & Jerry's is the biggest customer. As things stand today, we've created an additional demand for 300,000 pounds of rainforest nuts each year. Plus, in our first full year of operation, we'll be able to donate $25,000 to forest harvesters. It's a small part of solving a big problem, but it is building."

Newest Flavor Supports Native American Business

The Passamaquoddy Indians of Maine and Ben & Jerry's Ice Cream are doing business together to produce Ben & Jerry's latest feature flavor, Wild Maine Blueberry.

"Wild Maine Blueberry is another step in how we're defining what caring capitalism is all about," said Ben Cohen. "Our goal is to integrate concern for the community in every business decision we make. We're trying to develop a system that improves the quality of life through socially conscious purchasing of our ingredients. The brownies in Chocolate Fudge Brownie benefit the employment of underskilled persons, the nuts in Rainforest Crunch benefit the preservation of the rainforest, the peaches in Fresh Georgia Peach support family farms, and the blueberries in Wild Maine Blueberry support traditional Native American economy," Cohen said.

The Passamaquoddy Indians have gained national attention as a Native American community that has set up a diversified successful economy. Agriculture is a traditional element of the Indian economy, and when it comes to the Passamaquoddies, blueberries are a big part of that. Ben & Jerry's is making 80,000 gallons of Wild Maine Blueberry with over 50 tons of blueberries from the Passamaquoddy fields.

"And the great thing about mixing wild blueberries, which are sweeter than domestic, with Vermont's Finest All Natural, is that you get an incredible ice cream," Cohen said.

"It takes 400 to 600 rakers two to three weeks to harvest about 1,800 acres of wild blueberries," says tribal member and company manager Francis "Bibby" Nicholas.

The basis for these initiatives is better understood by looking to the underlying philosophies on which Ben & Jerry's was founded:

Chairperson's Letter[1]

The most amazing thing is that our social values—that part of our company mission statement that calls us to use our power as a business to improve the quality of life in our local, national and international communities—have actually helped us to become a stable, profitable, high growth company.

This is especially interesting because it flies in the face of those business theorists who state that publicly held corporations cannot make a profit and help the community at the same time, and moreover that such companies have no business trying to do so.

The issues here are heart, soul, love and spirituality.

Corporations which exist solely to maximize profit become disconnected from their soul—the spiritual interconnections of humanity. Like individuals, businesses can conduct themselves with the knowledge that the hearts, souls and spirits of all people are interconnected; so that as we help others, we cannot help helping ourselves.

It makes no sense to compartmentalize our lives-to be cutthroat in business, and then volunteer some time or donate some money to charity. For it is business that is the most powerful force in our society. Multinational corporations are the most powerful force in the world—stronger even than nation states.

---

[1]   Ben & Jerry's 1990 Annual Report.

So, if business is the most powerful force in the world, it stands to reason that business sets the tone for our society. No-profit organizations and charities cannot possibly accomplish their objectives if business does not use its power to help people.

The wonderful thing is that despite Ben & Jerry's avowedly and unabashedly populist leanings, you, our shareholders, continue to support us. I am proud to say that the employees of Ben & Jerry's are finding ways to help make money and help people at the same time. Once you start figuring out how to put these things together, the old way just doesn't make sense anymore.

We are grateful that you have invested your money in us, and we will do our best to make that investment a profitable one for all of us."

Conclusion

Ben & Jerry's is committed to making its social vision an integral part of the fabric of our day-to-day business mission. Social considerations are as important in its decision-making processes as are product quality and financial considerations. The goal is for all employees to own this idea and to be a part of the way the company makes decisions and plans. This mission encompasses everything from how one states what one believes about the great issues that face humanity to how Ben & Jerry's treats its employees.

To make this commitment a reality, companies need to be better at setting goals—social goals that are set in each department, as well as larger social goals for the entire company. By setting such goals, they can evaluate and hold themselves accountable for their performance, using agreed-upon standards of measurement.

Ben & Jerry's is also committed to the process of social performance reporting. It feels it owes it not only to itself, but to the public as well, to provide information that indicates whether it is succeeding at doing what it says it will. Its efforts at social performance reporting are imperfect—they reflect the need to develop specific goals in this area and to keep more useful records of work in the areas to measure performance.

As Ben & Jerry's social goals become clearer, everyone with a stake in this company—employees, customers, shareholders, suppliers, and the entire community—will share in the growing vision of business as a means to make the world a better place.

■ THE BODY SHOP

The power of believing is perhaps typified best by dynamic Anita Roddick, founder of The Body Shop, a model company that embraces myriad socially relevant issues. Anita's rags-to-riches rise to prominence is a marvel, but the how and why of The Body Shop's success is only part of the story.

Anita Roddick is one who would see the effect that the ocean tides have on ships—when the tide comes in, all the ships rise. Ms. Roddick has raised the tide of social consciousness in the entire business world. This outspoken advocate of change has clearly demonstrated that a company can be built not in spite of environmental consciousness, but because of it.

Anita is no latecomer to the area of corporate and social responsibility. She may even be the mother of it. In 1976 social responsibility was not in vogue. Quite the contrary. Most companies were fighting legislative mandates and controls, seeing only the threat of new costs related to compliance. While most looked at the down side, Anita saw only the up side. The spirit of "do it right," "do it first" did not frighten this housewife with two young children from the beginning of her adventure. Anita's success is based on common sense. She prides herself on being the consummate consumer—do what makes the most sense, don't oversell, don't make promises you can't keep, admit when you've made mistakes, and then fix them. Build in an approach to business that does not nag at your conscience, that is not destroying the planet, or its animals, that leaves people better off, and success is a given. This feisty entrepreneur decided to boldly go where most feared to tread. She turned a problem into a project.

The cosmetic industry seemed to be an unlikely place for Anita, with all its glitz, glamour, and promises of the fountain of youth. Anita's vision of the body led her to approach the industry from a different perspective. The Body Shop vision was to develop a full range of cosmetic products, including bath oils, milk baths, bath salts, shower gels, vegetable-based facial cleansers, sun screens, and fragrances—all to be made from natural, organic substances. A worldwide search for herbs and formulas was launched. Using natural methods to make cosmetic products fit nicely into a huge niche that women of the world were ready for. Anita carried this natural formula into every part of The Body Shop environment.

Anita's pursuit was more a statement of philosophy than a defined business plan, however. This philosophy would persist, overriding more conventional ways of conducting business. Her philosophy was coupled with typical first-phase business constraints, that is, capital, resources, credit, and specific knowledge. Anita was facing the realities every entrepreneur does, and the operative word for success is *resourcefulness*. With each step she defied conventional wisdom and solidified the strategy. Anita did not have the luxury of extensive planning or strategizing. She had to work through the process, so that she might discover who she could become and how this would shape the business of The Body Shop. Anita is not a glamour girl, so her business did not project or try to sell that image. Instead, her business reflected her values and approach to life. Building a business to make a profit and doing it in the way that allowed her to make a statement about her strong feelings led to success. Anita had engaged the concept of philanthropic economics. As her business formula took hold, so did her activism.

First on her agenda of challenges was her environmental mission. She wrapped herself and her business in the color green. She began recycling her plastic bottles with her customers; she would have them bring back empties and she would refill them. Paper recycling was next, as she wanted to find every creative way to hold down on paper use and waste. Today, The Body Shop utilizes handmade paper from Nepal, which uses materials like water hyacinth and banana to make paper, instead of the traditional tree. The project embraces traditional skill, provides employment in Nepal, and produces great products to sell.

Next were animal rights and animal testing. She refused to use products or by-products of animals in any of her cosmetic formulas; even the company's product testing would not include animals.

The rainforests are also a passionate concern of Anita's. The Body Shop linked with the British Trust for Conservation, and they had volunteers plant a tree for every bottle brought in to be refilled during a two-week period. By March 1991, 23,574 trees were planted. This carried into the U.S. mail-order business. Anita states her mission, "I think you can trade ethically, be committed to social responsibility and global responsibility, empower your employees without being afraid of them. I think you can re-write the book on the way a business can be run."

The Body Shop is a testament to one woman's vision and courage to pursue two goals at once—build a business and make a difference in society.

A Company Profile

Anita Roddick opened the first branch of The Body Shop in 1976 in Brighton, England. Today, there are more than 700 stores worldwide, from the Arctic to Australia, from Jeddah to Japan. They trade in 40 countries in 19 languages, and their numbers are growing.

About The Body Shop

- The company is based in Wick, England, near Littlehampton, West Sussex, where it operates from

320,000 square feet of warehousing and production space.

- It employs more than 5,850 people worldwide (1,850 in its own shops and offices; another 4,000 staff are employed by franchises).
- It expands through franchising. The first franchise was granted in 1977. Of 203 stores in the United Kingdom, 158 are franchises.

About the Products

- The Body Shop originally sold just 15 products. Today it sells more than 350, and the range is constantly evolving.
- Its color cosmetic range, called Colourings, was launched in September 1986.
- Mostly Men, a collection of skin and hair care products designed specifically, but not exclusively, for men, debuted in November 1986.
- Mamatoto, The Body Shop's comprehensive range of mother-to-be and baby products, was launched in the United Kingdom in September 1990 and in the United States in September 1991.
- Products that contain sustainable ingredients from the rainforests in Brazil are being developed and will be launched in 1992.
- The Body Shop has no advertising overhead and uses minimal packaging so the cost of the product is low compared with those products of similar quality and efficiency produced by other cosmetic companies.
- Unlike many major cosmetic brand-name products, The Body Shop's products contain a relatively high base of natural ingredients. For example, the Aloe Vera range contains as much as 98 percent pure aloe gel. Cocoa Butter Suntan Lotion is 13 percent cocoa butter.
- Anita Roddick and her anthropologists are constantly traveling, watching, and talking to women and men in other cultures to find out how they care for their

skin and hair. It is the combination of this traditional wisdom and modern scientific research that makes her work innovative and effective.

Profits

■ On April 16, 1984, The Body Shop went public with a placing price of 95p. On the first day of trading shares traded at £1.42. The company is known in the City, London's equivalent of Wall Street, as the "share that defied gravity."

■ Market value stands at approximately $850 million. Figures for the 12-month period ending February 28, 1991 show annual sales at $196.5 million (a 37 percent increase). Pretax profits rose 38 percent to $34.1 million.

Principles

The company's worldwide network is founded on a simple, honest approach to doing business. The company believes profit and principles must go hand in hand:

■ All the products do is cleanse, polish, and protect the skin and hair. The Body Shop makes no promises about rejuvenation; it promotes health rather than beauty.

■ The products are based on natural close-to-source ingredients whenever possible.

■ Ingredients or final products are not tested on animals.

■ The company operates under a strict environmental code. A refill service is available in every shop to conserve packaging and to promote reuse, all products are biodegradable, postconsumer waste is recycled, and recycled paper is used for everything.

■ Ingredients and products are obtained in an un-patronizing, nonexploitative manner.

■ The Body Shop has 475 community projects operating around the world.

■ Since 1976, 19 public education campaigns have been run in the firm's shops.

Awards

Anita and her company have won numerous awards: 1985 Business Woman of the Year; 1899 Anita Roddick OBE in the New Year's Honors List; 1988 Communicator of the Year; 1989 Retailer of the Year; 1989 United Nations' Global 500 Award; 1990 Queen's Award for Export; 1990 Sussex Business Awards' Company of the Year and Community Award; and 1991 Environmental Management Award, Better Environmental Awards for Industry.

The Body Shop at Home

■ The Body Shop invests time and resources to educate its staff as well as its customers. The company's London-based retail operations building is the site of its training school, founded in 1986. In addition to product, retail and communication training, the school promotes the company's values and motivates staff.

■ Soapworks is a 36,000-square-foot soap-making plant based in the Queenslie Industrial Park, Easterhouse, Glasgow. The Body Shop set up Soapworks to make the majority of the company's soaps. A trust fund was formed, and 25 percent of Soapworks' profits are plowed into the community. The factory currently employs more than 100 residents of the Easterhouse housing projects.

■ The company has created its own Community Projects Department to take action on a spectrum of issues connected with the environment in its widest sense.

■ The Body Shop employees and franchisees are encouraged to be active in their community by giving talks to local schools; helping out in hospitals; spending time with special groups of people, such as the elderly, the homeless, and the handicapped; and providing work experience for young people. Employees are allowed as much as a half day of company-paid time every four weeks to participate in these activities.

The Body Shop Abroad

- The Body Shop trades in the Third World in an unpatronizing and nonexploitative manner, encouraging local communities and developing countries to grow ingredients and make products for the company. This in turn provides employment and trade. Examples of "Trade not Aid" projects include a papermaking project in Nepal and an ingredient-sorting project in Brazil's Amazon Basin which will help protect both the rainforest and its inhabitants.

- The Body Shop has a larger presence abroad than any other British retailer.

- In November 1990, the company announced that, for the first time in its history, total retail sales from all shops in the United Kingdom were exceeded by retail sales in its overseas markets.

- The Body Shop's international business now provides 35 percent of group sales.

- The Body Shop has begun expanding into the United States. There are currently 78 U.S. shops, and this number is increasing rapidly. Sixty more are scheduled to open by November 1992.

The Future

None of the markets in which The Body Shop operates has yet reached the saturation point. The United Kingdom alone could support 250 outlets. On a global scale, the potential is virtually limitless. The concept of The Body Shop obviously crosses national frontiers with ease!

■ ESPRIT DE CORP

Esprit de Corp, one of the giants of the trendy clothes industry, was founded by two "children of the 1960s" and is now run by one of them, Susie Tompkins. It has a reputation as a socially responsible company, a reputation which has been strengthened by a recent advertising campaign. In a series of print and broadcast ads, average Esprit wearers respond to the question, "What would you do?" The company said that part of the purpose of the campaign was to involve young people in important issues facing the world. Esprit's mission sets the tone for all its activities: "Be informed. Be involved. Make a difference. The mission of Esprit is to live our values."

Esprit puts its money and time where its mouth is. It has a department called the "Eco Desk," which coordinates environmental and community affairs. The Eco Desk runs the Esprit de Corp, an innovative volunteerism program that matches employee time with paid time off. An Esprit employee can receive up to ten paid hours off per month to volunteer, provided he or she volunteers an equal amount of personal time. Employees can also apply for grants to the organizations for which they volunteer. On Earth Day, employees are given a day off from work in exchange for their time spent on volunteer projects, most focusing on Earth Day themes.

In addition to encouraging individual volunteer efforts, Esprit organizes groups to participate in community outreach programs. These range from environmental activities on Earth Day to renovating community centers. Esprit volunteers worked with the San Francisco Education Foundation to produce the 1991 "Circo della Terra," a show "starring 500 San Francisco school children." The "Circo" was designed to expose children to the arts and develop their creative abilities.

■ MCKESSON CORP.

McKesson is the nation's largest drug distributor. It also produces bottled water and owns a majority stake in Armor All car products. It has been involved with schools in the San Francisco Bay Area and has strong programs to encourage employee volunteerism, which it describes in the report "McKesson in the Community: Why We Do What We Do."

McKesson's Community Action Fund was established to "encourage employees and retirees to exert constructive influence in community affairs." All full-time and retired employees who have worked one year at the company are eligible if they volunteer at least 10 hours per month and have done so for at least six months. Spouses are also eligible if they put in 15 hours each month. Eligible employees and spouses can request funds from the McKesson Foundation to support the organization for which they volunteer. The foundation provides grants between $50 and $1,000 to be used for specific projects. Another program, the Community Action Team Fund Grant, gives from $500 to $5,000 to organizations for which five or more employees and/or retirees volunteer. McKesson also presents the Neil Harlan Award for Community Service to an outstanding employee volunteer. This award includes a grant of $300 to $5,000 to the employee's nonprofit of choice.

The other major part of McKesson's community involvement is the Youth Development Project. This project involves two local high schools, a Christian youth organization and McKesson employees. Alamo Park High School is an alternative school for students who have had academic or legal problems, and Mission High School has mostly Hispanic and Asian students from immigrant families, as well as students from "underemployed working class families." McKesson has demonstrated an interest in assisting these students in overcoming a variety of obstacles, including social and career problems. Some examples of this interest: the company organized an antidrug pledge for the class of 1990 at Mission High; the Learning Exchange, a tutoring/mentoring and cultural exchange program; and a summer hiring program. McKesson has also contributed funds to various Bay Area educational groups.

A local publication named McKesson one of "The Best Companies for Kids in the Bay Area," citing its community volunteers and education/training programs. In 1991, the National School Association honored McKesson with an Exemplary School Support Award, and California Business presented the company with an Excellence in Education award. The Drug Enforcement Agency recognized its antidrug efforts with a Certificate of Appreciation in 1990.

■ SALAD KING SALAD DRESSING

Among the pioneers to have their roots planted in cause-related marketing, before it was known as that, were Paul Newman and his wife Joanne Woodward. Their motives were incredibly unselfish. According to Paul Newman, the story goes that at the completion of the award-winning film, *Butch Cassidy and the Sundance Kid*, Paul received a recipe for salad dressing that was in Butch Cassidy's possession at one of his arrests, with a note from Butch himself that stated, "This stuff is so good it ought to be outlawed." Paul decided that he and an associate, writer A. E. Hotenner, would test the product under the label "Newman's Own" with the provision that all profits would go to children in need. Paul and Joanne's dream was to create a camp for children with life-threatening diseases, a place they could go and just be normal kids. The Newmans knew about tragedy. They had just lost their son, Scott, at a young age. The success of Newman's Own initially was thought to be just the curious shopper who loved the idea of Paul Newman's screen image. To the delight and maybe surprise of everyone, Newman's Own began to chip away market share from other more famous salad dressing brands. The media loved the story. Clearly, Newman's Own benefited from a public relations surge not provided to most new products. What was motivating the customers to buy Newman's Own? Was it the steely blue eyes of Paul Newman or the more meaningful mission he had embraced—the children?

Newman's Salad King of Westport, Connecticut, is now an extremely successful company whose roots were planted in a mission of hope and heart. To date, Newman's Own has contributed over $40 million of company profits to various children's charities throughout the country.

■ STONYFIELD FARM, INC.

Stonyfield Farm, Inc., was founded in 1983 with two goals: (1) to produce the purest, most natural and nutritious yogurts available and (2) to encourage consumers' support of family farmers and local agriculture in the northeastern United States. Stonyfield Farm signed the Valdez principles (a 1989 response to the Exxon Valdez oil spill, the Coalition for Environmentally Responsible Economies (CERES) established 10 commitments to a healthy and sustainable environment, and pledged to uphold the principles by using only environmentally friendly policies and methods, and to submit an annual progress report to the public) and participates in ACT-NOW (a group of companies working together to create positive social and environmental changes, delivering their message to consumers via product labels and packaging, promotional inserts, and space in mail-order catalogues). *Business Ethics* magazine awarded Stonyfield a Business Ethics Award in 1990 for its "commitment to nutrition, sustainable agriculture, and support of family farmers."

The company pays a premium for milk, helping to support local farmers. Stonyfield uses refillable containers for fruit, its yogurt cases are made from recycled fiberboard, and it estimates that 40 to 50 percent of the paper it uses is recycled. Although its yogurt containers are plastic, the lids are currently recyclable in many cities nationwide. The company actively researches developments in the plastic industry, discussing the dilemmas of providing environmentally friendly packaging openly with its customers through its company newsletter.

Stonyfield's company objectives include "serving as a model that environmentally and socially responsible businesses can also be profitable." It publishes a semiannual newsletter about nutrition, agriculture, and ecology.

The company also offers an "Adopt-a-Cow" program. A customer who sends in five Stonyfield Farm yogurt lids gets a picture of a cow, an adoption certificate, and a chance to visit the cow. The company sends a complete bio on the cow, how she's been brought up, who her parents are, what her farmers are like, what she eats, and what goes on in her life. Originally, this was an idea to teach children more about agriculture, but the program has been successful for people of all ages.

The company states that it would increase gross margins by 5 percent by using sugar in its product, but instead it sweetens its yogurt with fruit juice, which Stonyfield maintains is nutritionally superior.

■ AVEDA CORPORATION

Aveda Corporation manufactures skincare, haircare, and household cleansers, and is also one of the world's largest manufacturers of perfume, which they call Purefume.

All of their products are derived from 1,500 different species of plant essences and distilled flowers. Using organically grown materials, and their extensive clinical research, they were able to develop the first natural preservative. This patented preservative system is derived from specific plants and flowers that control bacteria, yeast, and fungus. They are the only company that can boast no petro-chemicals, which are very dangerous pollutants. They use all renewable resources for sustainable agriculture and growth. Their in-house corporation practices energy and waste reduction. The average company in America has 70 percent waste, while they are at 12 percent, trying to get to zero. Aveda was the first to sign the Valdez Principles.

Aveda's founder, Horst Rechelbacher is also the originator of "Give to the Earth Foundation," which raises $250,000 a year for environmental causes.

■ PATAGONIA

Since 1984, Patagonia, an adventure clothing company, has donated 10 percent of its annual pre-tax profits to selected environmental causes. It has given money to more than 300 nonprofit organizations, including the Audubon Society, the California Nature Conservancy, the Friends of Ventura River, and the Yosemite National Institutes. It also donated clothing to the needy and outfitted members of Greenpeace.

Yvon Chouinard, Patagonia's founder helped establish a corporate conservancy group, the Outdoor Industry Conservation Alliance, which develops programs and donates money for environmental issues. Some of the members of the group, which requires a $10,000 donation for membership, are Chouinard's chief competitors.

■ MATRIX ESSENTIALS, INC.

Matrix Essentials, Inc., a major manufacturer of professional haircare products headquartered in Solon, Ohio, has established policies based on concern for the environment. They believe in taking responsibility for our delicate planet because the future depends on it.

To offer relief to the nation's great woodlands, in 1991, Matrix joined forces with the National Parks and Conservation Association (NPCA), to launch the second annual Great Treesome—a national environmental restoration program to aid the nation's park lands. From February to April, 1991, Matrix made a donation to the NPCA for every purchase of a Matrix System Biolage product. The proceeds were used to plant and nurture trees in Redwood National Park.

"Thousands of trees were planted last year in Redwood National Park in California as a result of the 1991 Great Treesome program," said Arnold Miller, president of Matrix Essentials, Inc.

The National Parks and Conservation Association established in 1919, is the only group devoted solely to the preservation and protection of our nation's park lands. Matrix formed this partnership with the National Parks and Conservation Association to help heal our parks, which are being threatened by increased development activities.

Matrix created System Biolage, a botanically-based haircare line to tie-in both of these environmental programs. In keeping with its commitment to the environment, this haircare line is fully biodegradable, created with renewable resources, and is sold in recyclable bottles using the Plastic Container Code System to label all its containers for easy sorting when recycling. Matrix also does not animal test any of its products nor does the company use any animal by-products.

■ CONCLUSION

The role of the enlightened capitalist in American business is exciting. The strategies and tactics that help to build these businesses are definably socially driven. The business strategist should take note that in defining corporate strategy in the future, much can be learned by the examples illustrated in this chapter. I believe that the evolution of this strategy will create even tighter alliances between products and services, and causes.

As a consequence of this marketing evolution, in the future we may see the emergence of unique joint ventures and strategic alliance partnerships where popular causes will become private labeling devices for American business. Imagine, if you will, the Sierra Club franchise outlet that delivers a wide range of ecologically sound products to the consumer, incorporating health care, nutritional products, cosmetics, clothing, and food products directly to the consumer. I believe for such an enterprise to be initiated, the Sierra Club would purchase products directly from companies such as those illustrated in this chapter. The next evolution in marketing will promote capitalism and causes in this manner. The public is apparently ready to support such enterprises. The evolution of this new industry will require more Ben & Jerry's and The Body Shops of the future. There are 30,000 plus nonprofit organizations in the country that require ongoing financial support: These are the potential partners of the right enlightened capitalists looking to form new, cause-related joint ventures and strategic alliances.

For those of you who are inquisitive as to the tax structure and financial ramifications of such a move by nonprofits, rest easy. It is being done currently every day through licensing relationships with private enterprise.

6

■

Heart of the Deal
Investment Banking Connection to Philanthropic Economics

We have discussed the response of the American consumer in supporting various socially responsible corporations through their product purchases. This group of American consumers is also beginning to make its influence felt through the concept known as social investing. Money managers throughout the country are beginning to identify the correlation between the growing awareness of American consumers and their favor of companies that take a stance on social responsibility. Consumers are beginning to make investment decisions that affect their independent retirement accounts, pension plans, and investment portfolios. This group of consumers is recognizing that the socially responsible companies that demonstrate principles and values with which they identify, are more often than not beginning to financially out-perform those companies that aren't socially responsible. This facet of philanthropic economics will also become a powerful motivator for companies throughout the country to recognize the importance of a socially responsible rating.

This new investment concept is moving into investment banking criteria from the bottom up. Not only will established, publicly held companies benefit from this emergence trend, but privately help and start-up companies will also greatly benefit. The venture capitalist of the future will seek out small emerging opportunities of socially relevant companies more often than conventional companies —companies that incorporate not only socially correct principles, but companies that will develop products or services that will support the environment, impact education, improve health and nutrition, etc.

The investment banker of the future will be required to comprehend integrated political, social, and economic strategies. The likelihood of Wall Street becoming a kinder, gentler environment is almost a contradiction of terms. The 1980s and the Wall Street debacles have left a sour taste in the mouths of Americans.

The new enlightened investment counselors will represent a step in the right direction. In this chapter, The Heart of the Deal, we will highlight several companies that are defining a new beginning for the investment world.

■ SOCIALLY RESPONSIBLE INVESTING AND ITS RELATIONSHIP TO PUBLICLY TRADED COMPANIES

What is socially responsible investing (SRI)? Quite simply, SRI is the integration of both financial and social criteria when making investment decisions. The field can be broken into four parts:

1. Shareholder activism: Using stock ownership as a lever to encourage corporations to behave in socially responsible ways.

2. Guideline portfolio investing: Managing stock and bond portfolios within social constraints using "negative screens" to eliminate companies active in nuclear power, for example, or "positive screens" to include companies with proactive policies like employee ownership.

3. Community development investment: Meeting the needs of low-income communities through invest-

ments in intermediaries such as community loan funds, microbusiness funds, or housing funds.

4. Social venture capital: Investing in high-risk capital in young entrepreneurial companies that promise social benefit as well as financial return.

The SRI strategy asserts that investing is not value-neutral and that there are significant ethical and social consequences in how money is invested. It is a commitment, if you will, to achieving social good through investment.

■ THE HEART OF THE DEAL

The Calvert Social Venture Partners (CSVP), is the new wave of an old concept—venture capitalist (VC), only this time, the partners are just as interested in the companies' heart and soul as they are about the return on investment (ROI).

Traditionally, VCs have been viewed with cynicism and distrust by budding entrepreneurs. Sensitivity was not one of the VCs characteristics. The Calvert Social Venture Partners are the new breed. The founders are D. Wayne Silby, John Guffey, Michael Tang, and John May.

D. Wayne Silby, 42, is the chair of the Calvert Group of Funds, a multibillion-dollar series of public investment companies in Washington, D.C. He has committed himself to social investing as president of the $500 million Calvert Social Investment Fund and as co-founder of the Social Venture Network, a group of socially concerned entrepreneurs, of which the Calvert Social Venture Partners fund is a direct outgrowth.

Michael Tang, 36, has an extensive business background encompassing the management and acquisition of existing companies and investing in start-up ventures. He is CEO of National Materials, L.P., a diversified, family-owned Chicago company involved primarily in metals recycling, distribution, and manufacturing.

John G. Guffey, 42, is co-founder and partner with Wayne Silby at the Calvert Group and served as its president until 1987. His commitment to social change includes serving on the boards of Community Capital Bank of Brooklyn, New York, and the Coalition for Environmentally Responsible Economies. He is also vice chair of the Calvert Group of Funds and chair of the Calvert Social Investment Foundation.

John May, 43, is the managing partner of the firm. Since 1981, he has specialized in providing financial and management support to emerging growth companies. In 1986, he became managing partner of E. D. Wilt Investments, L.P., a small venture capital fund which is now fully invested. He enjoys working with entrepreneurs to grow their businesses.

Here is an introductory word from CSVP Chair Silby, excerpted from the company brochure:

Calvert Social Venture Partners was started from a vision: venture investments focused on the high purpose use of human talents. The founders, who also started a highly successful $500 million mutual fund, Calvert Social Investment Fund, were urged by their community of colleagues and entrepreneurs to bring socially responsible values into the venture capital community. Started in 1989, the fund is a vehicle where entrepreneurs can be seen for their social vision in addition to their ability to create successful businesses.

This is an overview to our extended community, about our work around a belief that for America to be a gentler nation in this emerging global era, investments must not only work for the investors but must also support the needs of a sustainable society and future generations.

A return to the industry's roots sets CSVP in search of early stage companies. Until this century, new ventures needed the permission of the community (by legislative incorporation or a royal charter) to come into being. Before a charter could be granted, the balance between the chartered company's benefits to society and the granting of special privileges such as limited liability, necessary for risky ventures involving many investors, was debated. Yesteryear's great American fortunes were made by groups of wealthy individuals pooling their excess resources to serve new market needs such as the railroads, electricity and the telephone.

Today those wealthy visionary individuals have been replaced by professional risk averse managers who, guided by pension fund "prudent man" rules, seek only financial return. Venture pools have been made larger to pay professional salaries, which makes the average investment size larger, often precluding early stage investments. Under these circumstances the professional managers have increasingly chosen later stage investments including bridge financing and LBOs. This creates a problem for early stage companies which have relatively modest capital needs but are the source of a society's future business vitality.

Calvert Social Venture Partners seeks to return to the traditional role of service to the community by nourishing the needs of budding enterprises that can make both economic as well as social contributions. Unlike most other venture funds dominated by institutional investors, Calvert Social Venture Partners is made up of a group of wealthy individuals who pool their money and talents to back emerging businesses. Yet in order to pay for the small office and staff, investments must be targeted where the prospects for a company to grow into a sizable enterprise are substantial. This does mean the fund must decline many socially worthwhile business opportunities where the potential for growth is limited. However, investing in companies with big prospects does involve greater risk. Although no one investment is certain to be successful, the pooling approach, which allows diversification (in Calvert Social Venture Partners case, 7–9 companies), is what has made venture capital funds appealing on a risk basis.

"THE EARTH IS NOT SOMETHING WE INHERIT
FROM OUR ANCESTORS, IT'S SOMETHING WE
BORROW FROM OUR CHILDREN."

■ MEET THEIR COMPANIES

The following is a list of companies that Calvert Social
Venture Partners has chosen to invest in. These companies,
products, and services contain highly socially relevant focuses.

Ecological Systems, Inc.—Clean Water

As the rivers, water tables, and oceans around the
world continue to absorb large amounts of toxic and pol-
luting compounds, clean water will become one of the
top priorities for the 1990s. One goal for our society must
be to decrease the amount of chemicals used in treating
water that is returned to our environment—this is the
goal of Ecological Systems, Inc. (ESI) located in Bethesda,
Maryland, one of the companies CSVP is backing. ESI
seeks to develop commercial applications of the Algal
Turf Scrubber (ATS), a technology which forgoes chemicals
in favor of nature's own natural process in treating water.
This company holds exclusive worldwide marketing rights
to this patented technology invented by Dr. Walter Adey,
director of the Marine Systems Laboratory of the Smithson-
ian Institute in Washington, D.C.

Although used only in closed aquarium systems over
its nine years of development, scientific evidence seems
to indicate that the ATS can be applied to a wide range
of water quality applications, where bacteria-based systems
are not completely successful. In the short term, ESI has
developed a marketable "Ecosystem," an aquariumlike system which can support an unheard of diversity of water
species for the educational marketplace, such as biology
classes in high schools. Longer term, the larger commercial
opportunities rest in waste water treatment. For example,
EPA regulations are restraining the development of aqua-

culture due to unwanted discharge into the environment. CSVP believes ESI's technology will make a significant breakthrough in the fish farming industry by permitting 100 percent closed-loop water systems.

Environmentally Safe Products, Inc.—Biological Pesticides

One of the greatest problems in commercial agriculture today is having to deal with the side effects of pesticides and herbicides necessary for high crop yields. One of the most promising solutions to this problem is to replace these chemicals with specially developed viruses which have no effect upon humans or animals, but are just as effective in reducing pest infestation. A leader in this evolving insecticidal virus products (IVP) field is another CSVP-funded company, Environmentally Safe Products, Inc. (ESPRO) located in Hanover, Maryland. ESPRO has had great success with GypCheck, used by the National Forestry Service to combat the gypsy moth, and a profitable Tussock Moth IVP product. CSVP's recent investment will allow ESPRO to expand sales of these two products, perform Environmental Protection Agency testing for new product registrations to combat the coddling moth and armyworm, and develop integrated ground support and logistical pest management services for municipal governments.

Katrina, Inc.—Food Quality

"Man is what man eats." Ensuring the quality of food in our mass consumer-oriented society is the mission of Katrina, Inc. in Hagerstown, Maryland, a third CSVP venture investment. Working with the patented near-infrared diode (NIR) technology, this company has developed a revolutionary on-line process sorting and control instrument which offers a wide variety of benefits for the food processing industry, including the ability to control production lines in real time; sort incoming fruits and vegetables on the basis of their internal quality; and accurately read the moisture content of dough, cheese, crackers, and other foods. CSVP's recent investment, along with a process control venture fund, will allow Katrina and its principal, one of the top three experts in this NID technology, to expand the company's start-up activities.

Shaman Pharmaceuticals, Inc.—Medicine and Cultural Survival

Protecting and honoring the wisdom of medicine men of remote forest traditions is important to global culture. The goal of Shaman Pharmaceuticals, Inc., in San Carlos, California, backed by CSVP, is to discover and develop pharmaceuticals known to medicine men, who are aware of the medicinal qualities of plants of places such as the Amazon, where it is estimated approximately one-half of all plant species can be found. The unique structural chemistry of these plants may lead to the discovery of new compounds which use receptors and body pathways previously undiscovered, thereby providing an alternative drug discovery route to mass screening and genetic engineering efforts. Already, Shaman has the unique distinction of moving its first product, an antiviral drug for children, into clinical trials faster than any other small drug discovery company in the history of the FDA. CSVP helped Shaman set up a foundation, "The Healing Forest Conservancy," with an emphasis on ethnobotany (the study of how traditional people use plants, particularly for medicinal purposes).

TireGator—Tire Recycling

Accumulation of used tires represents one of the more serious waste treatment problems facing the country today. CSVP-funded TireGator, a vertically integrated tire recycling company located in Texas, is capitalizing on an exclusive use agreement of an Air-Co Industrial Gases technology to convert this waste stream into a useful source of crumb and shredded rubber for use in tire derived fuels, asphalt highways, and recreational surface additives. The company currently has three main profit centers: tire collection and shredding in Dallas-Fort Worth; tire collection and shredding in Houston; and crumb rubber production in Mexico, Texas. A recent investment by CSVP will allow TireGator to expand its state-of-the-art cryogenic tire shredding plant to supply more crumb and shredded rubber to the expanding nationwide market.

LiteTrends, Inc.

Everyone has read about the dangers of excess cholesterol in the typical meat-packed American diet. But most people do not know that producing just 1 pound of meat uses 2,500 gallons of water and that for each acre of forest cleared for projects such as parking lots, houses, or malls, seven acres of forest are converted into pastures or fields for livestock feed. A meat-dependent diet harms the environment as much as the individual.

LiteTrends, based in Eldersburg, Maryland, is addressing these problems. Is has a unique process for texturizing and flavoring tofu to make it taste like meat. Although it will market first to institutional food service outlets, it plans to move eventually into the general consumer market. LiteTrends offers a tasty way to treat both our bodies and our planet with more respect.

ChekTec

Studies show that one in nine women will develop breast cancer over the course of her life. Yet despite progress in treating and preventing other cancers, the incidence of breast cancer in the United States continues to rise.

ChekTec is developing a series of invitro diagnostics to help physicians make cancer treatment decisions. One indicates whether chemotherapy is appropriate; another checks for cancer recurrence in recovered patients. Created by scientists at The John Hopkins University, these diagnostics have excited interest from SmithKline Beecham (their co-investor) and other major U.S. and Japanese pharmaceutical firms.

Duraplast

Some startling statistics have recently attracted attention to the pallet industry. The United States manufactures 500 million pallets for materials transport and storage every year, consuming 7.1 billion board-feet of wood and accounting for half of the hardwood cut in the United States yearly. These pallets are used an average of 1.7 times and then are discarded, producing 40 percent of our annual 6.3 million tons of waste wood.

Duraplast, located in Upland, California is developing a low-cost method for converting postconsumer plastic waste into lumber especially suited for pallets. The product should be less expensive, stronger, and thinner than previously available plastic lumber. Because several unexpected design modifications have been necessary and the board has not been perfected, CSVP has provided only a secured loan. However, CVSP is convinced that a strong market opportunity exists and is waiting only for the successful prototype to back Duraplast fully.

MEE, Inc.

One of today's most serious problems is the deterioration of life in our inner cities. As jobs and wealth depart for the suburbs, minority youth are left without positive role models or prospects for escaping the drugs, poverty, teen-age pregnancy, and violence that have become the norm.

MEE (Motivational Educational Entertainment, Inc.) in Philadelphia, Pennsylvania seeks to improve the quality of life for these youths through a dual focus on research and media production. It studies the kinds of media information to produce videos that will boost inner-city youths' self-esteem and inspire them with value-building messages. In addition, MEE uses its findings to produce market research reports for corporations seeking urban minority markets. MEE is CSVP's smallest investment, but it has the potential to make a significant contribution toward improving urban society.

■ OTHER SOCIAL FUNDS

The *Sand County Venture Fund*, Menlo Park, California, was founded by Michael Kieschnick. This $1.3 million fund invests in California environmental or human services companies. The fund is focusing on working with its current portfolio: Feeling Better Health Daycare, a start-up specialized day care provider taking care of mildly ill children, supported in part by employer subsidies; National Water Management, which uses a ozonization process to purify water in industrial cooling towers without the use of harmful chemicals and with dramatic water savings; Pure Harvest, which has developed methods of growing row crops without use of pesticides or herbicides and is bringing rice products grown without chemicals to the retail food market; and Zofcom, a rehabilitation device company serving quadriplegics.

Alterra Ventures,(formerly Highland Financial), Cambridge, Massachusetts, is a $4 million family-backed venture fund founded by Tim Joukowsky. The fund makes investments in the fields of energy, the environment, and social and health concerns and is currently raising expansion capital to make new investments and add growth to its companies, including Seventh Generation, the first ecological products mail order catalog company; Aqua Futures, an environmentally controlled recirculating fish farm which raises striped bass and hydroponic, organic vegetables; Pronatec, producer of a sweetener (Sucanat) that offers a healthful alternative to refined sugar; and Highland Energy Group, an energy management and service company which structures energy savings projects for property owners and state/federal agencies.

■ KINDER, LYNDENBERG, DOMINI & CO.

The Firm and Its Services

Of the various firms that are developing concepts and methodology for social responsibility, Kinder, Lyndenberg, Domini & Co. (KLD) has been around this subject matter since the beginning, and is recognized as the leader in this emerging trend. I have chosen to profile them as an example. It should be noted that during our research state, Peter Kinder was most responsive to our needs and shared openly with support from his staff.

Kinder, Lyndenberg, Domini & Co. in Cambridge, Massachusetts is a registered investment advisor providing social research on U.S. corporations in the investment community.

KLD maintains the Domini Social Index 400 (DSI). The DSI consists of 400 stocks of publicly traded firms that pass broad-based social screens. The DSI is both a benchmark for performance attribution for managers with social screened accounts and a resource for the social investment community. Its "Monthly Update" newsletter lists and analyzes the 400 companies in the DSI. Figure 6.1 provides sample pages from the DSI Monthly Update. Figure 6.1a is a partial listing of the 400 companies, with a categorical description of the type of business. Figure 6.1b lists business areas alphabetically and, within those areas, lists various companies and their market value in thousands of dollars. Figure 6.1c lists companies by market capitalization, in descending order of value. Figure 6.1d shows the stengths and concerns of the various DSI companies.

In the course of creating and maintaining the DSI, the firm has gathered extensive data on over 1,200 publicly traded U.S. companies. It has developed "Company Reviews" of over 800 of these companies (including all companies on the DSI and on the Standard & Poor's 500 Index). The reviews are one- to three-page profiles that highlight issues social investors may view as a major strength or concern for these firms. KLD's basic "Company Reviews" service includes hard copies of the reviews of the 650 companies in the DSI and the S&P 500. KLD's Social Investment Database offers access to all reviews KLD has produced through an on-line computer service. It also affords access to information not included in the reviews service, especially in the environmental area.

Figure 6.1

Stocks in the

DOMINI
SOCIAL
INDEX^{SM}
400

Monthly
Update
Subscription

As of:

February 28, 1991

Figure 6.1(a)

DOMINI SOCIAL INDEX 400

ACN	Acuson	Medical Equipment & Supplies
AMD	Advanced Micro Devices	Semiconducters
AET	Aetna Life & Casualty	Multi–Line Insurance
AFP	Affiliated Publications	Newspapers
AHM	Ahmanson, A.H.	Savings & Loan
APD	Air Products & Chemicals	Chemicals
ABF	Airborne Freight	Miscellaneous Transport
ALK	Alaska Air Group	Air Transport
ACV	Alberto–Culver	Home Products
ABS	Albertson's	Food Retailers
ASN	Alco Standard	Miscellaneous
AAL	Alexander & Alexander Services	Insurance Brokers
ALW	Allwaste	Pollution Abatement
AA	Aluminum Co of America	Metals
AZA	ALZA	Pharmaceuticals
AMH	Amdahl	Computer Manufacturers
AXP	American Express	Miscellaneous Financial
AGC	American General	Multi–Line Insurance
AGREA	American Greetings	Miscellaneous
AIG	American International Group	Multi–Line Insurance
ASC	American Stores	Food Retailers
AWK	American Water Works	Miscellaneous Utility
AIT	Ameritech	Telephone
AN	Amoco	Petroleum Products
AMP	AMP	Electrical Components
AMR	AMR Corp	Air Transport
APC	Anadarko Petroleum	Natural Gas Exploration & Production
ADI	Analog Devices	Semiconducters
AGL	Angelica	Medical Equipment & Supplies
APA	Apache	Natural Gas Exploration & Production
APOG	Apogee Enterprises	Construction Materials
AAPL	Apple Computer	Computer Manufacturers
AMAT	Applied Materials	Manufacturing
ADM	Archer Daniels Midland	Packaged Food
RCM	ARCO Chemical	Chemicals
ALG	Arkla	Natural Gas
ASKI	ASK Computer Systems	Software & Services
ATG	Atlanta Gas	Natural Gas
ARC	Atlantic Richfield	Petroleum Products
ACAD	Autodesk	Software & Services
AUD	Automatic Data Processing	Software & Services
AVT	Avnet	Miscellaneous
AVP	Avon Products	Home Products
BEZ	Baldor Electric	Electrical Components
ONE	Banc One Corp	Banks/Major Regional
BKB	Bank Of Boston	Banks/Other Major
BAC	BankAmerica	Banks/Other Major
BT	Bankers Trust New York	Banks/Money Center
BBI	Barnett Banks	Banks/Major Regional
BSET	Bassett Furniture	Furniture & Appliances
BMG	Battle Mountain Gold	Mining
BAX	Baxter International	Medical Equipment & Supplies
BDX	Becton Dickinson	Medical Equipment & Supplies
BEL	Bell Atlantic	Telephone
BLS	BellSouth	Telephone
BMS	Bemis	Miscellaneous
BJICA	Ben & Jerry's	Packaged Food
BNL	Beneficial	Miscellaneous Financial

124

BBC	Bergen Brunswig	Miscellaneous Health Care
BTV	BET Holdings	Entertainment
BETZ	Betz Laboratories	Chemicals
BMET	Biomet	Medical Equipment & Supplies
HRB	Block, H & R	Miscellaneous Financial
BOBE	Bob Evans	Restaurants
BORL	Borland International	Software & Services
BGG	Briggs & Stratton	Manufacturing
BU	Brooklyn Union Gas	Natural Gas
BG	Brown Group	Footwear
BR	Burlington Resources	Natural Gas Exploration & Production
CBT	Cabot	Chemicals
CRBN	Calgon Carbon	Chemicals
CE	California Energy	Miscellaneous Utility
CPB	Campbell Soup	Packaged Food
CCB	Capital Cities/ABC	Broadcasting
CPH	Capital Holding	Life Insurance
CAO	Carolina Freight	Truck Transport
CBS	CBS	Broadcasting
CTX	Centex	Housing Construction
CDVB	Chambers Development	Pollution Abatement
CHRS	Charming Shoppes	Specialty Retailers
CB	Chubb	Property & Casualty Insurance
CRCH	Church & Dwight	Home Products
CI	CIGNA	Multi-Line Insurance
CINF	Cincinnati Financial Insurance	Multi-Line Insurance
CMZ	Cincinnati Milacron	Machine Tools
CTAS	Cintas	Commercial Services
CC	Circuit City Stores	Specialty Retailers
CSCO	Cisco Systems	Computer Manufacturers
CITUB	Citizens Utlilities	Electric Companies
CLE	Claire's Stores	Specialty Retailers
CLRK	CLARCOR	Manufacturing
CKL	Clark Equipment	Manufacturing
CLX	Clorox	Home Products
KO	Coca-Cola	Beverages
CMCSA	Comcast	Broadcasting
CCLR	Commerce Clearing House	Publishers
CMY	Community Psychiatric Centers	Health Facility Management
CPQ	Compaq Computer	Computer Manufacturers
CA	Computer Associates Intn'l	Software & Services
CNE	Connecticut Energy	Natural Gas
CNF	Consolidated Freightways	Truck Transport
CNG	Consolidated Natural Gas	Natural Gas Exploration & Production
CPER	Consolidated Papers	Forest & Paper Products
CRR	Consolidated Rail	Rail Transport
CIC	Continental Corp	Property & Casualty Insurance
CBE	Cooper Industries	Electrical Components
CTB	Cooper Tire & Rubber	Vehicle Components
CSFN	CoreStates Financial	Banks/Major Regional
CPC	CPC International	Packaged Food
CPY	CPI Corp	Miscellaneous
NECC	Critical Care America	Medical Equipment & Supplies
ATXA	Cross, A.T.	Miscellaneous
CSX	CSX	Rail Transport
CUM	Cummins Engine	Vehicle Components
CYM	Cyprus Minerals	Mining
DCN	Dana	Vehicle Components

DH	Dayton Hudson	Department Stores
DAL	Delta Airlines	Air Transport
DLX	Deluxe	Printing
DVRY	DeVRY	Commercial Services
DEC	Digital Equipment	Computer Manufacturers
DDS	Dillard Department Stores	Department Stores
DME	Dime Savings Bank, NY	Savings & Loan
DNEX	Dionex	Pollution Abatement
DIS	Disney, Walt	Entertainment
DOLR	Dollar General	General Retailers
DNY	Donnelley, R.R., & Sons	Printing
DJ	Dow Jones	Newspapers
DIGI	DSC Communications	Telecommunications
EFU	Eastern Enterprises	Natural Gas
ECO	Echo Bay Mine Ltd	Mining
AGE	Edwards, A.G.	Miscellaneous Financial
EGGS	Egghead	Specialty Retailers
EGN	Energen	Natural Gas
ENE	Enron Corp	Oil & Gas Drilling
EQT	Equitable Resources	Natural Gas
FAST	Fastenal	Manufacturing
FJQ	Fedders	Furniture & Appliances
FDX	Federal Express	Miscellaneous Transport
FRE	Federal Home Loan Mortgage	Miscellaneous Financial
FNM	Federal Nat'l Mortgage Assoc	Miscellaneous Financial
FMO	Federal-Mogul	Vehicle Components
FNB	First Chicago	Banks/Money Center
FFB	First Fidelity Bancorp	Banks/Major Regional
FNG	Fleet Financial Group	Banks/Major Regional
FLE	Fleetwood Enterprises	Housing Construction
FLM	Fleming	Wholesale Food
FRX	Forest Laboratories	Pharmaceuticals
FULL	Fuller, H.B.	Miscellaneous
GCI	Gannett	Newspapers
GPS	Gap	Specialty Retailers
GMT	GATX	Miscellaneous Transport
GEC	GEICO	Property & Casualty Insurance
GCN	General Cinema	Miscellaneous
GIS	General Mills	Packaged Food
GRN	General Re	Property & Casualty Insurance
GSX	General Signal	Miscellaneous
GPC	Genuine Parts	Vehicle Components
GEB	Gerber Products	Packaged Food
GFSA	Giant Food	Food Retailers
GIBG	Gibson Greetings	Miscellaneous
GDW	Golden West Financial	Savings & Loan
GULD	Goulds Pumps	Manufacturing
GGG	Graco	Manufacturing
GWW	Grainger, W.W.	Electrical Components
GAP	Great Atlantic & Pacific Tea Co	Food Retailers
GWF	Great Western Financial	Savings & Loan
GWTI	Groundwater Technology	Pollution Abatement
HDL	Handleman	Leisure
HRD	Hannaford Brothers	Food Retailers
JH	Harland, John H.	Printing
HAR	Harman International	Leisure
HBOL	Hartford Steam Boiler Insurance	Property & Casualty Insurance
HMX	Hartmarx	Textiles

126

HAS	Hasbro	Leisure
HECHA	Hechinger	Specialty Retailers
HNZ	Heinz (H.J.)	Packaged Food
HP	Helmerich & Payne	Oil & Gas Drilling
HSY	Hershey Foods	Packaged Food
HB	Hillenbrand Industries	Miscellaneous
HD	Home Depot	Specialty Retailers
HONI	HON Industries	Office Furniture & Supplies
HI	Household International	Miscellaneous Financial
HUBBA	Hubbell	Electrical Components
HUF	Huffy	Leisure
HUM	Humana	Health Facility Management
HUN	Hunt Manufacturing	Miscellaneous
IDA	Idaho Power	Electric Companies
ITW	Illinois Tool Works	Machine Tools
IAD	Inland Steel Industries	Metals
INTC	Intel	Semiconducters
INDQA	International Dairy Queen	Restaurants
ION	Ionics	Miscellaneous
ISKO	Isco	Pollution Abatement
JR	James River Corp Of Virginia	Forest & Paper Products
JP	Jefferson-Pilot	Life Insurance
JPC	Johnson Products	Home Products
JOS	Jostens	Miscellaneous
KBH	Kaufman & Broad Home	Housing Construction
KELYA	Kelly Services	Commercial Services
KWP	King World Productions	Entertainment
KRI	Knight-Ridder	Newspapers
KR	Kroger	Food Retailers
KM	K-mart	General Retailers
LE	Lands' End	Specialty Retailers
LAWS	Lawson Products	Manufacturing
LEE	Lee Enterprises	Newspapers
LEG	Leggett & Platt	Furniture & Appliances
LGE	LG&E Energy	Electric Companies
LVC	Lillian Vernon	Specialty Retailers
LTD	Limited, The	Specialty Retailers
LNC	Lincoln National	Life Insurance
LIZC	Liz Claiborne	Textiles
LDG	Longs Drug Stores	Specialty Retailers
LOTS	Lotus Development	Software & Services
LLX	Louisiana Land & Exploration	Natural Gas Exploration & Production
LOW	Lowe's Companies	Specialty Retailers
LUB	Luby's Cafeterias	Restaurants
MGMA	Magma Power	Miscellaneous Utility
MNR	Manor Care	Miscellaneous Health Care
MHS	Marriott	Miscellaneous
MMC	Marsh & McLennan	Insurance Brokers
MAT	Mattel	Leisure
MA	May Department Stores	Department Stores
MYG	Maytag	Furniture & Appliances
MCAWA	McCaw Cellular Communications	Telephone
MCD	McDonald's	Restaurants
MHP	McGraw-Hill	Publishers
MCIC	MCI Communications	Telecommunications
MCK	McKesson	Miscellaneous Health Care
MEA	Mead	Forest & Paper Products
MX	Measurex Corp	Software & Services

MCCS	Medco Containment Services	Miscellaneous Health Care
MEGA	Media General	Newspapers
MDT	Medtronic	Medical Equipment & Supplies
MEL	Mellon Bank	Banks/Other Major
MES	Melville	Specialty Retailers
MST	Mercantile Stores	Department Stores
MRK	Merck	Pharmaceuticals
MDP	Meredith	Publishers
MER	Merrill Lynch	Miscellaneous Financial
MCRN	Micron Technology	Semiconducters
MSFT	Microsoft	Software & Services
MLHR	Miller, Herman	Office Furniture & Supplies
MIL	Millipore	Manufacturing
MODI	Modine Manufacturing	Vehicle Components
MMO	Monarch Machine Tool	Machine Tools
MCL	Moore	Office Furniture & Supplies
JPM	Morgan, J.P.	Banks/Money Center
MORR	Morrison	Restaurants
MII	Morton International	Miscellaneous
MYL	Mylan Laboratories	Pharmaceuticals
NEC	National Education Corporation	Commercial Services
NME	National Medical Enterprises	Health Facility Management
NSI	National Services Industries	Commercial Services
NBD	NBD Bancorp	Banks/Major Regional
NGNA	Neutrogena	Home Products
NEBS	New England Business Service	Office Furniture & Supplies
NYTA	New York Times	Newspapers
NWL	Newell	Housewares
GAS	NICOR	Natural Gas
NIKE	NIKE	Footwear
NDSN	Nordson	Manufacturing
NOBE	Nordstrom	Department Stores
NSC	Norfolk Southern	Rail Transport
NT	Northern Telecom Ltd	Telecommunications
NWPS	Northwestern Public Service	Electric Companies
NOB	Norwest Corp	Banks/Major Regional
NUE'	Nucor	Metals
NWNL	NWNL	Life Insurance
OMCM	Omnicom Group	Miscellaneous
OCQ	Oneida Ltd	Housewares
OKE	ONEOK	Natural Gas
ORX	Oryx Energy	Natural Gas Exploration & Production
GOSHA	Oshkosh B'Gosh	Textiles
PET	Pacific Enterprises	Natural Gas
PAC	Pacific Telesis Group	Telephone
JCP	Penney, J.C.	General Retailers
PZL	Pennzoil	Petroleum Products
PGL	Peoples Energy	Natural Gas
PBY	Pep Boys, The	Specialty Retailers
PEP	Pepsico	Beverages
PST	Petrie Stores	Specialty Retailers
PVH	Phillips-Van Heusen	Textiles
PIPR	Piper, Jaffray & Hopwood	Miscellaneous Financial
PBI	Pitney Bowes	Office Equipment
PNC	PNC Financial	Banks/Major Regional
PRD	Polaroid	Miscellaneous
POM	Potomac Electric Power	Electric Companies
PRE	Premier Industrial	Miscellaneous

128

Symbol	Company	Industry
PCLB	Price	Specialty Retailers
PA	Primerica	Miscellaneous Financial
PG	Procter & Gamble	Home Products
OAT	Quaker Oats	Packaged Food
RAL	Ralston Purina	Packaged Food
RBK	Reebok, International	Footwear
ROAD	Roadway Services	Truck Transport
RTC	Rochester Telephone	Telephone
ROUS	Rouse	Housing Construction
RDC	Rowan	Oil & Gas Drilling
RBD	Rubbermaid	Housewares
RML	Russell	Textiles
RYAN	Ryan's Family Steakhouse	Restaurants
R	Ryder System	Miscellaneous Transport
SAFC	SAFECO	Property & Casualty Insurance
SK	Safety-Kleen	Pollution Abatement
SFR	Santa Fe Energy Resources	Natural Gas Exploration & Production
SFX	Santa Fe Pacific	Rail Transport
SLE	Sara Lee	Packaged Food
SPP	Scott Paper	Forest & Paper Products
SEE	Sealed Air	Miscellaneous
S	Sears Roebuck	General Retailers
SRV	Service Corp International	Miscellaneous
SMED	Shared Medical Systems	Software & Services
SHX	Shaw Industries	Furniture & Appliances
SNC	Shawmut National	Banks/Major Regional
SHW	Sherwin-Williams	Construction Materials
SIAL	Sigma-Aldrich	Chemicals
SKY	Skyline	Housing Construction
SMCA	Smith, A.O.	Vehicle Components
SJM	Smucker, J.M.	Packaged Food
SNA	Snap-On Tools	Tools & Supplies
TWRX	Software Toolworks	Software & Services
SNG	Southern New England Telecom	Telephone
LUV	Southwest Airlines	Air Transport
SBC	Southwestern Bell	Telephone
SPEK	Spec's Music	Specialty Retailers
SMI	Springs Industries	Textiles
UT	Sprint	Telecommunications
SPW	SPX	Vehicle Components
STJM	St Jude Medical	Medical Equipment & Supplies
STPL	St Paul Companies	Property & Casualty Insurance
SREG	Standard Register	Office Furniture & Supplies
STH	Stanhome	Home Products
SWK	Stanley Works	Tools & Supplies
SRA	Stratus Computer	Computer Manufacturers
SR	Stride Rite	Footwear
STRY	Stryker	Medical Equipment & Supplies
SLM	Student Loan Marketing	Miscellaneous Financial
SUN	Sun Company	Petroleum Products
SUNW	Sun Microsystems	Computer Manufacturers
SNMD	Sunrise Medical	Medical Equipment & Supplies
STI	SunTrust Banks	Banks/Major Regional
SVU	Super Valu Stores	Wholesale Food
SYY	SYSCO	Wholesale Food
TMB	Tambrands	Home Products
TDM	Tandem Computers	Computer Manufacturers
TAN	Tandy	Specialty Retailers

TBY	TCBY	Restaurants
TEK	Tektronix	Electrical Components
TDS	Telephone & Data Systems	Telephone
TCOMA	Tele-Communications	Broadcasting
TLAB	Tellabs	Telecommunications
TANT	Tennant	Commercial Services
TMO	Thermo Electron	Pollution Abatement
TII	Thomas Industries	Furniture & Appliances
TNB	Thomas & Betts	Electrical Components
TMC	Times Mirror	Newspapers
TJCO	TJ International	Construction Materials
TJX	TJX Companies	Specialty Retailers
TR	Tootsie Roll	Packaged Food
TMK	Torchmark	Life Insurance
TTC	Toro	Miscellaneous
TOY	Toys 'R' Us	Specialty Retailers
TA	Transamerica	Miscellaneous Financial
TIC	Travelers	Multi-Line Insurance
USW	U S West	Telephone
UAL	UAL	Air Transport
UNM	UNUM	Multi-Line Insurance
FG	USF&G	Property & Casualty Insurance
USH	USLIFE	Life Insurance
USHC	U.S. Healthcare	Health Facility Management
VFC	V F Corp	Textiles
VALU	Value Line	Miscellaneous Financial
VDC	Van Dorn	Manufacturing
VFSC	Vermont Financial Services	Banks/Major Regional
VIA	Viacom	Entertainment
FW	Wachovia Corp	Banks/Major Regional
WAG	Walgreen	Specialty Retailers
WCS	Wallace Computer Services	Office Furniture & Supplies
WMT	Wal-Mart	General Retailers
WANB	Wang Laboratories	Computer Manufacturers
WGL	Washington Gas Light	Natural Gas
WPOB	Washington Post	Newspapers
WATTA	Watts Industries	Manufacturing
WLM	Wellman	Pollution Abatement
WFC	Wells Fargo	Banks/Major Regional
WSC	Wesco Financial	Savings & Loan
W	Westvaco	Forest & Paper Products
WETT	Wetterau	Wholesale Food
WHR	Whirlpool	Furniture & Appliances
WH	Whitman	Packaged Food
WMB	Williams Companies	Natural Gas Exploration & Production
Z	Woolworth, F.W.	General Retailers
WTHG	Worthington Industries	Metals
WWY	Wrigley, Wm.	Packaged Food
XRX	Xerox	Office Equipment
YELL	Yellow Freight Systems	Truck Transport
ZE	Zenith Electronics	Furniture & Appliances
ZRN	Zurn Industries	Pollution Abatement

Figure 6.1(b)

MARKET VALUE			% OF 400
APPAREL			**1.3%**

Footwear			
470.75	BG	Brown Group	
3602.98	NIKE	NIKE	
2359.48	RBK	Reebok, International	
955.82	SR	Stride Rite	
Textiles			
187.87	HMX	Hartmarx	
3994.33	LIZC	Liz Claiborne	
506.53	GOSHA	Oshkosh B'Gosh	
177.95	PVH	Phillips–Van Heusen	
988.79	RML	Russell	
478.47	SMI	Springs Industries	
1475.49	VFC	V F Corp	
15198.46		Group Market Value	

FOODS & BEVERAGES			**12.0%**

Beverages			
34966.84	KO	Coca–Cola	
25802.66	PEP	Pepsico	
Packaged Food			
6679.91	ADM	Archer Daniels Midland	
45.63	BJICA	Ben & Jerry's	
9188.51	CPB	Campbell Soup	
6116.02	CPC	CPC International	
8845.98	GIS	General Mills	
2265.36	GEB	Gerber Products	
9089.31	HNZ	Heinz (H.J.)	
3598.09	HSY	Hershey Foods	
4234.31	OAT	Quaker Oats	
5920.08	RAL	Ralston Purina	
7936.07	SLE	Sara Lee	
661.74	SJM	Smuckers, J.M.	
441.06	TR	Tootsie Roll	
2315.08	WH	Whitman	
2365.89	WWY	Wrigley, Wm.	
Wholesale Food			
1061.08	FLM	Fleming	
1917.17	SVU	Super Valu Stores	
3412.65	SYY	SYSCO	
641.41	WETT	Wetterau	
137504.85		Group Market Value	

Figure 6.1(c)

MARKET
CAPITALIZATION

40048.11	WMT	Wal-Mart
39562.06	MRK	Merck
34966.84	KO	Coca-Cola
28181.61	PG	Procter & Gamble.
26297.47	AN	Amoco
25802.66	PEP	Pepsico
24942.11	BLS	BellSouth
20937.28	ARC	Atlantic Richfield
19248.05	BEL	Bell Atlantic
19221.92	AIG	American International Group
17409.31	AIT	Ameritech
17081.73	PAC	Pacific Telesis Group
16400.42	DIS	Disney, Walt
16113.66	SBC	Southwestern Bell
15159.26	USW	U S West
11987.75	MSFT	Microsoft
11339.11	MCD	McDonald's
11125.75	AXP	American Express
10783.90	FNM	Federal Nat'l Mortgage Assoc
10681.97	S .	Sears Roebuck
9377.42	INTC	Intel
9188.51	CPB	Campbell Soup
9089.31	HNZ	Heinz (H.J.)
8930.38	BAX	Baxter International
8845.98	GIS	General Mills
8656.00	DEC	Digital Equipment
8539.30	JPM	Morgan, J.P.
8516.22	GRN	General Re
8458.63	LTD	Limited, The
7936.07	SLE	Sara Lee
7861.06	CCB	Capital Cities/ABC
7850.40	TOY	Toys 'R' Us
7139.11	NT	Northern Telecom Ltd
7110.11	NSC	Norfolk Southern
6995.29	KM	K-mart
6872.98	BAC	BankAmerica
6854.35	AAPL	Apple Computer
6808.01	MCIC	MCI Communications
6679.91	ADM	Archer Daniels Midland
6309.90	MA	May Department Stores
6267.24	JCP	Penney, J.C.
6250.25	NCR	NCR
6116.02	CPC	CPC International
6099.46	GCI	Gannett
5936.17	CPQ	Compaq Computer
5920.08	RAL	Ralston Purina
5691.67	HD	Home Depot
5486.93	MMC	Marsh & McLennan
5472.06	CB	Chubb
5442.44	AA	Aluminum Co of America
5253.80	UT	United Telecommunications
5253.80	TCOMA	Tele-Communications
5246.67	AMP	AMP

132

Figure 6.1(d)

STRENGTHS AND CONCERNS OF DSI COMPANIES

COMPANY	COMMUNITY	EMPLOYEE RELATIONS	ENVIRONMENT	PRODUCT	WOMEN/ MINORITIES	OTHER	MILITARY CONTRACTS	NUCLEAR POWER	SOUTH AFRICA
AMP				X			X		
AMR	X	X X			X X				
ACUSON									
AETNA	XX	X		X	X				
AHMANSON	X								
AIR PRODUCTS	X		XX X						
ALBERTO CULVER									
ALBERTSON'S		X X							
ALCOA		X	XX X				X		
ALLWASTE			X						
AMERITECH	X	X			X				

X = Concern or Strength
XX = Major Concern or Strength

Concern =
Strength =

Mar-91

133

KLD serves as a consultant to money managers, mutual funds, pension funds, and institutions practicing social investing. In this capacity, it develops social screens, applies the screens to investment universes, and monitors managers' implementation of client's social objectives.

The Domini Social Index

The Domini Social Index (DSI) is a market capitalization weighted common stock index made up of 400 U.S. companies that have passed multiple social screens.

In creating the DSI, KLD sought to construct a broadly diversified index within its social criteria. These criteria are both exclusive and inclusive.

KLD excludes the following from the DSI:

- Corporations with operations in South Africa, equity interests in companies doing business there, or arrangements that allow the South African government to obtain strategic products

- Military contractors that supply parts for nuclear weapons or that derive more than 4 percent of gross sales from conventional weapons

- Firms deriving over 4 percent of gross sales from gambling, distilling alcoholic beverages, or manufacturing tobacco products

- Companies owning interest in nuclear power plants, operating in the nuclear power industry, or producing any materials directly involved in the nuclear fuel cycle

- Corporations with notably poor records on the environment, employee relations, or community relations

KLD seeks to include the following in the DSI:

- Companies that are owned or operated by women or minorities or that have made substantial progress in affirmative hiring and promotion

- Enterprises that take a strong stance—backed by action—on the necessity for environmental responsibility, make products useful in maintaining a clean environment, and view energy production processes and consumption in an environmental context

■ Corporations that make exceptional efforts to treat employees fairly, promote employee involvement, and share ownership or profits with employees

■ Firms that emphasize the quality of their products and their relationships with consumers and customers

Through its original selection process, KLD eliminated from consideration those S&P 500 companies that did not meet its basic social criteria. Of the 500, approximately 255 passed DSI's social screens.

To the 255 S&P companies, KLD added 50 companies with notably strong social performance. KLD next looked at the largest corporations (in market capitalization) not on the S&P 500. From these, KLD selected approximately 95 corporations offering industry representation or substantial market capitalization. In selecting these companies, KLD favored firms that had positive social characteristics.

A company is dropped from the index and is replaced when its stock is no longer traded (usually as a result of a business combination) or when KLD determines that it fails a social or financial screen. In DSI's first year, fewer than two changes per month were made in the index.

Research Discipline

KLD maintains research files on more than 1,200 publicly traded U.S. companies. Over the course of a year, the firm examines approximately 1,000 companies and evaluates about 800. The evaluations are used to develop the firm's "Company Reviews" as well as to make portfolio decisions for the Domini Social Index. The following are among the areas in which it tracks corporations:

■ Company
■ Employee relations
■ Environment

- Product and consumer relations
- Women and minorities
- Military contracts
- Nuclear power
- South Africa
- Alcohol, tobacco, and gambling

The firm's research methodology incorporates three stages:

1. Basic data gathering
2. Literature reviews and company contracts
3. Stakeholders interviews

Basic Data Gathering (Stage 1)

KLD assembles basic information on a firm from public documents and business publications. This data is the foundation of the research and analysis that follows.

Every company analysis performed by KLD includes a review of the following documents:

- Annual report
- Annual report on Form 10-K
- Proxy statement
- Articles from daily newspapers and the business press
- Articles from trade journals

Literature Reviews and Company Contracts (Stage 2)

For firms facing particularly complex social challenges, KLD conducts comprehensive literature searches and makes direct contact with the company.

KLD uses many databases, including ABI/Inform, Infrotrac, Westlaw, Dow Jones, and NewsNet. The firm also uses specialized databases to obtain information on environmental and defense issues and subscribes to government watchdog and research services such as the Data Center. KLD also sends out detailed questionnaires requesting specific information for each screen.

When it first performs a stage 2 analysis, KLD establishes direct contact with the firm's investor relations officials. Company officials are usually asked to comment on KLD reports before the reports are submitted to the client.

Stakeholders Interviews: (Stage 3)

KLD frequently conducts stakeholder interviews to complete its picture of a company. These interviews include, but are not limited to, the following groups:

- Company managers
- Employees
- Customers
- Community groups
- Government regulators

Most firms considered for the Domini Social Index (about 50 per year) receive a stage 3 analysis. The number of additional stage 3 analyses varies depending on reported changes in DSI constituent companies and client demand.

Service and Publications

The KLD "Company Reviews" are one- to three-page profiles of the social accountability records of publicly traded U.S. corporations. The reviews are available for the 400 companies in the Domini Social Index, for the 500 companies in the Standard & Poor's 500 Index, and for more than 200 companies not on either index, for a total of over 800 companies. Reviews are available on a subscription basis for the 650 companies in the two indexes or at a premium on an as-needed basis.

The Social Investment Database Service provides online KLD's company reports coupled with an easy-to-use report writer. Its powerful word search function and sort programs allow the user to identify suitable companies and to design customized universes. KLD's Database Service includes all 800 plus reviews KLD has produced and provides access to information not included in the reviews service, especially in the environmental area.

The DSI Monthly Update is a 40-page pamphlet tabulating the index's performance and listing its constituent corporations. In addition, it indicates each company's particular social strengths or concerns.

The KLD Company and its Domini Social Index measure the share performance of the DSI against the share performance of the Dow Jones Index, and clearly the DSI companies have outperformed the larger Dow (see Figure 6.2).

The enlightened consumer is now also making investment decisions along with direct consumer purchases that reflect his or her social awareness. This is again another dynamic of *philanthropic economics*.

■ THE COVENANT PORTFOLIO

Another such investment advisory firm is the Covenant Portfolio. The Covenant fund is a diversified mutual fund which invests primarily in the common stock of American companies. Covenant's investment objective is to provide long-term capital growth, as well as current dividend interest. Covenant attempts to achieve this objective by investing in companies which meet the highest standards of social responsibility and business ethics. Their focus is on companies with high awareness in communities, competitors, customers, employees, environment, shareholders, and social issues and suppliers.

■ THE SOCIAL VENTURE NETWORK

Small to mid-size entrepreneurial companies that embrace the concept of social responsibility are finding each other in an effort to provide economic support and financial support, and information sharing. One such organization that is helping the emerging new start-up Ben & Jerry's of the world is a growing organization in San Francisco,

Figure 6.2

DSI 400 vs. S&P 500
Performance Since DSI Went Live

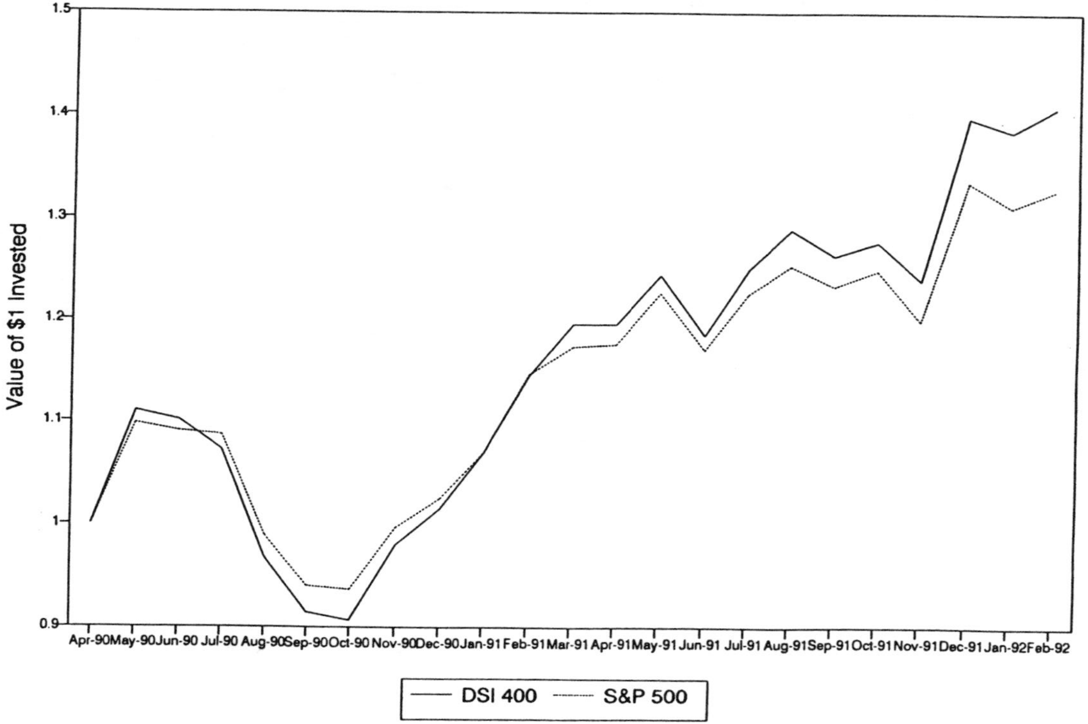

DSI 400 ———— S&P 500

139

California, the Tides Foundation, and its initiative is known as *The Social Venture Network (SVN)*.

The SVN, an amazing upstart organization founded in 1988, brings together all elements of philanthropic economics, the *enlightened capitalism*. The following pages contain commentary from the group's organizers.

Its mission is as follows: "We are a community of successful business and social entrepreneurs; our goal is to develop and advance commercial activity which integrates the elements of a just and sustainable society into day-to-day business ventures. We believe one cannot succeed without the other." The members' goal is to change the way the world does business. This dynamic and growing organization brings together like-minded business owners and executives into a network of responsible social activism. It covers all relevant social issues, including the development of information and products that underscore the concerns of the elimination of the rain forests, educational programs and entrepreneurial efforts to support AIDS research, the homeless crises, and so on. This dedicated network of 300 companies shares the same value structure and boasts names like Reebok, The Body Shop, Patagonia, Rhino Records, Microsoft, and Banana Republic.

The organization has also incorporated a venture capitalist feature into the network. Venture capital is provided to companies in early development stages that show promise as potential value-added contributors to society. Investment firms like A. G. Edwards, funds like the Calvert Social Investment Fund, and SVN are working on the creation of the High Social Impact Investment Fund (HSII) as a vehicle for investing in community-based loan and credit funds while providing the general public with investment opportunities with proactive high social impact. This organization attracts a wide base of social and business leadership over broad levels of influence.

At a recent network meeting, screen actor and community activist Richard Dreyfuss spoke of children's need to inherit clean air, clean water, and safe streets. He said, "We must reconnect with this country, support the community and infuse our children with a sense of virtues and a spirit of community service." Dreyfuss and his assistant are doing just that with their initiative, a community service clearing house in Los Angeles. The SVN seems to be in every sector of society—business, finance, writers, foundation development, and intellectuals—all in an effort to bring forth a message of doing well while doing good.

As this network evolves over the coming years, it will have a profound effect on how business is done. One valuable function of the SVN is the networking and strategic alliances that result. One meeting had a pronounced impact on a small company that was seeking an outlet for nuts imported from the Brazilian rain forest. The answer came from Ben & Jerry's Ice Cream; founder Ben Cohen produced a Brazilian nut-flavored ice cream. This kind of activity does not seem to be the exception, but the norm for this organization. Its members recognize that for these oftentimes struggling enterprises to survive with their ethics and values in place, it is imperative that they are assisted from time to time by larger companies in the network. SVN also has a mentoring program for these developing companies.

The network has instituted a next-generation program, known as "Bridges." The program involves instructing and nurturing the members' children, so they can carry on the values. This energized and optimistic spirit harkens back to the 1960s. In many ways, SVN members are not much different from activists in the 1960s, still wanting to change the world for the better. This time, however, they are better dressed and better financed with more focused goals—how they grew up! Not losing the dream and keeping the Great American Spirit.

The SVN program is clearly a result of the trend shifts in progress. More and more, companies will be enhanced by the connection of social good and personal and business success. Most significant is the willingness of large, successful companies and high-powered executives to take an active role with fledgling firms or embryonic ideas. This commitment illustrates why the trends will proceed forward—the Ben Cohens and Anita Roddicks, who have not lost sight of the rest of the world while pursuing their business goals.

Although membership to the SVN is by invitation only, and the cost is not inexpensive (though it is affordable), this group may be the social "young presidents" organization of the future.

■ CONCLUSION

The profiled companies and their various activities again illustrate the powerful and influential trend towards social responsibility. American businesses must quickly become aware of the economic impact of this trend. Unfortunately, small businesses will be the last to be informed, and with 93 percent of all of America's businesses categorized as small businesses, much work needs to be done. America's small to mid-size companies that are not yet enlightened need to be. No one organization is focusing yet on that fact. As a result of our research and the analysis of the growing need to inform and educate, we have created a new education and information center to bring the message to American business. Our workshops and seminars focus on how to make our existing corporate culture more responsible. We recently created the business association known as the American Business Coalition for a Better World. More will be discussed on this topic in Chapter 8.

7

■

America's Admired
How Big Business Is Assuming
National Leadership

It's fair to say that America and Americans are proud of their enterprise system, and we are most proud of our big business. In our changing society, they have begun to define the role they must play as leaders in the area of social responsibility. They are feeling the effect of the enlightened consumer, and the American public is requiring them to increase their role as global citizens. The companies profiled in this chapter are illustrative of how some of our most admired are conducting themselves as responsible companies, and a certain few are going far beyond the conventional business norms. Some may take exception with my choice of companies due to their products, but I have chosen this group primarily because they comprehend their roles as socially responsible companies.

    This chapter offers profiles of various companies with initiatives in areas defined as corporate social responsibility. The sources used in researching are varied, and in some cases, such as Johnson & Johnson and Merck, interview reprints and public speeches were obtained to present senior management's ideology.

There are other companies that one would question as to their role as socially responsible companies. One such company is the Adolph Coors Company. Typically alcohol-related companies are not included in a discusion of socially responsible enterprises, but I chose Coors because I believe it is much more than a provider of a product. Another notable in this class is the Anheuser-Busch. Several companies listed here have also been distinguished in *Fortune* magazine as the most admired companies in the United States.

■ SOME OF AMERICA'S MOST ADMIRED COMPANIES

Profiles of *Fortune* magazine's most admired companies and their respective initiatives and philosophy lend support to the pervasiveness of this trend. Bringing about significant social change via their leadership and commitment of resources typifies the new proactive practices being developed today.

■ IBM'S CORPORATE PROFILE OF SOCIAL RESPONSIBILITY

How big business sees this issue of social responsibility and its impact on their business is well defined in the opening statements from James P. Parkel, IBM's director, in his speech at the Keystone Conference in Golden, Colorado, October 1990. The conference brought together leaders from business and corporate America to discuss how to build a generation of MBAs skilled in solving social problems and enhancing American competitiveness. It was sponsored by the University of Denver College of Business, the Piton Foundation, the Adolph Coors Foundation and the Corporate Philanthropy Report.

SURVIVAL

Each of us has his or her own definition of corporate social policy. For some, it is philanthropy; for others, it is quality of life, or ethics, or corporate citizenship, or community action. The definition depends on one's perspective, but there is a growing recognition that the piecemeal approach to these subjects is not enough.

The prospectus for the October 1990 Keystone Conference put it this way: "Increasingly, American corporations are searching for ways to replace their piecemeal social initiatives with fully integrated corporate social policies—and to align them with business strategies in an inspiring way." Craig Smith, one of the spark plugs of the conference, popularized the phrase "corporate social policy" to describe this approach.

I would like to provide a mental image of corporate social policy. There are three types of corporations:

1. At the lowest level is the company that has a social policy only when it has a crisis—a product failure or a legal problem, for instance. When the crisis hits, the company rolls out a public relations program, utters some lofty thoughts, and does some good works. But when the problem goes away, so does the strategy. This corporation's social policy is essentially reactive.

2. At the middle level is the corporation with a tradition of philanthropy and good works perhaps going back many years. The chair is proud of his or her company's quality, its integrity, and its standing in the community, and he or she is generous in support of those qualities. The company's social policy, however, tends to be piecemeal. Many corporations are in this category.

3. At the top level is the corporation that will be needed in the future. It does not just react to crises

or "fly right" by instinct. Instead, it has a carefully thought-out social policy and a long-term strategy for implementing it. Its social policy is proactive.

Corporations are beginning to view social policy as something that is not simply "nice to have," but as a key element of success, even survival. Survival? That is a pragmatic approach to a noble problem.

Here are the harsh facts of life in this last decade of the twentieth century:

- Customers do not want to do business with companies that pollute the environment or are notorious for shoddy products and practices.

- Employees do not want to work for companies that have no social conscience.

- Nations and communities do not roll out the welcome mat for companies that take everything out of a community and put nothing back in.

- Students and faculty want to be a part of institutions that have a vision of the world as it ought to be, not just as they inherited it.

- Finally, voters and shareholders rally in favor of causes that are socially responsible—and powerfully against those that are not.

Organizations must either measure up to the rising expectations of these various constituencies, or they will not survive and thrive.

That is a challenge for today's business leadership and for the business schools educating the leadership for tomorrow. We need leaders equipped to balance the strategies of the future. But the reality is:

- In most corporations, social policy is not yet a significant element in the central strategy, not yet an integral part of the business process.

■ In most business schools, corporate social policy is not a part of the core curriculum on par with economics and finance, though it should be.

■ IBM'S APPROACH

I can't begin to answer for business as a whole, but I can explain IBM's approach to corporate social policy.

IBM starts with the benefit of an extensive network of programs already in place, built up over more than half a century. It still has a scratchy, grainy old film in which IBM founder, Tom Watson, talked to employees on the subject. He said, "Take time out from your IBM duties to do a good job in your community. Because no country can ever be better than the communities that make it. And the local community has to depend on the people who live there." His son, Tom Watson, Jr., defined corporate citizenship as one of the basic responsibilities of IBM.

The manager's manual reinforces the point: "We should accept our responsibilities as a corporate citizen in community, national, and world affairs; we serve our interests best when we serve the public interest."

IBM is the largest corporate giver in the world. Its worldwide philanthropic giving in 1989 was something over $135 million. Almost half of its employees in the United States volunteer their time to charitable causes.

John Akers, IBM's CEO, leads by example. In 1990, he began a two-year term as chair of the United Way of America. He is also a founding director of the Points of Light Foundation and the head of the Business Roundtable's education initiative.

This tradition—this infrastructure of people and programs—is the context for a major new initiative IBM launched in 1988.

*The Distinguished Corporate
Citizen Study*

IBM wanted to sharpen its focus on corporate philanthropic responsibility and the bottom line—meaning
the global strategy of the corporation. Therefore, a
study called "Distinguished Corporate Citizenship"
was launched.

A series of meetings was held in New York, bringing
together IBM's corporate social policy managers and
professionals from around the world. They came from
not just the United States, England, France and Ger-
many, but also from Japan, Korea, Brazil and Ar-
gentina—more than ten countries, small as well as
large. In parallel, IBM commissioned several external
studies and consulted with numerous outside experts.

Five countries in Europe and six in Asia were surveyed;
a thousand face-to-face interviews were conducted
in each country. The study found not only that
volunteerism exists, but that every country expects
it to increase. Especially in Asia, there is a strong
feeling that business should be still more involved
in volunteer efforts. In Europe, the surveys indicated
people felt corporate social policy activities should
be better publicized to build momentum.

Across the board, IBM noted growing activity, especially in Japan, reflected in the fact that IBM is
frequently asked to speak there. Keidenran, the Japanese organization for business, has established a
worldwide club, The One Percent NBT Club, to encourage Japanese companies to dedicate 1 percent
of their net (earnings) before taxes (NBT) to social
policy activities. One percent of NBT may not be
the best policy, of course, because it means that donations go up and down with profits, but it is a
step in the right direction.

Keidenran is also working to get tax exemptions for
Japanese companies giving abroad. Social responsi-

bility spending by Japanese companies in the United States is expected to reach $300 million this year. Honda owns the first Japanese foundation in Europe. In America, where the leadership in this area has traditionally been strong, IBM noted some slowdown because of mergers and acquisitions and the downturn in the economy.

One of the first conclusions of the study was that IBM should focus its efforts worldwide to achieve the greatest effect. Education and the environment are two such focuses. Both need sustained commitment and are key to many of the other issues confronting us. At the same time, IBM recognized that different parts of the world have vastly different needs. Therefore, there must be flexibility.

That leads to another conclusion, which is key to the management of corporate social policy in a firm like IBM: it is summed up in the phrase "Think globally—act locally." This addresses the old questions of centralization versus decentralization. A company as large as IBM, with 380,000 employees, has to establish clear goals, guidelines, and policies from the top, but then delegate responsibility as far as possible down the management chain to encourage local initiative. The principle holds true for social policy. What IBM is looking for is not to march in lockstep, but to encourage synergy. It wants to learn from different initiatives and share the best of them.

For instance, the principles of employee involvement are not unique to any one country. IBM has a program in place in 15 countries in which employees can get grants for any nonprofit organization in which they are personally involved. It is called the Fund for Community Service. In the United States in 1989, IBM gave $4 million in funding and equipment in this way.

Another conclusion from the IBM study was that a correlation exists between corporate social policy and the bottom line. Professor David Lewin of Columbia University's School of Business looked specifically at the correlation between corporate social policy and return on investment. His study covered 188 companies, assessing their community involvement in terms of people, money, and equipment and measuring that against the morale and productivity of their employees. The conclusions: Productivity is significantly better in corporations with a high rating on the community involvement index, and employee morale is three times better.

A final conclusion of the study was that IBM should apply standard business processes to corporate citizenship. Its executives believed the strategic planning and measurement disciplines used to run business could be adapted to social policy with positive effect. This principle has been applied to give a more unified structure to IBM's activities.

The Reorganization

In past years, IBM's corporate social policy activities had been split among several parts of the management structure: contributions used to be part of finance, university relations was managed by the chief scientist, and community programs were part of personnel. A reorganization grouped them together in one unit called Corporate Support Programs.

IBM's goal is to be a national asset, recognized as a worldwide leader in helping address societal issues in a way that is consistent with its business objectives.

The Need for Partnership

That is quite a challenge. IBM knows it cannot accomplish these lofty goals by itself. It needs partners.

IBM has partnerships with customers, suppliers, companies and communities. These partnerships exist for two pragmatic reasons: First, the computer industry is so complex and diverse that IBM knows it cannot meet all its needs by itself; second, it knows that long term, there will be no profit for IBM unless there is profit for its partners.

By analogy, the needs of society are so complex, diverse and pressing that IBM knows it cannot begin to solve them single-handedly.

The Role of Business Schools

That is what is meant by partnership, and it brings us to the second part of the equation mentioned at the outset: the role of the business schools. IBM is looking for a still closer partnership with them.

There are already some achievements to point to with pride. After the Wall Street scandals of the 1970s, 1980s, and early 1990s, an effort was made to instill a greater sense of business ethics in the new generation. The result was the funding, often with the help of corporations, of courses on business ethics in business schools.

However, a 1988 "Survey of Ethics Education in American Business Schools" (Ethics Resource Center, Washington, D.C.) brings good news and bad. Three quarters of the deans reported that ethics is a required part of both undergraduate and MBA programs, but only 20 percent of undergraduate programs require a separate course on ethics, and only 5 percent of MBA programs do.

Furthermore, we should keep in mind that ethics courses are usually no more than a subset of the larger issues of corporate social policy. In many schools, no comprehensive focus is directed at the connection between corporate strategy and corporate citizenship—the link between the bottom line not just of the corporation, but of the society in which corporations exist. We have a long way to go to make corporate citizenship a part of the core curriculum.

IBM would like to be partners with academics in finding solutions to that problem.

The Educational Initiative

Almost 22,000 IBM employees volunteer their time to developing quality education. One program combats functional illiteracy. IBM's educational task force is committed to bringing about systematic change in the U.S. public school system. IBM committed more than $59 million over a five-year period in grants of money, technology, and technical support to Kindergarten to Grade 12.

The Environment Initiative

Twenty years ago, IBM Chairman Thomas J. Watson, Jr., issued a corporate policy letter calling upon IBM managers to be continually on guard against adversely affecting the environment. IBM has taken the mandate seriously. It has invested more than $1 billion in capital equipment for environmental protection. In 1990, IBM received the World Environmental Center's gold medal for international corporate environmental achievement.

Health Initiative

The IBM focus in health initiatives is in areas of human misery and socioeconomic impact. AIDS and drug abuse are decimating entire communities and leaving death and despair in their wake. The World Health Organization (WHO) received a $1.5 million grant of equipment, software, and support for its efforts against AIDS. In France, the Pasteur Institute received $200,000 for AIDS research. In the United States, a $1.4 million grant was awarded for a project aimed at discouraging drugs and alcohol abuse among the young in eight U.S. cities.

Persons with Disabilities Initiative

The president's committee on employment of people with disabilities named David Schwartzkopf, an IBM employee from Rochester, Minnesota, the 1990 Disabled American of the Year. He helped IBM develop its affirmative action policy in the early 1970s. IBM has responded seriously and today is proud of the fact that 7,000 employees represent individuals with disabling conditions. To uphold the commitment, IBM is loaning $4.5 million worth of computer equipment systems to federally funded support centers for disabled workers being established across America through a program known as Disabled Assistance Network (DAN).

IBM has developed such products as a screen reader, speech viewer, and phone communicator for those with vision, speech, and hearing impairments. One of its most successful programs in this area has been computer programmer training for severely physically disabled persons, which now has centers in 30 U.S. cities. In partnership with community-based organizations and the federal government, the centers have provided training and job assistance in computer programming and data entry for more than 2,400 students since 1973.

The Disadvantaged Initiative

In 1989, IBM launched a $1.85 million initiative to aid homeless families in the United States. The program is designed to help the homeless become self-sufficient. It also addresses the special needs of children who face the prospect of growing up without the benefits of a secure, stable, learning environment. Grant recipients include United Way, the Enterprise Foundation, and the Better Home Foundation. IBM also sponsors about 100 U.S. job training centers in the United States for the disadvantaged through various nonprofit groups such as the National Urban League. More than 40,000 people have graduated from these centers since they began in 1976. The National Center for American Indian Enterprise Development received a grant from IBM to help more tribal and business enterprises get started as well as to expand.

IBM's international involvement is as far reaching as its domestic initiatives. IBM's global leadership and humanitarian efforts have led to a corporate culture which allows and fosters good works.

The Arts Initiative

IBM's broad-based support of the arts includes the underwriting of major cultural projects in virtually every area of the visual and performing arts. Altogether, IBM supports nearly 2,500 cultural organizations worldwide. The company's involvement is exemplified by the IBM Gallery of Science and Art in New York City. In partnership with cultural institutions throughout the world, it brings high quality science and art exhibitions to New York. On public television in the United States, IBM has underwritten cultural and educational specials. IBM was the sole underwriter of "Shape of the World," a six-part documentary devoted to mapping the globe. In conjunction with the series, IBM distributed social studies and science material to more than 200,000 teachers around the world.

Employee Involvement Initiative

Throughout IBM, employees are involved in their communities, contributing time and energy to everything from clean-up programs and blood donor drives in the United States to rice planting in Korea. The fund for community service programs encourages IBM employees to participate in community projects at the local level by providing cash and product grants to organizations in which employees volunteer their time. Grants for some 27,000 projects, totaling more than $44 million, have been made so far.

In addition to IBM directly supporting its employees, its charitable contribution campaigns in 1991 pledged $32 million to local United Way and other American health and human services agencies. The corporation's gift of $18 million in 1990 went to local United Way organizations in America.

■ JOHNSON & JOHNSON'S CORPORATE PROFILE ON SOCIAL RESPOSIBILITY

A statement from Johnson & Johnson's chair and chief executive officer, Ralph S. Larson, taken from Johnson & Johnson's social responsibility policy overview brochure, summed up his firm's role:

> For more than 100 years, Johnson & Johnson has made social responsibility an integral part of its business. Social responsibility takes many forms. It includes the manufacturing of high quality products, environment protection, an expansive corporate contribution program and the volunteer activities of our employees and retirees. Johnson & Johnson uses the time tested principles included in our credo as a guide post in making social responsibility as well as business decisions. We take pride in the thousands of Johnson & Johnson employee and retirees who converted our social responsibility beliefs into action. These people are truly making a difference.

Larson goes into more depth in a follow up interview:

Q. How does Johnson & Johnson define social responsibility?

A. As a leader in health care, we believe we have a special responsibility to enhance the quality of life for our customers, employees and the community at large. This responsibility goes beyond producing high quality products. It also involves conducting our business in accordance with the highest ethical standards, treating our employees sensitively and fairly, and helping to meet critical community needs.

Q. How important is social responsibility to Johnson & Johnson?

A. We take our responsibilities to society very seriously. It is a concept which has become ingrained in our corporate culture and strongly influences

the way we do business. We would not consider
ourselves successful as a corporation if we were
to fall short as a good corporate citizen.

Q. How do you instill the importance of social responsibility throughout the Corporation?

A. Our Credo is the main instrument of communication about our social responsibilities worldwide.
It is more than a statement of our principles.
The Credo is at the center of our business management process at Johnson & Johnson. So we
are continuously monitoring our performance at
all levels on social responsibility issues.

Q. What makes Johnson & Johnson different in its
approach to social responsibility?

A. The commitment we make to our Credo, and
the investment of resources we place behind that
commitment, is perhaps our greatest distinction.
We assign philanthropy a high priority. Our most
senior people are involved in setting directions
for this program and in carrying out its objectives.

Q. How is corporate philanthropy used to advance
the Corporation's overall social responsibility obligations?

A. This program is carefully managed to help improve
the quality of life, particularly in those communities
where we have a presence. Our contributions program addresses broad concerns, but gives priority
to health care interests. We make major contributions to programs that target health and the
environment, the family values, education and
employment.

Q. How does volunteerism factor into Johnson &
Johnson's commitment to social responsibility?

A. Many of our employees and retirees around the
world give of their personal time and talents to
voluntary activities. We encourage and empower
our people to be active in their communities, in

part, through a matching gifts program, and by recognizing their valuable contributions.

Q. How does the Corporation's commitment to social responsibility benefit its stockholders?

A. We feel social responsibility is crucial to our long-term business success. Shareholder value is greatly enriched because of our reputation as a caring company, and the high priority we place on social responsibility. It is a vital part of who we are.

The internal wellness program, "Live for Life," is a comprehensive wellness program helping employees maintain and improve their health. Many of the company's philanthropic programs are directed toward meeting community needs. One such program is the Christmas in April program, which brings an early Christmas to community elders and handicapped homeowners through a volunteer effort in which free home repairs, maintenance, and cleaning are provided to homeowners who can't afford to do the work themselves.

Johnson & Johnson believes greater support from the private sector is needed to preserve or reestablish an acceptable quality of life. Corporations like Johnson & Johnson can make a difference through partnerships with the public sector's coalition of business and independent projects that can enrich the community, safeguard the environment, and improve the quality of life. No limit is placed on the volunteer activities of the current and retired Johnson & Johnson employees. Volunteerism is encouraged by the example set by senior executives.

Special Constituencies

Johnson & Johnson supports the community which allows people the opportunity to create their own success. This initiative is extended to women, minorities, and people with disabilities. In recognizing the need for talented people, Johnson & Johnson has made its work sites accessible to individuals with disabilities. In addition, operating companies have redeveloped programs to train and hire the physically challenged. Their outside vendor policies call for contract work with organizations of people with disabilities as well as women- and minority-owned businesses.

Environment

Johnson & Johnson developed a special initiative in 1979 when its Credo was modified to include a responsibility to protect the environment and natural resources. Two cross-sector environmental task forces led by senior executives have since been formed to supervise environmental policy implementation worldwide. One effort—recycling—is saving 370,000 trees a year.

Special Philanthropic Initiatives

Many of Johnson & Johnson's operating companies conduct their own philanthropic activities. One such company helped launch the National Safe Kids Campaign, which seeks to reduce the 16 million preventable injuries and 8,000 deaths that children suffer each year. Johnson & Johnson also supports the LEAD program, which encourages young people of color to choose business careers. Its unique employment initiative, Bridge to Employment, provides at-risk youths with skills needed to enter and remain in the workplace. Johnson & Johnson is in partnership with the National Alliance of Business Head Start pre-school and day care program designed to reach children early with a strong support structure. Drugs and alcohol abuse have devastated the lives of far too many young Americans and their families, and in its commitment to education and the community, Johnson & Johnson is funding an effort to address this tragedy. The Live for Life school nurse fellowship program is based on the pivotal role of the school nurse in identifying students with substance abuse problems. The Worldwide Child Survival Program addresses another critical issue. Each year, 15 million children in underdeveloped countries die before the age of 5 because of malnutrition and preventable diseases. The Johnson & Johnson Worldwide Child Survival Program is dedicated to reducing these deaths. Johnson & Johnson is in partnership with United Nations Children's Fund (UNICEF). The key to the program's success is the involvement of Johnson & Johnson's managing director and employees in the targeted nations. In 1990, Johnson & Johnson contributed $26 million in domestic cash contributions, $15.9 million in domestic product contributions, and international cash gifts of $4 million.

■ NIKE'S CORPORATE PROFILE ON SOCIAL RESPONSIBILITY

The goal of Nike's corporate giving program is twofold: (1) to enrich the communities where its employees live and work through support of educational, social service, cultural, and environmental concerns and (2) to enhance the lives of children in major urban areas of the United States by supporting grass-roots organizations that provide unique educational opportunities.

Nike has teamed up with the National Foundation for the Improvement of Education (NFIE), a private foundation established in 1985 by the National Education Association, the nation's largest teacher's union, to create a $1 million "Just Do It" grants program for teachers. The "Just Do It" grants program with NFIE is part of a two-pronged stay-in-school campaign that includes a series of television ads featuring athlete superstars Bo Jackson, David Robinson, and Michael Jordan promoting the value of education to the country's youth. Nike provides $250,000 annually in "Just Do It" teacher's grants for grass-roots dropout prevention programs.

The CEO and founder of Nike, Philip Knight, cited the powerful effect which the company's "Just Do It" campaign has had in motivating the general public to engage in personal fitness programs. Knight said he has high hopes that the "Just Do It" grants "will similarly stimulate teachers to come up with creative grass-roots programs to motivate kids to stay in school."

Based in Beaverton, Oregon, Nike is the world's leading manufacturer of athletic footwear, apparel, and accessories. Three-fourth's of the company's philanthropic budget is dedicated to inner-city youth programs, with particular emphasis on education. It selected NFIE to administer the "Just Do It" grants because of the foundation's expertise in the area of dropout prevention programs, a prime example of the public and private sector working together.

"We're delighted that Nike has taken the posture that mental fitness and academic achievement are as important as physical fitness and athletic prowess. It's an important message which Nike is delivering through some impressive role models. We're pleased that the company is lending its creative advertising resources as well as providing funding for teacher's grants to help solve the dropout problem," said NFIE Executive Director Donna Rhodes.

The Nike ad campaign features athletes Bo Jackson, who is finishing a degree in child and family development at Auburn University; David Robinson, who graduated from the U.S. Naval Academy with a degree in mathematics; Michael Jordan, who went back to school to finish his degree in geography at the University of North Carolina; Georgetown University basketball coach John Thompson; and award-winning filmmaker Spike Lee.

"The Nike funds," said Rhodes, "provide a margin of difference for students who are on the verge of mentally or physically checking out of school. And they represent an important investment in this country's future."

The "Just Do It" program focuses on bottom-line results: proposals designed and implemented by teachers; programs that encourage students to take responsibility for their own learning, initiatives that challenge teachers to find ways of creating supportive environments to foster academic success; and efforts that tie self-esteem activities to academic achievement. "We'll be looking for projects that can make a real difference in the lives of students," Rhodes said.

Ghostwriter! Children's Television Workshop

The Ghostwriter project is a unique, multimedia project launched in fall 1992. It is the brainstorm of Children's Television Workshop, producers of Sesame Street, 3-2-1 Contact, The Electric Company, and other highly regarded children's television programming. Directed primarily at urban, low-income, 7- to 10-year-olds, the project combines a television program, a nationally circulated magazine, and national syndicated newspaper column, all designed to reinforce literacy skills for children. The "Just Do It" fund has provided a $5 million grant for this project.

Boys & Girls Clubs of America

Nike believes learning opportunities exist for children at play and is a major sponsor of the Boys & Girls Clubs of America. The Nike Cross Training Challenge program offers five athletic and academic challenges during the year for the clubs' 1.4 million members.

Scholarships/Internships

Nike offers minority scholarships through a variety of programs, including the United Negro College Fund, the Hispanic College Fund, the Urban League, the "I Have a Dream" Foundation, and others. It also provides support for education conferences and symposiums. Additionally, Nike has a summer internship program for college-level students.

Community Programs

Nike supports education, social services, civic and cultural events, and environmental projects in their hometown communities of Portland, Oregon; Memphis, Tennessee; and Greenland, New Hampshire. The organizations which benefit from Nike's support, both through grants and in-kind contributions of Nike products, are too numerous to list, but include gang intervention programs; minority youth programs; arts and cultural events; homeless relief programs; and support for the elderly, the handicapped, and the disadvantaged. Employees of Nike help direct the company's giving program through the Nike Employee Matching Gift Program, through which employees gifts are matched dollar for dollar by the company. In addition, Nike encourages employees to volunteer their time with community groups.

■ MERCK PHARMACEUTICAL'S CORPORATE PROFILE ON SOCIAL RESPONSIBILITY

The president and CEO of Merck, P. Roy Vagelos, M.D., in 1990 addressed the University of Michigan's new MBA students, and the following are selected excerpts of that speech. His address, "Global Citizenship: Serving Society Through Innovation, Superior Products and Social Responsibility," offers a vivid and encompassing account of a firm's response to the driving forces in today's society:

> I believe that Corporate Citizenship (whether it's global or local) is not something companies should practice *ONLY* in their spare time, *ONLY* through voluntary efforts and/or charitable giving.

> I believe that corporate citizenship begins with delivering valuable products or services which serve society and fulfill human needs. The strongest global citizens serve society through continual innovation which results in superior products that help people around the world.

> In the final analysis, companies rise and fall based on how well they serve society. If competition does it better than you do, they win and you lose—which is why serving society is the true foundation of our free enterprise, capitalistic system.

Not to imply that conducting business in a complex society such as ours is a simple matter—especially in a global marketplace. Business does not operate in a social vacuum, and corporations must respond to many different publics, which often have conflicting interests.

That means none of these publics will ever be satisfied perfectly; and corporations must balance their conflicting interests against economic, political and competitive realities.

First among these publics are customers. In Merck's case—since our business is healthcare—our customers are physicians who prescribe our medicines and patients who take them.

In my opinion, Merck is *most fortunate* in that our business is saving lives and fighting disease. That is citizenship of the highest order because we measure our success by how much we help people around the world. . . .

. . . As a result of our approach to business—as a responsible and successful corporate citizen—Merck has received awards based on our work around the world:

- In *Fortune* magazine's annual poll, we've been named "America's Most Admired Corporation" for the past five years in a row;

- *Forbes, Fortune,* and *Business Week* have praised us for our innovative products and management;

- *Sales & Marketing Management* ranked our sales force number one in the pharmaceutical industry;

- *Black Enterprise* magazine said that we were one of the "50 Best Places for Blacks to Work";

- *Working Mother* magazine has named Merck one of the best employers for women and working mothers for the past five years;

■ The Business Enterprise Trust—a non-profit organization headed by business, media, and labor leaders—called us one of the "Heroes of American
Business" based on one of our product donation
programs, which I'll describe later.

As I'm sure you know, *Fortune* conducts its "Most
Admired Corporation in America" competition every
year. And, in terms of corporate citizenship, it is
interesting to note a change in the recent voting.

Speaking of the most recent poll, *Fortune* said: "The
judges are increasing their emphasis on product quality
and corporate responsibility. . . . The number of re-
spondents citing responsibility to the community and
environment as the most important standard for judg-
ing a corporate reputation has doubled."

Last year, however, we issued a global environmental
policy with goals that exceed the standards established
by the Environmental Protection Agency. The goals
of our policy are:

■ By the end of 1991, to reduce worldwide air emissions of known and suspect carcinogens by 90%;

■ By 1993, to eliminate these emissions altogether,
or apply the best technology;

■ By 1995, to reduce by 90% worldwide releases of
all toxic chemicals.

We are on track to accomplish every one of our
goals. *Industry Week* magazine said: "Merck's commitments to the environment can serve as a role
model for corporate environmental commitment . . ."
and said our policy was one of the "Gutsy Decisions
of 1990." We think it was just good business.

Underscoring the importance of the environment to
Merck, I've agreed to serve on the President's Commission on Environmental Quality, made up of 25
environmental, business, and academic leaders. The

purpose is to "assess opportunities that address critical environmental challenges" and to balance the goals of the environment with economic growth and quality of life.

The commission is charged with a number of critical environmental issues, including pollution prevention, managing natural resources, and global conservation through international cooperation.

In addition to producing valuable products and our concerns for the environment, Merck also donates money and products to help people in need. We give to help the poor, to artistic and cultural programs, and to education. Our total donations—cash and products over 5 years—will have grown from slightly more than $18 million in 1987 to nearly $41 million this year.

According to survey reported in *Business and Society Review*, when our product and cash gifts are combined, Merck is one of the top 10 corporate givers in this country.

More than half of our cash contributions goes to education in the United States. As you can see, of the $13 million we gave to education in 1990, 67% went to programs in postgraduate education, 23% to undergraduate education programs, and 10% to pre-college education programs. We can't possibly support every worthwhile project, so we've decided to target our giving primarily toward programs that prepare students for careers in science and medicine.

In the last couple of years, however, we've supported more programs at the *pre*-college level to help address the crisis in education in the United States.

These statistics were compiled by *Fortune* magazine and they're horrible: every eight seconds of the day a child drops out of school; on international tests, U.S. students score at the bottom, or near the bottom in science; and every year 700,000 youngsters graduate from American high schools who can barely read their diplomas. A survey of 160 large corporations found that a growing number of U.S. companies—nearly 20%—have trouble finding workers who read well enough for the lowest level entry positions. Almost half of the companies said that up to 35% of their employees could not handle more complex tasks.

Given these trends, how can the United States ever expect to compete in a world marketplace that is increasingly technical?

There are, of course, many efforts under way to address our crisis in education. One is the Education Initiative of the Business Roundtable. Under direction of the BRT's Education Task Force—of which I am a member—we have enlisted the support of more than 170 chief executive officers of major corporations across the country.

Our objective is to work with governors in all 50 states to help address the problems, define the role business can play in solving them, and help to revitalize education across the country. The companies are devoting executive leadership, money and human resources in a 10-year effort. Thus far, BRT initiatives have been launched in 33 states.

We are working with Governor Florio [New Jersey] and the Commissioner of Education on several fronts. We studied all 555 school districts in our state and compared their financial, staffing and scholastic performance in school district "Report Cards."

At Merck, we launched an internal communications campaign so that our employees can see how dissatisfied they *should be* with the quality of U.S. education.

The themes we're using to make the point that our school children are not achieving the way they could or should. I think the message is pretty clear.

We're encouraging other New Jersey companies to launch similar "dissatisfaction campaigns." If they do, we can reach more than 100,000 New Jersey residents who work for BRT companies alone.

Another example of Merck's citizenship is the grant that we gave in order to build The Children's Inn at the National Institute of Health in Bethesda, Maryland. The facility is fulfilling a real need, and it is serving as a home away from home for seriously ill children who are treated at the NIH.

For many years, these children and their families had to find their own accommodations—often in hotels and motels miles away from the NIH campus—while the youngsters were being treated for life-threatening diseases.

Merck donated $3.7 million to construct The Children's Inn. It is a 32,000 square foot facility with bedrooms, kitchens, playrooms, family rooms—all the comforts of home—for these children and their families.

Inside, The Inn is spacious and comfortable, with plenty of room for children and parents to relax, to prepare meals and to share warm, personal moments.

One of the great things taking place at The Children's Inn is the support that the families are giving to each other while they all stay there.

When we opened The Inn, we expected the adults to support one another—but based on reports we are getting—it is surprising how *the children* are reaching out and giving each other so much empathy and support. Parents report that this personal contact is having strong therapeutic effects on the kids.

In one year, over 700 children have stayed at The Children's Inn. They have made more than 2,300 visits, and they've come from 49 states and 16 countries.

In July, to help celebrate the one-year anniversary of The Children's Inn, Merck gave an additional

$500,000 challenge grant to establish a "Friends Fund" to help sustain The Inn's future operations.

As a company, Merck is pleased that we have been able to find meaningful ways to demonstrate responsible global citizenship.

I'm also pleased that you're beginning your business education with projects to demonstrate a commitment to community service. Your experience should give you lasting satisfaction.

My father used to say that we are put on this earth to help others, and I firmly believe that. It's true of individuals and corporations. I hope the program here is the beginning of many years of commitment and corporate caring for the needs of others around the world.

■ KELLOGG COMPANY'S PROFILE
ON SOCIAL RESPONSIBILITY

The company is deeply committed to being an economic, intellectual, and social asset in each location where it has business operations. This commitment is firmly grounded in the belief that Kellogg people, products, financial resources, and technologies can, and do, make important contributions to the quality of people's lives.

Each business unit of Kellogg Company independently plans its own social responsibility initiatives and is held accountable for helping the company meet ambitious goals in this area. Kellogg employees are encouraged to be active in community affairs and are recognized for the contributions they make. Corporate support, local implementation, and employee participation ensure that the company's resources are directed in ways which truly make a difference.

Company founder, W. K. Kellogg, once declared, "I'll invest my money in people." This vision of corporate social responsibility led to the establishment of the W.

K. Kellogg Foundation, which, although legally separate, is Kellogg Company's largest stockholder. As a result of the Foundation's substantial holdings in the company, roughly one-third of all the company's dividends are distributed by the Foundation to charitable endeavors.

Kellogg Company's corporate contributions help charitable organizations and groups improve opportunities for fuller participation in our diverse society. Examples include:

- The United Negro College Fund (UNCF) Telethon, which Kellogg Company has sponsored since 1986 with annual contributions averaging over $1 million. The company has also organized Celebrity Tribute fund raisers for the telethon. More than 300 Kellogg employees and family members volunteer during the annual telethon. Kellogg Company's support for the telethon and other UNCF activities exceeded $900,000 in 1991.

- The NAACP's nationwide ACT-SO competition, which encourages and rewards scientific achievements by minority youth is also supported by Kellogg Company.

- Since 1983, Kellogg has sponsored Public Broadcasting's Reading Rainbow program, a highly acclaimed children's television program emphasizing the importance of reading for children.

- Annually, Kellogg funds a scholarship program— Youth for Understanding, to enable children of Kellogg employees in the United States and Canada to take part in a unique exchange experience with a family in another country. Thirty students are selected each year.

- Kellogg Company initiated and led a fund-raising effort to establish a math and science educational center for Battle Creek, Michigan area students.

- Kellogg Company sponsors the Kellogg International Student Scholarship Program (KISSP) which supports four international students each year at Kalamazoo College.

- Kellogg Company is the founder and co-sponsor of the World's Largest Breakfast Table held in Battle Creek, Michigan each year.

- Kellogg Company is the major sponsor of the Battle Creek International Hot Air Balloon Championship.

- Kellogg Company strongly supports local United Way efforts; SER Jobs for Progress, community economic development; international, state, and local Special Olympics, Junior Achievement; Student Expos; and a wide variety of health and wellness initiatives.

- Kellogg Company supports several job training initiatives, including: Opportunity Industrial Centers; Urban League targeted job training programs; Jobs for Progress.

Kellogg Company's commitment to responsible corporate citizenship has been recognized by many organizations. The Council of Economic Priorities, an independent social advocacy group which evaluates corporate social responsibility, has consistently awarded Kellogg Company its highest possible ratings in the areas of corporate giving, advancement of women and minorities, contracting, disclosure of information, community outreach, and environmental protection. In 1990, the Council named Kellogg one of the top five companies in the United States in the environment stewardship category, and in 1991 awarded Kellogg Company top honors in the employee responsiveness category.

National publications such as *Black Enterprise, Hispanic, Working Mother,* and *Ms.* magazine have also given Kellogg Company superior ratings.

Kellogg Company is intensely focused on the future success of its business, understanding that continued profitability and growth are the most important contributions Kellogg Company can make in any community. This focus on future success is evident in its commitment to capital improvements. Over the last three years, Kellogg Company has invested more than $1 billion around the world in facility and technological developments. These investments will contribute to Kellogg Company's worldwide growth and make it possible to continue its long-standing commitment to be an economic, intellectual, and social asset wherever it does business.

■ THE PRUDENTIAL INSURANCE COMPANY OF AMERICA'S CORPORATE PROFILE ON SOCIAL RESPONSIBILITY

Prudential Insurance Company has been nominated for its efforts to rescue Newark, New Jersey. Since, 1976, Prudential's Social Purpose Investment Program has targeted worthwhile social projects that might not otherwise qualify for loans because of their size, the risk involved, or the actual location of the project.

Separately, the company's investments through the Social Purpose Investment Program, operated through the Corporate Social Responsibility Division of the Public Affairs Department, totaled $30.4 million in 1990. These are divided among three main program areas: affordable housing, economic revitalization, and health care cost containment. Investments include a $15 million investment in the $63 million National Community Development Corporation. The program is aimed at stimulating affordable housing and economic revitalization in Newark and a number of other cities where Prudential operates.

Prudential also has a volunteer recognition program called Prudential Partners in Community Service, which gave $1.2 million in 1990 to nonprofit organizations for which employees volunteer. The company's foundation's giving totaled $16.3 million in 1991.

Prudential was the long-term lender, providing a 20-year mortgage for Community Service Corporation for a joint venture between Supermarkets General Holdings Corp. and a local nonprofit, New Community Corporation, to develop a shopping center in the Central Ward of Newark, the first since riots destroyed the neighborhood in the 1960s. New Community's quest for support from other companies was fruitless. In contrast, Prudential proved eager to work with the group.

172   *Chapter 7*

Andy Ditton, executive vice president of Local Initiatives Support Corporation, another group which Prudential has long supported with low cost loans, said "The telling characteristic of Prudential's involvement in community development is their staying power." Over time, almost all major insurers have left the business of offering below-market community loans. Prudential, in contrast, is as active as it has always been.

In Newark, Prudential also operates a program called READY (Rigorous Educational Assistance for Deserving Youth). If the student completes high school, READY will pay the student's college expenses or offer equity in operating businesses that are started in Newark. One of the key components is the READY mentoring program, whereby Prudential employees work with Newark students to help them achieve their goals.

■ ADOLPH COORS COMPANY'S CORPORATE PORFILE ON SOCIAL RESPONSIBILITY

The Adolph Coors Company, founded in 1873, is included among the largest U.S. corporations in *Fortune* magazine's rankings. The company operates businesses in brewing, aluminum rigid container sheet, ceramics, folding carton and flexible packaging and biotechnology. The company employs more than 11,700 people, and has shown its commitment to the community.

In 1990, for example, Coors Brewing Company, the largest subsidiary of the Adolph Coors Company, announced plans to donate $40 million over five years through its Foundation for Family Literacy for programs aimed at improving family literacy. More than 40,000 people have been helped to date through the combined efforts of Coors, its distributors, and nonprofit literacy partners.

Charitable Giving

In 1991, the brewing company budgeted nearly $4 million for charitable giving (including in-kind contributions).

Volunteerism

More impressive is the brewing company's commitment to volunteerism. Its employee volunteer group—the V.I.C.E. (Volunteers in Community Enrichment) Squad—donates thousands of hours to volunteer service every year. In 1990 alone, more than 3,700 employees—more than a third of the Coors work force—donated more than 36,000 hours of service to 123 different projects. In fact, the V.I.C.E. Squad received the prestigious 1990 Volunteer Action Award from President George Bush.

Employee Wellness Center

In 1981, Coors opened a 25,000-square-foot wellness facility at its Golden, Colorado, plant. The Wellness Center was the brainchild of William K. Coors, CEO of Adolph Coors Company. His goal was to have "the healthiest employees in the Rocky Mountain Region." The mission of the Wellness Center is to provide fun, cost-effective, state-of-the-art health promotion, screening, testing, and education programs to enhance positive life-style changes.

The Center, open 97 hours per week, is available free of charge to employees, retirees, spouses, and dependents (12 years or older). The Coors Wellness Center has received national recognition from the Association for Fitness in Business and Kelly Communications for its emphasis on providing information and opportunities to employees to promote healthy living. The Center also serves as a role model to other corporations in developing their own employee wellness programs.

The Center provides classes and health education in the following: fitness classes (50 plus per week), cardiovascular exercise equipment, strength training machines, free weights, stress management, anger management, orthopedic rehabilitation, smoking cessation, cholesterol education classes, supermarket savvy, individual nutrition counseling, cancer support groups, smart heart, wellness counseling, cardiac counseling, alcohol awareness, pre/postnatal, parenting, well back clinic, health risk appraisals, lifesteps, and weight management.

In addition, the following screenings and evaluations are offered: cholesterol screening, blood lipid testing, body fat evaluation, submaximal exercise evaluation, mammography, maximal GXT, skin cancer screening, and blood pressure tests.

Environment

Coors has made tremendous strides in environmental management. In fact, in 1991, the company was recognized for environmental excellence by the National Association for Environmental Management.

However, Coors is the first to admit that the company is not perfect. Coors has made some mistakes in the past and is working diligently with the regulatory agencies to correct them and, more important, prevent them from happening in the future. The company's focus is on pollution prevention, and in 1992, it hopes to complete at least three pilot programs in pollution prevention throughout the Coors companies.

Coors received recognition in 1991 from the National Association of Environmental Management for its recent accomplishments.

Coors' Product and Social Responsibility

Coors Brewing Company derives the majority of its revenues from the sale of beer. The recent trend has been for society to promote and even legislate responsible drinking. As the nation's third largest brewer, Coors has a strong and vested interest in seeing that its products are enjoyed responsibly. Coors has made major investments in programs which address the problems of drinking and driving, substance abuse, and so on. It supports community-based programs to promote healthy life-styles and foster responsible decisions about drinking.

Prevention Programs

Alcohol, Drugs, Driving, and You (ADDY) is a comprehensive education program designed to reduce alcohol-

and drug-related auto accidents among teenage drivers. Coors provided the initial funding for ADDY in 1983 and has continued to support the development and distribution of the program. ADDY has been cited as a model educational driving program by the National Safety Council. Coors and 80 of its distributors have been recognized by the National Highway Traffic Safety Association for their role with ADDY at the local level.

National Organization of Student Assistance Programs and Professionals (NOSAPP) takes the success of employee assistance programs to the schools to help youth deal with the stresses of adolescence. Student assistance programs are effective in preventing and reducing student problems such as alcohol and drug misuse and abuse, teen pregnancy, delinquency, suicide, and school dropout. NOSAPP has planned a significant role in the rapid spread of student assistance programs across the country by serving as a clearing-house of information and providing technical assistance in starting and growing student assistance programs. Coors was instrumental in forming NOSAPP several years ago and has been a major supporter in years since.

Partners for Youth Leadership (PYI) is a national program that promotes, supports, and reinforces youth involvement and leadership activities. The program, which provides training for school and community organizations, has been implemented in school districts across the country and has involved more than 100,000 students.

Higher Education Programs

National Collegiate Alcohol Awareness Week (NCAAW) is an annual event held in October on more than 3,000 college campuses around the country. The purpose of NCAAW is to encourage on-campus activities and community participation in alcohol education. Each year, Coors awards scholarships to the six colleges that develop the most innovative alcohol awareness and education programs.

Coors is involved with the *Inter-Association Task Force on Campus Alcohol and Other Substance Abuse Issues,* which represents student affairs professionals across the country. One purpose of this organization is to address alcohol policies and alcohol education programs being developed on college campuses.

And, as do other major brewers, Coors supports *Boost Alcohol Consciousness Concerning the Health of University Students (BACCHUS)*, a national student organization with more than 335 affiliated chapters of colleges across the country. Students involved with BACCHUS encourage their peers to develop responsible habits and attitudes toward alcoholic beverages. The organization promotes respect for state legal age laws and campus policies.

Responsible Advertising

Coors also works to build awareness of the issues surrounding the misuse of alcohol through advertising, public service announcements, posters, and other materials. One of the first steps Coors took to increase awareness was the placement of the "Drink Safely" logo on all Coors packaging. In 1986, Coors became one of the first major brewers to develop a television advertisement to encourage responsible drinking.

Coors Brewing Company is firmly committed to marketing practices that demonstrate responsibility and concern for the safe enjoyment of its products. It encourages only legal and responsible use of its products and adheres to the Beer Institute Advertising Guidelines set forth for the brewing industry, as well as those of the Inter-Association Task Force. Coors' policies state that Coors' advertising and other marketing efforts should be directed only to those of legal age of purchase. It avoids glamorizing excessive consumption and portraying unsafe behaviors. In May 1991, Coors voluntarily agreed to remove the slogan "Won't Slow You Down" from national advertising and promotional efforts. Moreover, Coors has led the fight for the right to inform consumers of the alcohol content of beer. It has gone to court to try to provide consumers with that information.

On December 11, 1991, the U.S. surgeon general and executives of some of the nation's leading wine, beer, and distilled spirits companies met to discuss and address the problem of illegal underage drinking. In a joint statement issued by Surgeon General Antonia Novello and members of the alcohol beverage industry, both parties stated that they were "encouraged by the steady decline in illegal underage drinking at the high school level, and in the decreasing number of traffic fatalities involving teenage drivers as documented in recent studies. The efforts of the private sector and the family [that]have led to the improved awareness of this problem are recognized and supported."

Sponsorships

Coors Brewing Company sponsors many programs, including cultural events and sports individuals, teams, and leagues. These sponsorships enhance the quality of life of its consumers and others who enjoy watching these activities. Many of these events would not take place without Coors' sponsorship, and Coors believes sponsorship of community events does not cause misuse or underage drinking. In fact, Coors involvement with sports provides many opportunities to convey meaningful moderation messages to a broad public audience through signing and other appropriate vehicles. Coors' relationship with celebrities also provides a vehicle for them to promote safety, including legal and responsible decisions about drinking.

Coors' "Literacy. Pass It On" Program

In 1990, Coors launched a five-year, $40 million program committed to reaching 500,000 adults with literacy services. In two years, Coors' "Literacy. Pass It On" achieved the following:

- Donated $2.25 million to local, regional, and national nonprofit literacy organizations.
- Generated more than 45,000 calls to the Coors' Literacy Hotline from people who wanted to learn to read or help teach someone to read.

- Reached 201,000 new adult readers with literacy services.

- Provided substantial national support to Laubach Literacy Action (LLA), Literacy Volunteers of America (LVA), Opportunities Industrialization Centers of America (OIC), and SER-Jobs for Progress to expand their literacy services.

- Donated a portion of the proceeds from children's book, *Ira Wordworthy*, by Stephen Cosgrove to Wilder Opportunities for Women. Some $750,000 will provide literacy training for 20,000 low-income women in the United States.

- Was honored by First Lady Barbara Bush with a Certificate of Appreciation for support of the Third National Adult Literacy Congress, a Washington, D.C., conference for new adult readers.

Program Overview

Coors' "Literacy. Pass It On" program is the only comprehensive, long-term commitment by an American corporation which addresses all levels of the national illiteracy problem: raising awareness, recruiting volunteers, supporting a hotline, and generating funds. The program began in March 1990, when Coors Brewing Company launched a national $40 million program to reach half a million people with literacy services by the end of 1994. Coors formed partnerships with four national literacy organizations to accomplish this goal.

Public Awareness Campaign

A major element of this program is an extensive public awareness effort. The multimedia component of the program entails newspaper, magazine, radio, and billboard advertising, as well as direct marketing to promote solutions to illiteracy. Other program components include advertising and public relations programs targeted to the general market, African-Americans, Hispanics, and women.

In addition to advertising, special events and programs are planned to heighten awareness of illiteracy and its presence in the community, as well as generate funds to combat the problem on a local level. To help spread the word locally, regionally, and nationally, the program includes celebrity spokespersons such as film star Danny Glover, recording artists Jeffrey Osborne, Lisa Lisa, and Vanessa Williams, and author Stephen Cosgrove, who will be making special appearances at the events.

The Coors Literacy Hotline

Coors' "Literacy. Pass It On" program includes the Coors' Literacy Hotline, a toll-free number (800-626-4601) to help direct nonreaders and volunteer tutors to programs in their local areas. The hotline operates seven days a week at 8-hour-plus days. Both English- and Spanish-speaking operators answer this number daily, while interpreters for other languages and dialects are available on request.

The hotline database contains information on 18,000 literacy programs and approximately 60,000 human services programs throughout the United States and its territories.

Coors' "Literacy. Pass It On" Celebrity Spokespeople

The caliber of celebrities involved indicate the stature of Coors' literacy program.

■ Actor *Danny Glover* is the celebrity spokesperson for Coors' "Literacy. Pass It On" program. Known in Hollywood as the man who "is always doing something for underprivileged people," according to co-star and friend Mel Gibson, Glover has dedicated his life to helping others.

"The issue of family literacy is an important one to me personally. I have worked to inspire a love of reading within my own family," says Glover. One of Hollywood's most versatile and respected actors, Glover has gained international star status for his box office busters *Lethal Weapon, Lethal Weapon 2, Lethal Weapon 3,* and for his recent hit *Grand Canyon.*

■ Singer *Jeffrey Osborne* has dedicated the last two years to helping Coors with the battle against illiteracy. "I've spent many years making music. With Coors' 'Literacy. Pass It On,' I hope to make a little magic," says Osborne. He began as a lead singer and occasional songwriter with the band L.T.D. In 1990, after a two-year absence from the recording studio, Osborne returned with a powerful album, "Only Human," and a national tour.

■ Singer/entertainer *Vanessa Williams* has also campaigned with Coors against illiteracy. "I know that nothing is more important to personal growth, success and self-esteem than literacy," says Williams. Williams has proven this statement through her success in theater, television, and motion pictures, and she is committed to helping others succeed through promoting literacy.

■ Performing artist *Lisa Lisa*, of Lisa Lisa and Cult Jam, believes "You can't be a singer or an actress or a baseball player, or anything at all unless you can read," she said. This is why she has made a commitment to the Coors' campaign against illiteracy. "I know that if I couldn't read, I wouldn't be here today," says Lisa Lisa. Her fourth and most recent album "Hell's Kitchen" is named for the tough New York neighborhood where she grew up and still resides. This performer knows that one of the best avenues to rising above such an environment is education—and education is based on basic reading skills.

National Literacy Partners

Coors has joined the fight against illiteracy with four national literacy organizations. Laubach Literacy Action, Literacy Volunteers of America, Opportunities Industrialization Centers of America and SER-Jobs for Progress have been able to reach more nonreaders and expand existing adult learning programs with donations from Coors. Since 1990, Coors has donated a total of $2.25 million to these groups.

Laubach Literacy Action

LLA is a nonprofit, educational corporation founded in 1955. With established programs both nationally and internationally, LLA recruits volunteers and sponsors numerous projects to enhance volunteer literacy programs. It has 1,000 affiliates across the United States.

In 1991 alone, LLA's army of volunteers contributed more than 6.5 million hours of service to help teach more than 100,000 adults listening, speaking, reading, writing, and math skills.

Literacy Volunteers of America

Founded in 1962 and based in Syracuse, New York, LVA's mission is to use volunteers who provide a variety of services to enable people to achieve personal goals through literacy. Over the years, LVA has proven how effective volunteers are in the fight against illiteracy.

Its volunteers, supported by professional staff, serve as tutors, tutor trainers, secretaries, administrators, planners and communicators and in other functions necessary to achieve its mission. LVA has 450 affiliates across the country.

Opportunities Industrialization Centers of America

Founded in 1964 and based in Philadelphia, its national network of 70 community-based organizations is dedicated to providing training and educational and employment opportunities to anyone who is unemployed or underemployed.

OIC recognizes that employment and social opportunities are directly related to the ability to read and comprehend. Through its community-based Learning Opportunities Centers, OIC offers self-paced, computer-assisted educational programs that allow the entire family to increase reading and math proficiency.

SER-Jobs for Progress

To address the needs of the Hispanic community in the areas of education, literacy, job skills training, and employment, SER-Jobs for Progress was founded in 1964. Based in Dallas, the organization currently operates 111 programs in 83 cities across the country.

In 1986, SER initiated Family Learning Centers to combat the growing illiteracy rate among Hispanics. These centers have three components: an automated learning environment; community volunteer "literacy councils" that join parents, educators and private sector supporters to help educate minority students; and SER Care, a child care program designed to enhance children's educational development while their parents receive basic skills instruction.

Coors' Environmental Initiative

Adolph Coors Company, in association with the Center for Resource Management (CRM), established an innovative Clear Creek Watershed Improvement Initiative (CCWIIN), designed to provide leadership and coordination of ecological and recreational improvements in the Clear Creek Basin.

The initiative will address the impact on Clear Creek caused by intensive use of dozens of municipal, industrial and agricultural water rights holders along the entire basin. Improvement programs will focus on four areas: public access and utilization, including trails and greenbelts; water quality, including both point and nonpoint pollution sources; fish and wildlife, including riparian habitat improvement; and stream flow augmentation, examining innovative exchanges resulting in increased flows available for wildlife.

The program will operate under the direction of William V. "Jack" Hibbert, newly appointed water projects manager at Coors, who will be assisted by CRM, a nonprofit organization specializing in building alliances that encourages environmental stewardship. Adolph Coors Company also has a Clear Creek Technical Advisory Committee. The purpose of the committee will be to recommend a comprehensive improvement plan and facilitate improvements to the basin.

"A number of Adolph Coors Company operations are located in close proximity to Clear Creek," said Sandra Woods, principal environmental officer for Adolph Coors Company. "Coors is well positioned to take a leadership role in creating a community of interest in this watershed and we believe this initiative will enable Coors to encourage the development and focus of substantial resources on the improvement of the Clear Creek Basin for all users."

"This is an exciting and innovative program," said Terry Minger, president of CRM. "By bringing together all of the diverse members of the community who have a stake in Clear Creek's future, we believe we can achieve significant progress toward restoring the basin to ecological health. This initiative may well provide a model that can be replicated nationwide in other endangered watersheds."

■ LEVI STRAUSS & CO.'S CORPORATE PROFILE ON SOCIAL RESPONSIBILITY

Mission Statement

Levi Strauss & Co. is a firm that illustrates a socially responsible approach to business. Levi Strauss includes in its mission statement a section regarding this approach: "We will conduct our business ethically and demonstrate leadership in satisfying our responsibilities to our communities and to society. Our work environment will be safe and productive and characterized by fair treatment, teamwork, open communications, personal accountability and opportunities for growth and development."

Historical Commitment

Throughout its 142 year history, Levi Strauss & Co. has maintained a strong commitment to corporate social responsibility. This commitment is underscored by its progressive business practices, leadership initiatives in corporate philanthropy, and contributions to community-based organizations. Levi Strauss & Co. has set a leadership standard in the apparel industry by providing year-round employment and offering health care, profit-sharing, and retirement benefits to employees. In addition, Levi Strauss & Co. is committed to enhancing the competitiveness of U.S. operations by upgrading the skills of its work force and instituting alternative manufacturing methods. It was ranked among the Top Ten of America's Most Admired Corporations by *Fortune* and is often cited by both the business and nonprofit communities as a model of corporate social responsibility.

Social Investment

Levi Strauss & Co. traditionally sets aside 2.5 percent of pretax earnings annually to be used for charitable contributions through the Levi Strauss Foundation (LSF). The foundation's philanthropic contributions are specifically targeted to two key areas: (1) AIDS education and direct services for high-risk and under-served populations and (2) economic development programs that benefit low-income persons. In 1991, LSF and Levi Strauss & Co. made contributions totaling approximately $7.5 million to support nonprofit, community-based organizations and employee volunteer efforts on a worldwide basis.

At Levi Strauss & Co., employee involvement in volunteer and philanthropic activities is encouraged and supported by foundation contributions. Today, there are over 80 "Community Involvement Teams" of employee volunteers in plant communities worldwide. These local employee CITs volunteer time to work on community projects that address social issues such as homelessness, drug abuse, or the environment. CITs are also empowered to make grants to nonprofit organizations in their own communities.

In 1991, employee CITs awarded grants totaling nearly $1.8 million.

The foundation also administers a merit and need-based scholarship program for children and/or dependents of Levi Strauss & Co. employees. Approximately $275,000 is awarded annually in scholarships that can be used for study in two- or four-year colleges or for vocational training.

Levi Strauss & Co. has also been awarded recognition for its efforts in the area of corporate social responsibility. In 1991, the Levi Strauss Foundation received the Edward Brandt award from the National Leadership Coalition on AIDS for leadership in AIDS funding. In addition, Levi Strauss & Co.'s AIDS education efforts were the subjects of a case study published by the Harvard University School of Business in 1991. Recognition also came from the Hispanic community. Levi Strauss & Co. has been among the top 100 firms named in *Hispanic* magazine as "doing the most to provide opportunities to Hispanics."

Diversity

In the 1950s, before the passage of civil rights legislation, Levi Strauss led the industry in integrating its manufacturing plants in the southern United States. Today, Levi Strauss demonstrates its commitment to equal employment opportunities and affirmative action by recruiting and advancing people of color to positions of responsibility in the company.

In 1991, 35 percent of 1,429 Levi Strauss managers and supervisors were ethnic/racial minorities, and 50 percent were women. At the senior management level, the percentage of minorities and women in key positions has continued to increase. Racial/ethnic minorities represent 14 percent of senior managers, up from 9 percent in 1990; the share of women rose to 30 percent from 28 percent two years ago.

In addition to specifying diversity as a key value in the company's mission and aspirations statements, Levi Strauss & Co. promotes workplace diversity through a supportive corporate infrastructure:

- *Diversity training*: Diversity training is part of a comprehensive management development program that includes courses on values, leadership, and ethics. Managers are required to attend the four-day diversity program to learn ways in which diversity can be an asset to the company.

- *Employee associations*: Levi Strauss & Co. actively encourages and supports four associations that serve as informal corporate networks that offer professional development and mentoring opportunities to employees. The organizations are Asian/Pacific Islanders Employee Association, Black Professionals Organization, Gay/Lesbian Employee Association, and the Hispanic Leadership Association.

- *Minority purchasing program*: Levi Strauss & Co. has been a leader in promoting the use of minority- and women-owned/operated businesses. In the last four years, the company has purchased over $160 million in goods and services from minority business enterprises.

- *Project change antiracism initiative*: The Levi Strauss Foundation has contributed $3.3 million to Project Change, a Levi Strauss & Co. initiative aimed at helping communities reduce racial prejudice and improve race relations. Pilot efforts have begun in three Levi Strauss plant communities: Albuquerque, New Mexico; El Paso, Texas; and Valdosta, Georgia.

- *Extension of medical benefits to unmarried couples*: Consistent with its nondiscrimination policies, Levi Strauss & Co. recently extended medical and dental benefits to unmarried couples.

- *Physically/mentally challenged employees*: In response to passage of the Americans with Disabilities Act, Levi Strauss & Co. has formed a task force to seek ways to enhance company programs relating to physically/mentally challenged workers.

- *Workplace literacy*: Levi Strauss & Co. has established a continuing education initiative at all domestic facilities to improve employees' basic literacy and English as a second language (ESL) skills. The Basic Education and Learning (BELL) program offers funding for each facility to use in tailoring a basic education program to meet employees' needs.

■ *Work/family initiatives*: Levi Strauss & Co. has launched several initiatives promoting a better balance between work and family life. In addition to instituting flextime and child care subsidies for employees, Levi Strauss & Co. has established a Child Care Fund to increase the supply and improve the quality of child care services available to employees and communities in which their plants are located. This year, the Child Care Fund will make grants to nonprofit organizations in four pilot communities: El Paso, Texas; Knoxville, Tennessee; San Antonio, Texas; and Fayetteville, Arkansas.

■ *Environment action group*: Representatives from domestic and international divisions serve as members of this important Levi Strauss & Co. task force. The EAG makes recommendations to senior management regarding environmental policies and guidelines for action on environmental protection issues on a worldwide basis.

■ COCA-COLA'S CORPORATE PROFILE ON SOCIAL RESPONSIBILITY

The Coca-Cola Foundation is committed to serving communities through education. Its $50 million pledge toward improving education during the 1990s will support a broad spectrum of innovative approaches to the challenges in education.

The foundation supports programs for early childhood education, elementary and secondary schools, public and private colleges and universities, teacher training, adult learning and global education programs, among others.

Coca-Cola believes that the foundation has a responsibility to support education programs specifically for minority youth. By the year 2000, minorities will make up approximately one-third of the American population and an even greater proportion of public school students. Coca-Cola is committed to preparing this generation of young people for the enormous challenges awaiting them in an increasingly complex and interdependent world.

Because education is a continuum stretching from preschool through adult life, the Coca-Cola Foundation offers comprehensive support for broad-based educational initiatives. In 1990 alone, it awarded $5,073,067 in grants to over 140 programs in the United States and abroad.

The foundation's focus on education is consistent with the Coca-Cola Company's more than a century old commitment to social responsibility through corporate philanthropy. Indeed, the foundation is merely one aspect of the Company's system-wide support for education. For example, in 1990 the Coca-Cola Company contributed more than $1 million to educational institutions through the matching gifts program. Additionally, the company's operating units and the locally owned and operated bottling companies support education at the grass-roots level by sponsoring programs such as the Coca-Cola Scholars and "We Mean Business" Scholarships.

In 1991, in support of the national education agenda forged by President Bush and the nation's governors, the Coca-Cola Company established with other leading corporations the Coalition on Educational Initiatives. This coalition sponsors a monthly editorial forum in which parents, educators, students, and others share opinions and information about education programs that work.

Quite simply, they believe that American business must stand behind American education now as never before. A healthy business climate cannot long co-exist with an ailing social environment. Strengthening both has become the goal of its corporate philanthropy.

Communities at home and worldwide must be prepared for a more dynamic tomorrow. As one business committed to doing its part, the Coca-Cola Foundation is addressing high-quality educational opportunities for all people. The Coca-Cola Foundation's comprehensive commitment to education becomes a reality in diverse ways across a continuum from early childhood education to lifelong learning programs.

Entering the decade of the 1990s, the foundation stepped up its support of educational initiatives to address pressing needs in areas such as teacher training, minority education, innovative urban programs, and literacy initiatives. They also increased instructional support for kindergarten through grade 12, math and science education, health education, arts education, and college preparation.

It is no coincidence that the foundation's initiatives are consistent with the national priorities set at the 1989 Education Summit. They intend to help raise academic achievement—especially among low-income students—to help reduce dropout rates and to ensure an adequate supply of good teachers.

The following programs are part of the Coca-Cola Foundation's investment:

- *Early Intervention: An Ounce of Prevention*: Recognizing that early intervention can prevent a multitude of problems, especially in low-income families, the Coca-Cola Foundation supports several early childhood development programs.

- *Young People Helping Young People*: This year alone, almost a million young people will quit school before graduation. This dropout rate, one of the greatest threats to education in America today, has reached crisis proportions.

- *Bridging the Math/Science Gap*: As technology is integrated ever more thoroughly into people's lives and work places, public school systems struggle to keep pace in teaching math and science to young people.

- *Arts for More than Arts' Sake*: Integrating the arts into education can lead to significant improvement in students' overall academic achievement, as demonstrated by the success of the A+ Arts Infusion Program of the Greater Augusta (Georgia) Arts Council. A+ Arts teaches drama, music, dance, and visual arts, and it incorporates these arts into other academic subjects ranging from math to language to science.

■ *Filling the Teacher Pipeline*: Recognizing that tomorrow's leaders will be only as good as today's education, the Coca-Cola Foundation supports innovative teacher training programs.

■ *Filling the Student Pipeline*: By the year 2000, a majority of all new jobs will require postsecondary education, but growing high school dropout rates and high levels of illiteracy are taking a huge toll on college enrollment figures, especially among minority students. In fact, 82 percent of today's American colleges and universities must offer basic remedial instruction.

■ *Advancing Literacy*—Last year alone, high school diplomas were awarded to half a million functionally illiterate students. During the 1990s, the ability to read at the 12th grade level will be a prerequisite for entering the work force. Clearly, illiteracy is one of today's most pressing educational challenges.

The foundation supports a variety of literacy programs, including those conducted by Literacy Volunteers of America, Literacy Action, SER's National Hispanic Literacy Initiative, and Project READ in Atlanta.

■ MCDONALD'S CORPORATE PROFILE ON SOCIAL RESPONSIBILITY

McDonald's Corporation has been at the center of social responsibility for an extremely long time. The success of McDonald's is a twentieth-century fairy tale. In the early days of its entrepreneurial existence, it fought hard just to stay alive.

The children who fell in love with Ronald McDonald's found the love was returned threefold. It was McDonald's that answered the call for help when a Philadelphia Eagles' football player's young daughter was stricken with cancer. The player and his wife wanted to be with their child during treatment and found it nearly impossible. The hospital had no way of accommodating the family. The Eagles' team management and ownership heard of the hardship and, along with a local doctor, decided to create a residence close to the hospital that would allow families to be near their hospitalized children: a safe refuge, a place that felt like home. The team approached just one organization for help, and help they got. The first Ronald McDonald's House was created. Today, more than 150 Ronald McDonald's Houses bring families together, and the list keeps growing.

The corporation has also formed the McDonald's Charities Group whose focus is on children's educational issues. It also joined with professional golfer Greg Norman in supporting his golf tournament "The Shark Shoot-Out," which raises money for children's causes.

In recent years, McDonald's has developed initiatives to support black history education. On the environmental side, it has again been a leader. Its rain forest policy #5 states, "Tropical rain forests play an important role in the earth's ecology, and their destruction threatens the delicate environmental balance of our planet." As a result of this policy, nowhere in the world does McDonald's purchase beef raised on rain forest land or rain forest areas recently deforested. In fact, McDonald's has a strict corporate policy against using rain forest beef: "It is McDonald's policy to use only locally produced and processed beef in every country where we have restaurants. In those isolated areas where domestic beef is not available, it is imported from other countries. In all cases, however, McDonald's does not, has not, and will not permit the destruction of tropical rain forests for their beef supply. . . . This policy is strictly enforced and closely monitored. Any McDonald's supplier who is found to deviate from this policy or cannot prove compliance with it will be immediately discontinued."

McDonald's uses only 100 percent pure U.S. domestic beef in America, only 100 percent pure Canadian beef in Canada, only European Economic Community grown and approved beef is used in Europe. McDonald's will continue to monitor its beef suppliers and adopt policies and practices aimed at protecting the global environment on which the children of this world depend.

In addition to its rain forest policy, it announced in 1990 its McRecycle USA Program. It included a public commitment to purchase $100 million worth of recycled products each year for the construction, remodeling, and equipping of its restaurants. This figure is in addition to the millions its spends every year on recycling paper products for its offices and restaurants. McRecycle USA was created to reinforce support of recycling and is designed to stimulate the market for recycled materials. McDonald's recognizes that it takes an active market for recycling efforts to succeed, so it is trying to help. Watch for more and more McDonald's restaurants being built, renovated, and equipped with recycled materials.

McDonald's is building in elements to service other people's needs besides children's. It introduced the first braille menus for sight-impaired customers and a new picture menu designed for customers with speech or hearing difficulties. McDonald's continues to demonstrate the trend theme of doing well while doing good.

■ HERMAN MILLER CO.

Herman Miller, a furniture maker in Zeeland, Michigan, no longer uses tropical wood, such as rosewood from endangered rain forests, in its office desks and tables. Instead, he uses cherry, which does not come from endangered tropical areas. CEO Richard Ruch said he thought first of the environment aspects, and then he wondered what impact it would have on sales ($869 million in 1990). In fact, it added luster to Herman Miller's already shining reputation. Inspired by Miller's success, the Business and Institutional Furniture Manufacturers Association now urges all its members not to use tropical woods from endangered forests.

■ RECENT WINNERS OF THE COUNCIL ON ECONOMIC PRIORITIES AWARDS

The following companies received national awards from the Council on Economic Priorities at the awards ceremony in April 1992. This year's recipients are as follows:

Environmental Stewardship

■ *Church & Dwight Co., Inc.*, based in Princeton, New Jersey, won in the large company environmental category. Judges approved of the company's successful efforts to promote baking soda as an environmentally safe alternative to harsh household chemical cleaning products. In addition, Church & Dwight, the manufacturer of Arm & Hammer baking soda, is developing baking soda-based technologies to treat smokestack emissions and waste water. Church & Dwight sponsored both the original Earth Day in 1970 and the 20th anniversary celebration in 1990. Church & Dwight was the first company to introduce a phosphate-free detergent.

■ *Conservatree Paper Company* of San Francisco, California, earned the Environmental Award for small companies. The company is the largest wholesaler of recycled paper in the nation. Conservatree was recognized for its lobbying efforts on behalf of pro-recycling legislation, including a stronger Environmental Protection Agency definition of recycled paper, so consumers would be informed of the breakdown of recycled content origin.

Equal Employment Opportunity

■ *General Mills, Inc.*, of Minneapolis, Minnesota, earned the award in the category of Equal Employment Opportunity. The company's board is 13 percent women and minorities. Four vice presidents at the corporation headquarters are women and 3 are minorities, and some 36 percent of managers and officials company-wide are women and minorities. The company has an impressive record of purchasing from minority-owned businesses, and this year it launched a minority vendor program as well as an informal mentoring program.

Responsiveness to Employees

■ *Donnelly Corp.*, of Holland, Michigan, earned an award for responsiveness to employees. A leading manufacturer of automotive mirror and glass supplies, the company began involving employees in formulating policy making decisions as early as 1952. Profit sharing covers all employees, work teams elect their own leaders and set their own production goals, and employees serve on committees that are empowered with decision-making authority on matters including grievances. The Donnelly Committee, the pinnacle of this structure, determines policy on issues such as drug testing. This committee vetoed management's choice to drug test "for cause," instituting, instead, random testing to avoid bias.

■ *Lotus Development Corp.* of Cambridge, Massachusetts, earned a special citation in the responsiveness to employees category for an innovative benefits program.

Lotus, a producer of computer software, recently expanded its benefits programs, despite financial difficulties, to include homosexual partners of its employees. Lotus is now the largest for-profit company to provide benefits to gay partners, whom it refers to as spousal equivalents. One of the initial obstacles to be overcome in implementing this far-reaching program was the concern of insurance providers about costs. Lotus spent a significant amount of time convincing insurance carriers that the AIDS liability risk was comparable to other risks already covered for legal spouses, and therefore should not significantly change premiums. Moreover, Lotus seeks to provide a tolerant employment atmosphere for homosexuals who have made important technical contributions to the company.

Charitable Contributions

- *U S WEST, Inc.*, of Denver, Colorado, earned this year's award in the category of charitable contributions. Serving 14 western states, the regional telephone company has committed itself to economic development in rural areas. It is credited with helping indigenous Americans build self-reliant communities through job and educational assistance. The REVIVE program (Rural Economic Vitality Initiative), part of U S WEST's overall Economic Independent Initiative, focuses on microenterprise development, small business research and innovation, and training assistance, in rural areas.

Richard McCormick, CEO of U S WEST, was recently honored by the Sioux nation and the Lakota tribe at a traditional Lakota naming ceremony. He was given the Indian name of Wambli Ohitika, which means "eagle who cares." The 51-year-old executive received this highly unusual honor for his firm's contributions to Native Americans. Under McCormick's direction, U S WEST (estimated 1991 revenue of $10 billion) has given a total of $1.3 million to the American Indian College Fund and 21 tribal colleges. McCormick has said Native Americans respect the "right stuff," including traditions, family, and the environment. Some 650 Native Americans work for U S WEST, approximately 1 percent of its employees. McCormick's goal is to increase that number, particularly at higher management levels. As he pointed out, roughly half of the country's 2 million Native Americans live within his firm's 14-state service area.

■ *Tom's of Maine,* located in Kennebunk, Maine, won a charitable contribution award for small companies. This maker of natural and cruelty-free health care products exceeded the 10 percent limit on tax deductibility of corporate charitable gifts, a threshold few companies have crossed. Some two percentage points of the grant money is set aside yearly for employees to allocate via balloting. Staff members are permitted 5 percent of their paid time to do volunteer work. In 1991, the company donated to a charity that develops hiking trails along the Portland waterfront. It has also supported Maine Audubon and assisted the town of Kennebunk in expanding its recycling program by providing bins, which qualified the town for state pickups of recyclables. The firm also supports nonprofits that integrate the disabled into society and aid Native American causes.

Community Outreach

■ *The Prudential Insurance Company of America,* headquartered in Newark, New Jersey, and *Supermarkets General Holdings Corp.* of Woodbridge, New Jersey, jointly won in the category of community outreach.

■ *Supermarket General,* which operates supermarket and drugstore chains, including Pathmark and Purity Supreme, was praised for opening stores in Newark, New Jersey, and the Bedford Stuyvesant section of Brooklyn, where urban decay left residents nowhere to do basic shopping. In Newark, the store is co-owned with a nonprofit agency, the New Community Corporation. New Community hires the employees, ensuring that local residents have access to good jobs and training programs. Free health tests are administered at the pharmaceutical counter, also in conjunction with a local nonprofit agency. The company also employs mentally challenged adults in some of its stores, assisted by the Association for Retarded Citizens.

■ CONCLUSION

American big business is oftentimes slow to respond to emerging trends and conditions. However, American big business has continually demonstrated the charitable side of its nature with a long history of corporate giving. The new ideology in American business is to embrace a greater sense of commitment other than direct economic support. The various initiatives and programs being directed and funded by these companies go well beyond the concept of charity. These leading companies fully embrace the concept of philanthropic economics, of caring and sharing.

The workplace of the future is being defined as an extension or reinforcement of family values. The employees of these companies will receive the benefit of the enlightened thinking of management. As business turns the corner and moves beyond the restrictive end, and towards the caring and empowerment phase, it will enjoy greater loyalty from its customers and employees. The American dream still encompasses the idea of enjoying your work, being proud of the company you represent, and in turn having the company recognize your value and contribution.

A strategist's perspective: companies that sell or provide service to major socially responsible companies will be initially motivated, and subsequently required to demonstrate the same ideology and behavior as the larger companies (i.e., their customers), in order to retain their supplier status. The burden clearly is on the small companies who sell to the larger companies to recognize the leadership principles of their customers, and to modify their sales, marketing, corporate cultures, and practices to become socially responsible themselves and to follow the lead of their customers.

Eventually, big businesses will scrutinize their suppliers as a defensive tactic. For example, a large food processing company that determines that it is purchasing raw materials from a supplier that has a poor reputation in the areas of human rights, environmental disruption, and unethical hiring practices, to name just a few, will remove that supplier from its approved list. The economic might and muscle wielded by big businesses is a powerful determinant on many of their suppliers.

8

■

Philanthropic Economics in Motion

Based on the suppositions and conclusions of the ultimate impact that would be felt on small businesses brought about by customer or public pressure, it was our determination to focus our strategic thinking into the business to business marketplace.

We determined that if we could integrate the concepts of social responsibility with clearly defined tactics, we could encourage small business corporate cultures to espouse philanthropic economics. We believed in the viability of this strategy. We knew, however, that if we conducted this study purely as a consultant, the real business practitioners would find our conclusions oddly suspect. Therefore, I made the decision to engage the strategy as a working business model. We believed that if we were to become credible as socially responsible consultants to businesses, we would have to do more than theorize the ramification of this strategy. We decided to take this step of enlightened capitalism. We could develop a working model that significantly altered these preexisting cultures.

Establishing ourselves as a working model of enlightened capitalism was not in itself enough: we had to actively educate our small business clients about the benefits and power associated with socially responsible strategies. Our small and medium size business clients tended to think of the term "philanthropic economics" as ad-hoc giving, loss of control, and being targets for every charity in the community. In educating this group, we needed to move slightly beyond next weeks payroll considerations. Small and medium size businesses are burdened with a crisis management mentality. Therefore, discussions of long-term gains and economic stabilization are oftentimes discarded as a pure luxury. In recognizing the problems of the small and mid-size businesses, we also recognized the solution. Those that maintain the current mindset of crisis management are simply allowing their business to be moved in a reactive fashion. The option of a proactive strategy would in fact do no worse than the current crisis management scenario, but could very well provide an opportunity for a unique differential advantage, and the probability of being perceived as a higher value added supplier. The operative world became *change*.

We asked this group of small and mid-size companies to measure the effectiveness of a socially responsible strategy against the following criteria:

- Do the trends, conditions, and data supplied provide sufficient evidence that the American public and segments of American business are moving in this direction? (This is our intellectual discussion.)

- Has it been demonstrated to your satisfaction that the companies that subscribe to this ideology and business practice are oftentimes becoming industry leaders and enjoying the financial gains associated with such? (This is our financial discussion.)

- Have we demonstrated that contributing, sharing, involvement, and commitment with workers, customers, and the community, is not only personally satisfying, but also demonstrates the opportunity to get something back beyond direct compensation? (This is our emotional discussion.)

When we receive an affirmative to the above mentioned analysis and strategy plan, we then recognize a candidate who may be able to subscribe to the concept of enduring change.

In selecting the industries to which we would promote this strategy, we tried to focus on industries whose products and services were being purchased directly by a business, rather than a consumer. We wanted industries whose products and services were used in abundance by the general business community. We wanted to start with the typical supplier to big business.

The criteria that we would use to choose the industries we would develop was:

1. Find an industry that fits into almost every corporate setting as a supplier.
2. Find an industry whose total sales with the industry equal at least $10 billion.
3. Find an industry that is dealing with overcapacity or declines in gross margins.
4. Find an industry that sees itself in trouble (those that are in trouble will listen better).
5. Find an industry we know something about.
6. Find an industry that is used to large capital requirement to operate their business.
7. Find an industry that is primarily privately owned.
8. Find an industry that has lots of competition.
9. Find an industry that the consumer goods and package goods companies rely on for service.

The process of elimination and criteria measurement was endless. Once we had several industry candidates in focus, we began the design of a program. In the case of our first vertical test, we needed to build a model that was virtually airtight from conception to installation and, ultimately, to implementation on the side of our client. This meant that in most cases we would be asking companies that sold services to their current customer in one fashion, now to do it in a totally different fashion.

The issue was to become one of determining factors of whether our candidate industry could place some emphasis on marketing themselves versus simply being a low-cost provider. The issue of converting corporate culture would go far beyond the ideology of philanthropic economics; it would come down to sales tactics and business development practices. It seemed the further we got, the tougher it would be to pull together. Everything was a supposition. No one knew for sure.

What is it we wanted our intended clients to say to their customers? "If you purchase your products or services from my company, at the same service standard and quality standards you already require, and at the competitive price you deem fair, my company is prepared to contribute a percentage of that purchase to a charity or socially responsible initiative you have underway, in your name."

Initially, we would create a strategic partnership with the customers, who now receive a value extension from an ordinary business expense stream. Then we would help them accomplish their goals. Depending on the total dollars spent from this expense area, thousands of dollars or more can be contributed directly from the supplies to business. The benefit to our client would be the value-added social responsibility feature, plus, in the test market, which we will discuss in detail, additional public relations value would be provided to the corporation who placed the order.

■ PHILANTHROPIC ECONOMICS IN MOTION: THE USA COMMUNICATIONS PRINTER PROGRAM

Our first targeted industry (the first of 56 such industries) was to become the fifth largest industry in the United States, with a total of $134 billion in gross revenues, representing as much as 3 percent of the gross national product.

Our program was designed for the commercial printing industry, a highly capitalized cottage industry. Of the approximately 58,000 commercial printers in the United States, most are family-run businesses. The industry has several segments:

1. The traditional storefront quick printers that prefer to be known as business printers. Their primary focus is on small business with one- and two-color printing. This group represents approximately $1 billion in annual sales.

2. The commercial printers whose focus is on large corporate customers. Their equipment is designed for longer and more sophisticated work. This group is generally in the $5-40 million class of annual sales. This group represents approximately $40 billion in total sales and is the primary focus of our marketing effort.

3. The forms manufacturers who have annual sales in the $7-10 billion area.

4. The total represented segments of this industry equate to more than $135 billion in combined sales and services. Almost 3 percent of the gross national product is print related.

In developing our first business-to-business program and to engage fully philanthropic economics, we had to determine why a company's traditional marketing wasn't working and how to correct it. The questionnaire I created for myself was the first step. Returning to my force level analysis, I applied the same technique and asked, "What drives the printing industry?"

The driving force had been the growth of business itself. As business cycles ebb and flow, printing rises and falls along the same predictable curve. Printing is incorporated into various internal and external communication requirements of the business. Therefore, as business is experiencing a strong sales surge, business will naturally produce more advertising and promotional material. As more and more printers began to purchase larger and larger equipment to be better positioned as suppliers to the larger corporations, the printers' corporate pie became smaller. The printers believed that their investment in larger formatted equipment would provide them with a unique differential advantage over their competition.

Initially the strategy proved viable, but as time progressed, overzealous equipment manufacturers began to create financing programs that allowed almost anyone to secure larger equipment. The dynamic that was to follow was simply one of overcapacity, that is, too many presses, too few customers. Business was quick to take advantage of the highly competitive market. This allowed business to shop for the best price possible, and printers, with their equipment sitting idle and lease payments due, were motivated to do a job for little or no profit. The great squeeze had begun, and pricing pressure bore down on the entire industry. As a result, more and more printing firms began to collapse. Major firms attempted to buy smaller ones in a mad dash to pick up corporate accounts. The slowdown in the general economy, combined with the overcapacity, had a doubling effect. Add the recession to this scenario, and the results were catastrophic.

■ APPLYING CAUSE-ALIGNMENT TEST

This industry best fits a strategist's model for a theory of consolidation under a value-added umbrella. The external and internal trends affecting this industry made it obvious that a value-added concept, associated with cause-aligned reasoning, would be a powerful motivator to the printer's customers, that is, corporate America. The entire concept of philanthropic economics is one of serving the interest of the customer through closer ties to the values of those customers. Therefore, the corporation would be better prepared to continue to support the customers' causes through a printer's contribution formula program. The printer could now assist the corporation in a very direct fashion using a cause-aligned concept.

■ TARGETING A MARKET

Corporate America buys a tremendous amount of print every single day. No one program would fit 58,000 printers, so a printer segment had to be selected. The trends best positioned themselves for a printers' program of consolidation. In other words, the issue of total available market share left us only one alternative, to move existing market share into less fulfillment sources. In positioning this industry, it was clear that some segment would show up as the logical choice. The research indicated that a "no man's land" existed for the commercial printer. This printer was too big to be small, and too small to be big. A target group was chosen of firms doing between $5 and $20 million in annual sales. Typically, they were not able to downsize and were not big enough to attract serious outside corporate-financed interest. This target group was chiefly privately owned and closely held, and was also the most susceptible to changing their corporate culture to accommodate the shift of positioning. My proposed culture shift would be nothing short of a 180-degree market repositioning.

Printers rely solely on selling, and define that as marketing. We needed to define the difference between sales and marketing. Selling is an artform, marketing is a science. We knew we could prove to them that strategic marketing was dependent on statistical trend shifts and business analysis, and thus could begin to educate and modify their thinking. Easy to say, difficult to do. My target group showed signs of initially accepting the concept of change, at least intellectually. These printers agreed that their current tactical selling efforts were subject to the will of the marketplace and all the unknown variables that surround vendor selection. They recognized that they were virtually out of control. Customers were no longer loyal, instead they shopped hard and long. Consumers demanded better service, quicker turnaround, tighter control, extended payment terms, and increased flexibility. The printer had to perform under the burden of ever-declining margins. Constant reinvestment into state-of-the-art technology was a competitive requisite. This industry pays on a straight commission basis, so the pressure imposed by sales or management to buy bigger and better equipment is constant. In addition, qualified salespeople are difficult to find and keep in this industry. The print sales force is hard to motivate and just as difficult to control. Larger firms have the capital and market presence to invest more directly in people, their training, education, and so on, which gives them a greater hold on employees. Small companies with less than $5 million in sales have the owner, a top salesman, and maybe another relative. Survival is the controller and motivator. Our target group was the one with all the problems and in a no-win situation. They would listen to an alternative.

Add the printer's dilemma of adverse selection due to overcapacity and the lack of a measurable form of creating value-added service to the print order (no method for differentiation), and a graphic picture exists for a strategist. The perfect model is set for strategic alliance via cause-related marketing. The fact analysis is simple:

- Fact 1: Corporations buy printing.
- Fact 2: Corporations have customers.
- Fact 3: Customers' values are now important to corporations.
- Fact 4: Printers print.
- Fact 5: Printers need corporate America.
- Fact 6: Printers offer incentives to corporate customers that enhance their value directly to their own customers.
- Fact 7: A cause-related alliance is obvious.

■ IDENTIFYING A CAUSE WITH WHICH TO ALIGN

The program I developed incorporated ideas from many sources. My role was to integrate easily understood sales and marketing tactics to create a unique cause and effect relationship. My task initially was to identify a program that possessed *real value* for all concerned.

None of the parties associated with my developing concept would settle for anything less than tangible and measurable results. Hype or concept would not play out well with this critical audience. As a strategist, my activity was focused on selecting the right cause category. Random focus studies were initiated, attempting to pull samples from various life-style groups and the ultimate end user, the customer, to define what issues/causes they felt the strongest about. After several months of sampling, it was determined that although the survey group had dozens of real concerns, the top-ranking issue in a random pattern questionnaire always placed children first as the strongest and most emotional factor. We attributed this to the fact that a larger percentage of the sample can directly relate to the issue versus, as an example, homelessness, AIDS research, or environmental concerns.

Once we understood the primary focus, the picture began to take shape. Our study indicated that the total child was important, including health, education, safety, and so on. Affiliating with well-known organizations that dealt with specific illnesses or specific trauma was too vertical an application. We needed an affiliation that covered the specific as well as the broad-based care of children. The answer was discovered in the numerous children's hospitals through the country and their increasing commitment to caring for children. A point of real distinction for the children's hospitals is that *no* child is ever turned away for care. The various children's hospitals care for over 5 million children each year and from all national and socioeconomic categories. This focus group touches 200 million Americans directly or indirectly.

■ BUILDING A STRATEGIC ALLIANCE

In 1982, an organization was developed to assist the local hospitals raise dollars to offset their ever-increasing cost. The Children's Miracle Network (CMN) was developed with the assistance of founders Marie Osmond, John Schneider, and honorary chairman Bob Hope. The concept was a national event that joined together hospitals and local television stations with a telethon. The program was unique in two ways. First, each market would hold its own local telethon, so local corporations supporting this social cause could benefit from local media coverage and public relations. Additionally, and most important, every dollar raised on a local basis stayed in the local community: there would be no administration chargebacks. The media forum that was created via the telethon format was the perfect tool to encourage corporate America to support the Children's Miracle Network.

When all 185 television markets are tied together, the telethon reaches 93 million viewers directly each telethon year. This vast audience provides real motivation to advertising-driven corporate America. The Children's Miracle Network has attracted national sponsors like Wal-Mart, Hershey Foods, Dairy Queen, Marriott, and Johnson & Johnson to this dynamic forum by encouraging the corporate sponsors to develop and drive cause-related marketing programs themselves. The sponsors developed various themes ranging from coupon redemption that provided a revenue source to the hospitals, to discount special events, and traditional fund raisers. Each corporation benefits economically, but so do the hospitals and the children. Corporations enjoy greater sales using a cause-related affiliation with CMN. It was clear to me that the very same corporations aligning themselves with CMN as national or local sponsors *all bought a lot of print*!

■ DETERMINING A COMMON BOND

If we could develop a program that allowed corporations to *increase* their *contributions* or *create a contribution* to CMN, *without spending any new dollars*, we would have a unique value-added feature. The method was simple. Corporations already have a preexisting print need and budget. What this scenario created was the beginning of a new strategic alliance that would benefit all concerned. With corporations already committed to this high-profile media event, and having identified children as the cause, we now had a valuable formula for the printing industry.

The CMN world was populated with all the right factors, including national celebrities like Mary Hart, Merlin Olsen, Marilyn McCoo, Bill Cosby, Kenny Loggins, and honorary chair Bo Jackson, to name just a few. CMN itself had grown in just ten short years. Last year alone it raised more than $100 million, making it the largest telethon in the world.

Printers are not marketers. For the most part, they see themselves as custom manufacturers. They sell printing by providing *price, service,* and *quality.* To alter the culture of this industry would not be easy. First, they did not practice marketing in a conventional sense. What would they know about the latest method known as cause-related marketing? The method I developed and the model that was created is as follows:

The first was to see the CMN marketing people at the national headquarters in Salt Lake City. The meeting took place at 6:00 A.M. in a local hotel. Our meeting was with the vice president of marketing and the vice president of public relations; neither knew who we were or what we were about, yet they had the foresight to allow us an opportunity. In other words, they were open to new ideas. I came to this meeting armed only with a concept. My expectations were limited.

The idea I presented to Jay Vestal, vice president of marketing, and Steve Williams, vice president of public relations, was direct. My plan was to create the first business-to-business cause marketing program, one that would benefit CMN by incorporating the printing industry into a national network of independent printers who would hold a designation in their local markets as the official printer to the Children's Miracle Network. This 200-member network of printers would offer to corporations in their market a simple and straightforward proposal. Assuming the printer met a corporation criteria of price, service, and quality, for the right to be the corporation's printer of choice, the printer would contribute to the local CMN-affiliated hospital 3 percent of the gross amount of any printing order fulfilled by the printer. A trust fund would be established at the hospital in the name of the awarding corporation, that is, philanthropic economics.

■ **INCORPORATING VALUE-ADDED BENEFITS**

The benefits to the corporation were dynamic. Printing is a necessary business expense, so no new funds needed to be generated. By selecting a member printer, a philanthropic contribution was generated for the corporation. This dollar amount would be redeemable come telethon time the same way any other dollar would be redeemable. Each local telethon has thresholds of contributions, categories that entitle the corporation to various promotional features. One of those features, as an example, is the right to an on-air appearance for check presentation of the gifting corporation. In most markets, the minimum on-air criteria is about $3,000. A corporation that buys print repeatedly throughout the course of a year may buy as much as $1 million or more. If that firm elects to use one of our network printers, and take advantage of the 3 percent contribution, $30,000 in the company's name is given to the local CMN hospital. A donation of this value would place this corporation in the top 10 percent of givers in the local market and allow it to benefit from airtime, logo use, and many other promotions valued more than 3 times the amount of the contribution, all generated simply through the print purchase.

Skeptics will raise their hands to ask how the printer can afford this amount off the top, unless it was really built back into the price somewhere. First, corporations that would consider this program have the most sophisticated purchasing system that always receives a number of bids or quotes on any print project. This buyer would know from the start if the cost of the program was buried in the cost of the job. Next, the printer who used that ploy would lose that business. Still, how can printers afford the program? Several suppositions justify the 3 percent contribution.

The belief in the translated value to the corporation in very real value, presented a cause and effect factor for a new business capture. I believed that this economic proposal is compelling to a corporation, especially in tough economic times. The dollar stretching cannot be ignored for a fiscally sensitive corporation. This translates into an account development profile for the printer to be highly improved as compared to its conventional selling practices. This factor alters a major component known as a quote-to-hit ratio. As a result of the cause marketing program, the ratio improves, and the program has real economic value. Assume the industry average is 1 print order in 20 quotes for conventional selling. If, through this value-added incentive program using cause marketing, that ratio becomes 1 job out of every 5 quotes, this factor would influence the sales and general administration costs of the company. This would translate into new dollars for the printer.

Next, assume that the improved selling climate translates into more volume, filling up available plant capacity. This distributes the total fixed overhead cost over a greater volume, making printers extremely profitable when they fill available capacity. The most measurable aspect is the unique partnership printers enjoy with their suppliers of products such as paper, ink, film, chemicals, and equipment. The program we designed encourages and motivates the suppliers to take a direct role by offering the printer discounts on raw materials. Naturally, the printer spends millions on consumable supplies.

What would motivate a supplier to support this program, other than the obvious charity affiliation of the Children's Miracle Network? The business issue is straightforward. The printer now has a method to grow business over the normal competitive restraints. This translates into more purchase of supplies to offset the cost of the 3 percent donation: Once again, philanthropic economics in action.

■ SETTING UP THE PROGRAM

The specifics of the program, designed for printers with the help of the Children's Miracle Network, are simple. My company established a national master license agreement that provided us the authority, in conjunction with the member hospitals, to designate an official printer to the Children's Miracle Network in virtually every U.S. city. The license provides us with a vehicle. The program, however, needed to be clearly defined. It had to consist of a marketing plan, a sales plan, a public relations plan, and various sales and marketing support programs, including logo and promotion materials, customer videos, meeting and information systems, and so on. To build the network was the first step; city by city we traveled the country to meet the candidates.

As candidates converted to members, we began to create what is known as *critical mass*. Each member's equipment was similar yet dissimilar enough to provide full coverage of every graphic arts requirement, from the smallest presses to the largest. The value of this critical mass, in theory, made every member equal in all aspects to provide the print customer control over all print needs, not just what the local printer could manufacture. The great equalizer in that members can exchange job requirements and needs over our own on-line telecommunication link provided by Printer's Periscope in Pennsylvania.

With this unique concept now being positioned, the next step was to create a national buying co-operative. When completed, this network will represent over $2.5 billion in annual supply needs. Once the network exceeds over 100 members, forecasted in 1993, we will begin a top level national sales development effort. The members of this first business-to-business program are excited and motivated to be a vital part of their communities. The network's contribution potential for the hospital is outstanding. Two hundred members contributing at least $20,000 per market would generate $4 million a year—raised out of a source that did not exist two years ago—philanthropic economics.

In recent months we have begun to add further value for our network members by showing them exciting ways to use their printing capacity to help the kids, with custom-designed products created by our team. The purpose of this in-depth discussion is not to boast, but to encourage. We have identified over 56 other industry groups that could benefit from exactly the same strategy, and they will, it is hoped, become more branches on the tree, helping us recognize the reality of the American Business Coalition for a Better World. Our program has now grown beyond children's issues, but it continues to support them. We believe we need to provide the benefiting corporate customer greater latitude in dealing with this total issue of social responsibility.

It is our corporate customers—along with us—that make the principles come together. Therefore, we have broadened the scope to take into consideration any worthwhile social issue to use in this same supporting partnership philosophy. We will not dictate to a corporation what cause they should support, and as a strategic partner, we will do our best to support any initiative the corporation deems socially relevant.

Eventually, our attention will most assuredly cover environmental issues. To that end, we will be encouraging the printer network and their suppliers to be environmentally smart, including the use of recycled paper and soybean-based inks in their business. It is our hope that the entire industry will embrace the strategy, along with our efforts to show them how they can take a leadership position.

In that regard, we have much work to do. We have begun to model a center here in Arizona that would ultimately be used to expand the philosophy.

Philanthropic economics was developed only after the entire issue of corporate social responsibility had a foothold in corporate America. I credit those who came long before me in the pursuit of this marketing success story, one of the few win-win situations I have ever seen.

■ THE AMERICAN BUSINESS COALITION FOR A BETTER WORLD

The role that USA Communications may assume in the future is that of a teaching practitioner. Every day more is learned about how companies are creating and developing initiatives in the area of social responsibility. Our organization receives calls from all types and sizes of organizations seeking information, knowledge, insights, and research into this incredible trend shift. Given the demand for information sharing and development of strategic positioning, USA Communications is taking the necessary steps to create the framework that will provide a clearing house and service center to companies of all sizes. Thus, organizations seeking to focus on social responsibility as a major thrust to their enterprises will have a resource.

This center, which will open in 1993, will be located in Phoenix, Arizona. It will provide an ongoing meeting and networking center for information, co-operatives, and business plan development. It will directly interface with dozens of socially active organizations and deal with topics ranging from AIDS to drug abuse, education, health care, conservation, the environment, animal rights, human rights, Third World issues, and so on. The center will work with a number of business schools as well as all segments of corporate America. The primary mission is to provide those companies already committed a social relevance with programs and initiatives via feedback sessions, surveys, research, and program enhancements. The center will offer companies the opportunity to educate themselves on the subject of corporate social responsibility. The center will assist in plan and program development for the entrepreneur who is creating products or services that have social relevance.

This association will become a reliable clearing house for information gathering and sharing. Major corporations will find a high level of creativity and innovation in the center. Nonprofit organizations will be able to locate corporate support for their programs. The small business sector will find both network affiliations and models to build their businesses. The center is an exciting concept, and although the seed was germinated at USA Communications, it is a center that belongs to all the companies that have and will come to embrace social responsibility.

Our critics will say that the concept of this form of philanthropic economics is exploitative. Our response is: of the vast array of social problems that face our society every day, each solution is contingent upon economics. Our government system is no longer adequate to manage effective social programming. Our personal and business tax structure cannot be burdened with the weight of billions of dollars of socially needed capital. Our society's infrastructure is business. Our economy's lifestyle reflects accurately how well or how poorly business is doing. There is a direct correlation between business, the American people, and our social requirements. What's good for business can now be logically converted through this philosophy into being good for society.

The cost associated with the solution to just one issue is monumental. If American business can benefit by this initiative and share the wealth proportionately, then theoretically, everyone wins. In developing marketing strategies that incorporate cause consciousness, we feel we have taken a responsible step. The effectiveness of the strategy is measured directly by each company involved and the various causes they support. The reality of personal giving and corporate giving is now in a highly competitive state. I've had the opportunity to sit in dozens of corporate foundation's offices and see first hand the volume of grant requests they receive each week. Corporate America, facing its own highly competitive environment, finds more difficulty with the concept of taxation in direct giving. They do favor and support the concept of win-win, which allows them to develop cause initiatives that directly or indirectly help to build positive consumer relations, profits, and earnings for the benefit of their employees and shareholders. The purists who consider the strategy to be exploitative need to provide an alternative to their method of direct giving.

Competition is the operative word in American business. This strategy helps to make more companies competitive. My motivation in writing the book was that more, or even all, companies found a strategic opportunity in their businesses that would give back more to society and at the same time, make their business a more secure employer for the American worker.

9

■

Initiating a Philanthropic Economic Business Strategy

No matter what the business and what its size, one basic thing is required—management.

Management will determine whether a business succeeds or fails, is profitable or not. Management allows a firm to take on and run a successful socially responsible program and fit it into the business. Management is the most overlooked word in business and also the most misunderstood. In my training days of executive development programs, I would always start by asking my students (who were already senior managers of large companies) one question, "What is management?" This highly paid audience had some interesting responses. Engineers would define it in planning terms, coupled with cost containment, finance executives would define it in profit and loss terms, administration would define it in people terms, and sales would define it in market share and competitive terms. Each was narrowly correct, yet many times mutually exclusive of the other. No one could give me a complete and generic answer because these managers were what I like to call the hole diggers, vertical thinkers who have little or no instinctive vision. There are two distinct forms of thinking: vertical thinking, which fits most professionals, mobile managers, and lateral thinking which incorporates and encourages creative thought and the ability to recognize cause and effect reasoning over an entire sphere of influence. Lateral thinkers do not possess what one would define as expert knowledge in any one area, but they do possess the ability to understand interaction.

■ SOCIAL ISSUES AS PART OF STRATEGIC PLANNING

Cause alignment should not be considered until managers fully realize how this ideology, implanted into the company, will affect the corporate culture. The issue of management is most critical and the core of every business. Therefore, I encourage you to learn and exercise our definition of management: "Management is the guiding and directing of the human and physical resources of the company into a dynamic organizational unit that accomplishes the *specific* objectives of those being served (customer) with a high degree of morale and satisfaction on the part of those performing the service (employees)." This basic concept is often overlooked in the development of a strategic plan. As a strategist, my job is to develop strategic thinking first, the plan second. That cannot be done if the audience is tightly locked into a vertical bias, unless the vertical biases are relaxed. It is extremely difficult to alter or improve corporate culture.

Strategic thinking is not some mystical art form. It is, however, usually different from task management processes that vertical managers develop. All strategic thinking processes focus on the concept of defining the trends and cultural climate into the heart of the plan known simply as the "mission statement." The mission statement is critical to a company and absolutely necessary when beginning cause consideration. Every firm, whether it plans it or not, has a company culture which often reflects the company founder, president, and employees. This culture precedes involvement with causes. Executives must be sure what signals the current culture is projecting before trying to wrap itself in the warm and glowing cocoon of cause alignment. A firm can do irreversible damage to itself if the cause-consciousness it espouses appears to be exploitative rather than a sincere attitude and real commitment. There is nothing worse to see than full-page newspaper advertisements taken out by oil companies showing themselves in harmony with wildlife and nature, and then two pages later in the same newspaper, read a story of an oil tanker that has run aground and killed thousands of animals. Ask executives of such a firm's involvement with a cause program and the managers will look puzzled and say they had not heard about it. Nor should a company whose employees cannot read and that has no company-sponsored program to help, promote a literacy program. Cause alignment works well, but a firm cannot move before examining its company culture.

■ THE ENLIGHTENED CEO

With the success now being seen at both ends of the business world (that is, large multinationals and smaller entrepreneurial companies that designed their philosophies of principles and profit from the start), the next likely group to be affected will be the thousands of established companies in the middle. This vast arena will slowly yet surely be integrated into the movement of socially responsible companies.

The manner in which they become enlightened may not always be proactive. Companies may find that to compete, they must subscribe to the new ideology. Companies that supply industry directly may encounter resistance from their customers unless they meet new emerging criteria.

The unenlightened will need to examine how they do business. The decontamination will be a mandate in the near future. This process may be painful and costly, but the alternative is pure suicide. A corporation's entire culture should be examined from the ground up. A new model will have to be created and implemented over time. Old beliefs must be challenged and reexamined in a new light. Management will be measured against the new philosophy. Employees and workers' relationships will be redefined. Attitudes will change or the people will change. A facade of social responsibility cannot be presented to the public when behind the walls of that company, management practices from the Dark Ages are being carried out. Family owned and operated businesses will have tougher times than those midgroup companies that are public or a division of other companies. Unenlightened entrepreneurs will also find it hard to compete unless they differentiate and embrace the concept of social responsibility.

Companies will fall into two areas of reactive planning:

1. One group will do it by default—they feel they must do it.
2. The other group will do it by design—they will subscribe to the general principles of the philosophy.

The first one will approach the issues with the mind-set of compliance. This "do and say the right thing" approach is a preplanned roll-out strategy which basically states, "Use it when the need fits and put it away when it doesn't." The *appearance* of a plan is effective only as long as the company can keep the facade alive. The danger is being exposed, which is inevitable. In that case, it would have been better not to have had a plan at all. The commitment of management for real change must be in place. Once set forth on this path, there is no logical retreat. It is like the dentist's office, it may hurt, but it will be worth it in the long run—the operative statement being *long run.*

This is not a short-term fix; the company that embarks on this journey is ultimately going to prevail over ones that do not. Hundreds of companies throughout the United States are deeply involved in the concept of quality improvement. The functional side of quality improvement deals directly with statistical controls. The human dynamic is the people who maintain those controls. People are at the center of all quality programs. The goal of business is to have the worker share in the company's quality values to become a pro-active, solution-oriented force. The preponderance of evidence in this book should illustrate that the need for change is now.

There is no simple way to accomplish this task, but each journey begins with a first step. In that regard, one must ask the following question, "What message do we send to our customers?"

- Do they see us just doing our jobs?
- Do they see us as being responsible to the environment?
- Do they see us as being concerned, local corporate citizens of the community?
- Do they see us as being concerned employers that seek to enrich our employees' life-style beyond their paychecks?
- Do they see us as being involved and interested in global and local issues?
- Do they see us as being better than our competition or less than our competition in socially relevant areas?
- Do they see our executives and senior management as being actively involved in socially relevant areas?
- Do they see that we encourage our employee involvement through volunteer initiatives?
- Do they see our support for education, human rights, and conservation in our actions and deeds?
- Do they see our products or services as being ecologically sound?
- Do they see our recycling and using of alternative raw materials programs?
- Do they see our reinvestment in society?
- Do they see our suppliers and our services selected as being based on how they measure up as socially responsible citizens?

- Do they see our educational commitment to teach our employees methods of involvement?

- Do they see our mission statement of social responsibility?

- Do they see our employees committed to our mission statement?

- Do they see our recognition as industry leaders in social responsibility?

- Do they see shareholder or owner support for our mission statement?

- Do they see our long-term vision and our short-term plan to make a positive impact?

If your answers are "yes," welcome to the world of enlightened capitalism. If you answered more than 25 percent "no" or "I don't know," it may be time to make a decision. Consider this. Can your company afford to answer "no" to any of the questions?

The definition of leadership is to show the way, to guide, to direct, to persuade, and to proceed.

To proceed means now—start, move. Firms cannot wait to develop the perfect plan before beginning. Managers should begin by thinking in socially responsible terms, thinking how it would affect them, their family, their co-workers, their friends, and their associates. They should ask, "Do I like the way I might become? What would I do? What area of social issues affects me emotionally the most? What would I *like* to do about it? What *could* you do about it? Could I find the time?" Questions are the same whether the person is the president of the company or a line employee. To change a company, an employee might have to change himself or herself.

The corporate culture is made up of years of attitudes, styles, policies, guidelines, emphasis, tactics, training, doing, feeling, thinking, selecting, choosing, taking on, and letting go. Knowing right from wrong and doing both, being on time and late, being ahead and behind, never down and never up, winning and losing. All the things and all the times have created a foundation to a firm's philosophy.

This foundation is hard fought with many casualties along the way. To disregard the history of a business and assume that one can begin with a clear slate would be naive.

Therefore, all is relevant. The issues associated with this strategy must take into consideration not only past history, but also the future. The question firms ask most is, "How do you keep the mission alive when your company is barely active itself, during the bad times when success seems so far away?" The answer I give is the one I try to live by. The world will go on without me or my company, and if I or it fails at the business at hand, I still will live to see another day, and my principles, ethics, and values can never suffer or lose unless I choose to let them. Managers should never let a bad situation dictate what they know is right. If it is only right in the good times, it is a fool's fancy. If a company is on top and doing well, it should start a plan. If a company is in a down cycle, it *needs* a plan. In either case, the very best time is now. To begin, take stock of whom is chosen within the company to be the architect of the company's image. Then, what does the image say about the company? "I don't know" is totally unacceptable because that translates into "I don't care to know." Even a poor image is better than an uninformed one. Managers need to ask somebody. They will at least have an opinion. There is no easy way to ask these questions, but it must be done.

Whatever personality, reputation, friends, values, and family are to a person, that is what a company's image is to it. It is the definition provided to the world. A good image is built on good works, while a bad image is build on bad works or no works.

Some managers do not know the difference. They have been backstabbing others for so long and getting rewarded for it that to them bad is good and now it is second nature. That was then and this is now. Those people are in the shrinking minority, short termers, and they will never be convinced there is a better way. Even wolves in sheep's clothing eventually behave like wolves: a good predator will not be kept down forever.

After surveying the landscape for wolves, find an enlightened person who will recognize the importance of having a company that stands for something. The enlightened people will fight to the end for what they believe in. These are the ones filled with belief; the loud and boisterous often vanish at the first sign of battle.

Corporate communities within a company will have both wolves and enlightened. The wolves will see this as threatening to their territory and fight to defend antiquated turf. Every step along the way, they will defend the old practices and policies. They will define social relevance as a passing fad, no more worthy of consideration than any other fad that they can conjure up from the past. They will say that the only things that matter to customers is price, and the only thing important to employees is their paycheck; that use of company funds or resources on charitable issues is really the government's job; and that a company can never succeed where the government gave up. They will say that if the disadvantaged really wanted to work, they could; that AIDS is God's way of getting even; that environmental issues are media hype; that human rights do not belong in the workplace; and that work is hard, that's why they call it work. They will argue that economically the firm cannot afford it and that this business is different from the ones in the book. They believe that even the Republicans know that the "Thousand Points of Light" was the result of the explosion brought about by the federal deficit. But the wolves can be penned with facts, data, logic, and exposure. Then a company can begin to shape its corporate culture into the twenty-first century.

Companies are adept at planning. A socially responsible plan is an extension and integration into a preexisting business plan. The role is still to inform, educate, and motivate, to determine what employees should know. Once this has been answered, the company will have just laid pen to the beginning of its new mission statement.

Now let's shift the focus to business personnel to determine the effects of philanthropic economic *thinking*.

■ THE ENLIGHTENED MANAGER

It is obvious from the profiles of enlightened companies that there is a sureness and certainty in their missions, that they are not whimsical fads or fancys. They are direct and forthright and, more important, supported by the resources of the company. The corporate culture is infected with decency, the operative word for contemporary management. To the new managers and their new management styles of empowerment, caring and concern is a far cry from the theory X days. Enlightened managers, for the most part, have been given the green light. There are several new books on the market that attempt to define the new management philosophy and styles. They all use the latest buzzwords of "management with compassion."

In a recent *New York Times* interview, Harriet Rubin, executive editor of The Doubleday/Currency line of business books, stated, "The new business books that are crossing my desk tell me that traditional management ideas may no longer be relevant. The marketplace says traditional ideas about business management don't excite much *passion* anymore. Among the thinkers I have been talking to, there is a deepening suspicion of what is tangible in business. The intangibles are feelings, perceptions and attitudes." Several books come to mind that clearly state that management is in transition: *The Executive Odyssey* by Frederick G. Harmon (New York: Wiley, 1989), *Beyond the Trust Gap* by Thomas R. Horton and Peter C. Reid (Homewood, IL: Business One Irwin, 1991), *Good Intentions Aside* by Laura L. Nash (Harvard Business School Press, 1990), *Managing from the Heart* by Hyler Bracey (New York: Delacorte Press, 1991), and *Love & Profit: The Art of Caring Leadership* by James Autry (New York: Morrow, 1991).

The new management theorists clearly have recognized that the management edict in the next century will be kinder and gentler. Companies clearly will require that managers relate to the corporate ideology that they are nurturing and instilling. The only way leadership can anchor this new philosophy is to make it *believable to all*.

"All" in this case implies customers, employees, suppliers, and the public. Managers asked to carry out corporate policy on company-based initiatives must and will demonstrate legitimate empathy and passion for the corporate goals that include all their direct philanthropic directives. The new management styles will require the manager to be enlightened. The self-actualized manager will require department heads and supervisors also to be invested in a new, enlightened way of thinking.

People have a caring and loving side, but management's basic distrust of employees, and vice versa, has not brought forth a sense of shared values and beliefs. Managers in the future will be developed based on models that influence and inspire rather than control and dominate. These influential managers will communicate with employees through *common stake* approaches, both groups clearly vested in well-defined *"joint" goals and objectives*. The enlightened manager will chiefly direct corporate missions and personal missions to assure that each may benefit from the other. The most powerful tool in the manager's work chest will be the ability to empower the employee both singularly and as a group. Empowerment is seen as a first step toward trust, and trust is the basis which will alter corporate culture in a positive direction. Trust is a critical first step. Once trust is established, respect will follow. With respect comes pride, and with pride comes passion. There is nothing more powerful than a passionate employee, be it a manager or an entry-level employee. The secret ingredient for all entrepreneurs is passion!

The enlightened manager will nurture personal goals and value objectives. The company that creates a mission statement that closely resembles its work force mission will win and win big. Old forms of motivation, such as the carrot-and-stick approach, will be placed on a shelf. Employees will be seen as the engine that drives, the wings that lift the company, not the other way around. Managers will still be accountable for profit contributions or losses as in the past, and profits will not take a back seat to feeling good. It will be seen, however, as *part* of the responsibility of management, not its only responsibility. This is the significant difference for the managers of the future.

Profit at what price will be the measurement, not at the price of the manager's personal ethics or the company's ethics. The concept of profit at all costs is dead. So is the highly mobile impersonal manager, the skill-driven creator of the 1970s and 1980s. Interpersonal skills were once believed to be an elective; new managers will be multilevel literate in interpersonal skills, which means they must be able to relate and communicate through all levels of the company, from factory worker to senior management, not solely on their peer level. Managers' good works will be evaluated inside the company as well as outside. Leadership will best be assessed by its ability to generate followership. Transitional managers will find the new corporate culture difficult to deal with. Transitional managers will find themselves on the outside looking in unless they can assimilate into the new management framework. Emotional resignation or withdrawal into safe niches within the company are not reasonable alternatives.

The new manager will also be blessed with empowerment, in essence an entrepreneurial freedom within the organization. Risk will be seen with greater tolerance. Creativity and innovation will be underwritten within the corporate guidelines, which will allow people to fail without total job jeopardy. Managers will foster better planning processes; they will be more sensitive with resources. They will incorporate more challenge into solutions with greater rewards for success. Career logic planning will continue to be relevant, but less ridged and structured in vertical applications. Engineers, chemists, and scientists will be integrated into the total corporate environment. Senior management candidates will hold a global overview of the company's place in the community and society in general. The enlightened executive-level managers will be universal in their application of management practices. As companies embrace this philosophy beyond total quality management (TQM) style, there will not be a laissez-faire attitude. It will be all business, but all business will encompass a much greater dimension than ever before. If a company believes it must address a specific issue that is affecting society, such as adult literacy, its approach to this concern will be dealt with as if it were central to the firm's financial statement.

Social responsibility specialists will begin to develop. Apple Computer, as an example, has a position known as a "green manager." These specialists will become part of the corporate landscape. Quality and service will not be replaced by "feel goods," but by this time everyone should have figured out how to build and service products right the first time. This translates into a new scenario where quality and service are no longer distinguishing characteristics for a company to exploit. The time and the technology will come when building right will be an exact science. The American consumer will accept nothing less. Managers of these companies will be charged with finding and developing important new roles for the companies to distinguish themselves.

The enlightened manager will live the life of his or her business and profession. Sound family health care and health education, as well as fitness and nutrition, are areas that may be covered by a statement of "in the company's best interest strategy," to make sure that managers are doing the right things at home.

Recently, Adolph Coors created its Wellness Center (described in the Coors profile) for the benefit of employees and families. This is much more than a gym; it is a health care, counseling, and education center. The economic benefit to Coors has been to lower their loss/claims ratio on health insurance.

Corporate ladders will be filled with people who are being freed from routine tasks to be used better as field intelligence sources. It is logical progression. Managers cannot be expected to relate to a problem that they are removed from. The higher up, the farther from structure. The new manager will be a consultant to his or her own company, reporting to a receptive and reactive core center. Philanthropic economics will drive the philosophy that all elements will go from "my" concern or job scenario to *everyone's job* scenario. When manufacturing perfection takes place, all cost variables will virtually go away, that is, waste, spoilage, or bad parts. This means maintenance sectors will change from full-time to occasional. Better product forecasting will occur, requiring less inventory and stock, warehouse space, or chance of loss. Loss prevention comes down to better quality and better warranties. Better warranties equal less risk of litigation. The companies will make less and keep more and have greater staying power with less critical economic swings.

The area for growth for many may be found in the very causes being addressing today. There is much to explore in the infrastructure of our society: health care, aging, disease, education, the environment, and nature with her mysteries. There is much to do. The most obvious is "This only applies to the major corporations or companies that service the general population, right?" Wrong. Whether a person is a gas station owner, local franchise general manager, or the private golf club manager, he or she will have a vested interest in this style of thinking and managing. It is simply a matter of perception of values and how they translate into a business.

The good news for the enlightened manager is that he or she will be compensated well for the time away from the office, and this will not be seen as an intrusion. Quite the opposite is true. It will be sought after in the new terms; managers must begin to think in horizontal terms. They must find creative and innovative ways to save the planet; teach the illiterate; save the disadvantaged; volunteer to help the homeless; and teach their children about AIDS and sex education, drug addiction, alcohol, street gangs, staying in school, and safety. The enlightenment has begun.

Wal-Mart, for instance, has the most excited associates ever seen. This electrifying group wants to stand for something. They do their jobs as if they are the most important jobs in the world, and they do them while they help the local community they serve. The vast power of a company working with their employees will make a huge impact in the future.

■ THE ENLIGHTENED EMPLOYEE

The future enlightened employee will in one way or another have already been affected by the outreach of corporate America's socially responsible initiatives. The impact may be through direct support of their educational assistance or community programs that have affected their local community or indirectly with support of immediate family or friends. This will act as a conditioning of social activism for those employees who have not experienced the benefit of the strength or role that American business has played in their lives. Upon employment, they will have extensive indoctrination into social awareness by their employers. Training and skill development will be expansive and encompass hobbies and areas of general interest. All parts of an employee's skills knowledge information will be encouraged. This will be done mostly so that employees could be called upon to tutor, mentor, motivate, or in general contribute to the betterment of their community and fellow workers.

Empowerment will become the great equalizer for the employees' career goals, and personal goals will be encouraged through the enlightened companies. Employees will find and develop common community-based programs in partnership with their company. Future employees will feel a sense of oneness with their employer, as a part of their identity and value structure. When one is fully in line with one's personal mission statement, there is a sense of all things being in harmony. The company of the future will become an extension of the process. Employees will be enriched by the companies they work for in this manner.

■ SMALL BUSINESS—THE GROUP THAT CAN PERHAPS BE THE MOST CREATIVE

The previous examples are just a few on an ever-increasing list of the business community's proactive response to social challenges. The key to this phenomenon is that all parts of the general business society are being touched, from the smallest to the largest.

Small business today is in a favorable position to develop strategies that it can implement quickly. The benefit to small business is their ability to create or enter into the *strategic alliance*. Small-business owners can become major players in cause-conscious community relations and can position their businesses or business services as being valuable to the businesses they target as prospects. Small-business owners should seek charitable organizations that have strong following of interest and then develop a plan that shows the charity it has a real service and can create value for the charity's customers by aligning with the company. Be prepared to make certain guarantees to the charity; they are not an entrepreneurial environment. The most valuable assets charities possess are their reputation and logo. They are not very inclined to give up either to a half-baked concept or a purely exploitative scheme. Develop a reasonable plan with a start, middle, and end; detail promotional concepts; allow charities the approval of written or printed material that incorporates their name or logo. Show them a plan that focuses initially on the existing customer and then shifts to a new business development agenda. Ask to be included as a member of their corporate board.

■ THE RESULTS OF SOCIAL VENTURING

Reputation—A Firm's Most Valuable Asset

American business partnerships with their customers will affect everyone positively. The business that chooses to become aligned with the strategy will begin to experience a sense of value beyond the bottom line. The concept of "goodwill" has always been part of the financial analysis of a company's valuation. This oftentimes abstract number is applied without the benefit of real measurement. In the very near future, goodwill will become a central consideration in not only financing valuations, but also the very core of a deal. Business will move from "the art of the deal" to the "heart of the deal."

A company's reputation and image is all it really has. It is the reputation that holds up the image, and it is the image that holds the value. Case in point—Exxon will not fully recover from the Prince Williams Sound incident for an extremely long time. Customers will not support a company with a poor image or reputation, and good employees are also hard to find. Today's consumers are the most intelligent in the history of business. They possess a keen sense of insight into a firm's agenda. If it is merely hype, customers will flush it out in a heartbeat. Sincerity will be measured and reported by direct results. Accountability is the operative in this sector of business initiatives. The American public needs to know of a firm's efforts and involvement.

Reputation Tied to Social Responsibility

Managers need to look at their businesses and ask several questions:

- What can we do that will make a difference to society?
- What can I do, use, buy, sell, service, create, build, or promote that can be applied to a socially responsible action or activity?
- What resources that are not being fully exercised could be put to work on social good?
- Who in my organization could champion an initiative?
- Which suppliers would likely join such a program?
- Which customers would benefit?
- How would employee morale be affected?
- How would the sales force perceive a program as benefiting the customers and the community?

■ How will shareholders react to a socially responsible corporate initiative?

These questions and a dozen more constitute the model of a supposition—the "what if" scenario. Customers are becoming more aware each day of the role firms are playing in our world. Although it is hard to measure the impact on the public when a company joins the pact of social relevance, it is much easier to measure the effect of companies that do not.

The future is a blending of conventional and unconventional tactics. Corporations will take on a greater role in areas of education, as an example. Conservation, environment, and health care areas, once left to government and special interest groups, will be met by American businesses seeking solutions and results. The skills and intelligence are resident in business to improve on how these social areas are managed, controlled, and developed. Therefore, American business would rather take direct ownership to certain problems so that it might have a direct influence rather than rely on a tax structure that forces business to be passive in its involvement, yet do all the funding. "Privatization" is more than a concept; it is becoming a reality. State and local government will begin to find ways to create more private sector incentives from which their local constituents will benefit. The format of most economic development authorities (EDAs) could be restructured to improve the concepts of enterprise zones or minority business ventures, to expand into socially relevant and locally based programs run by the private sector to improve public sector programs. Work-start programs, technical training centers, research grants, day care centers, self-insurance programs, medical reimbursement, partnerships with education, housing, health care, and environment are all realities today. A corporation's mission is to develop a mission.

Cause-aligned social responsibility builds a better company and creates more revenue. This is a business decision, not a giving decision. The first step is to determine how the business fits into the picture. Is the customer a retail end-user or a supplier? Is the product soft or hard cost? Is it a consumable or a fixed purchase? The rationale here is that an industrial-based company will develop a different program from the retailer, service companies look different from manufacturers, and so on.

Following is a basic model to work against. To begin the task of assessment and evaluation, think in a pattern that allows and encourages plan success. Remember, to achieve one needs measurable results. Build and design in such a way that *results* can be seen from efforts, not simply effort. This will motivate you even more. Build on success as is done in the primary business. Keep the vision fresh. Demonstrate to others the plan success. Lead the company into a sense of shared values and concerns.

Mission Statements

Take a look at how IBM approached its social responsibility mission statement in Chapter 7.

Perception is reality. No matter what one believes to be true, if others see it another way (be they employees, managers, or customers), it is *their perception that matters!*

I dwell so much on management because these are the people who must be held responsible. Cause alignment is not an overnight fix. It is however, a fix, if truly adopted. It will bring more business than any strategy I have seen if it is incorporated as a philosophy of the business and not just a short-term tactic or promotional strategy. Management, for my discussions, must fit the previously examined definition if a firm is intending to move in the direction of philanthropic economic reasoning. The mission statement of the company is like a navigational system on a boat or aircraft; it defines, clarifies, directs, and moves the company on a course. The mission statement is visible to all, internally and externally.

Missions are much easier to write than live up to! When management sits down to define as a company how it should be perceived, the key is making it believable so that others will lay claim to it as if it were their own. Ownership by the people in the company is important.

It is they who give the company heart and soul. Developing the mission statement is a process of discovery and analysis, not just writing words that are full of adjectives that sound good. To begin, the mission itself has three distinct elements: (1) direction, (2) the vehicle, and (3) the identity. Direction is where the firm is going. The vehicle is how it will get there. The identity is what it will look like when it arrives. This process can be applied to a company, a product, or a service. The direction is the hard-edged side of this process. Defining direction is more than saying up, down, east, or west—it is a complex analysis. It is here, right at the beginning, that management usually loses interest in strategic thinking, when it finds out that it is hard and not easily done. Direction is full of all kinds of facts, forecasts, and reflection.

Business Life Cycles

The phase of a development cycle the company is in will define much of the directional information. Industries, like companies, like products, have cycles.

The cycles can mean a product's useful life or even a company's useful life. Carriage makers are not needed today as they were in 1890. Some companies and industries are in their free-fall decline phase, others are in their growth stage and still defining themselves, still others have matured into stable companies and products that enjoy the slice of the market. Companies and products mirror each other in amazing ways. Years ago business cycles were defined in the following ways:

1. The wonder period
2. The blunder period
3. The thunder period
4. The plunder or sunder period

This descriptive assessment is still current in its definition of phases. People seem to forget that every business in this country started as a small business. Ford Motor Company started in Henry's garage. Some ideas will become big ideas, and some little companies with big ideas will become big companies someday.

A company's phase can clearly help to define the directional element of the mission statement. Seeing how cause concepts fit a company's current perceptions can be useful. Doing a comparative study on a competitor to see how to counter the move of a competitor who employed the strategy first is instructional. This approach helps keep the issue on track. The goal is to go through the entire process as if a competitor launched a program of cause alignment and how its customers view it, how the employees would handle it, and what benefits were gained or lost. Management will be able to see how it might fit its company and what it would do to competitors. It will also help define an anticipation strategy of how competitors might act to a firm's beating them to the punch, so to speak.

Direction and strategy go hand in hand. As the mission statement begins to take form, it will focus more and more directional qualities into the desired strategy. The goal is to have the mission reflect the perceptions of the customers and employees. By visualizing, management allows itself the process of horizontal thinking, creating the vision necessary to shape a company's culture. Whether this is a full session in which all the king's horses and all the king's men and women begin, or the lonely entrepreneur with a dream sitting alone late at night, the thinking must take place.

Cause-Alignment Planning

The mission requires the most attention and management of direction and will be joined now with a vehicle of some sort in cause-alignment planning. It is at this point that employee and customer concerns are sorted through. What causes seem to fit the characteristics of the company, the culture that is beginning to be defined? The mission statement that developed should be as broad and far reaching as practical. This is the vision component. Once management knows how it wants to be known, the next step is to define what it will take to get it there.

Once the mission statement describes the business, values, culture, and commitment, the next word is "responsibilities." The next step is to determine what responsibilities are created or generated by the mission statement. Some of them will fall right out of the statement itself; for example, if a mission states a firm will have 100 percent satisfied customers and customers are number one, management must determine how many unsatisfied customers exist and why they are unsatisfied. That's a *responsibility*.

I remember Fred Smith, chair of Federal Express, describing his company's statement, "When you absolutely, positively have to get it there overnight, use Federal Express." The strength of that statement is powerful. It was determined that in fact Federal Express had an approximate 98.9 percent on-time rate. Most companies would be delighted with this percentage; not Federal Express. The 1.1 percent that got away meant over 16,000 promises it did not keep that day, and to Fred Smith, that was totally unacceptable. When a claim is made in a mission statement, it will translate right into a responsibility that must be *managed*.

Over the years, I have met dozens of dedicated business managers, executives, and owners. Unfortunately, dedication is not enough. The famous cliff divers of Mexico demonstrate a clear image of dedication and commitment visually to me, as they climb the face of the cliffs. I define that as dedication. Once they're standing on the top measuring the surf movements, that's analysis. When they step off, that's commitment! That is the word that drives Fred Smith. That is the word that has to be understood to define responsibility.

An analysis of responsibilities begins to form the outline of the next part of the strategic plan, the objective stage. Many planning processes start at this level, with no regard for the mission statement or the responsibilities that follow. For those very reasons, most plans fail. They are not properly anchored with a commitment. *The objective stage* is easier to deal with now. Milestone charts can be developed, tasks are isolated, personnel identified, training designed, and so on. The objectives' layout plan can be accomplished in a fairly short period. Objectives must become manageable and not too far removed from current reality to appear obscure. Once the objectives are defined, the daily action plan of task assessment and evaluation is prepared. The concept with this method of strategic planning is to anchor the commitment ideals firmly and then to have them supported by the daily action plan. The process should be so close to what a firm wants to become as a company that the employees' day will be defined by the tasks that are in direct alignment with the objectives, which in turn support the assigned responsibility, all tied into the mission. This forces a company to live it.

MISSION STATEMENT

RESPONSIBILITIES

OBJECTIVES

ACTIONS

The strategic planning process and the mission statement process are the superstructure needed to develop the ideology for the corporate culture. Small to midsized companies have perhaps the best and easiest time in implementing this process. Large corporations have a much easier time implementing *tactics* than they do strategies. Large companies have led the way with cause alignment to date, but for the most part have deployed it as a promotional tactic. This is not to say that they will not convert their culture over time. It just takes longer. Smaller companies have a great opportunity to leap ahead into the next generation.

Incorporating Cause-Related Marketing and Charitable Enterprises

The time to incorporate cause alignment into business is now, as Ben & Jerry and Anita Roddick have done. This is the right time to distinguish a business based on cause-related marketing. The strategy available for the small undistinguished company is to align itself with the right cause, one that helps promote its business in a way that allows it to trade off of the public relations value of the cause alignment. If a company has the right cause and principles and fully grasps the concept of business-to-business cause marketing, it can achieve great success. Many firms are not yet there. We hope they will be soon; then the national organization can be helpful in placing them into a network of senior executives of major companies that would be impossible to meet through normal business channels. This is the *real* benefit of strategic alliance.

This strategy can be engaged in many ways. Some companies use a promotional format. This heightened promotional period, a typical cause-related marketing promotion to test the reception of customers, may run only a few weeks or up to a year. Most retail programs can be deployed more easily. One must decide whether to offer a discount, a redemption, or an incentive to the customer that will be converted to cash for the charity. Many companies offer a fixed percentage of total sales, some of targeted sales or certain customer classifications. The design of the sales and marketing plan has much versatility. In exchange for a financial commitment, firms will be given certain public relations opportunities via the charity. This promotion exchange needs to be communicated to a business' audience for it to do any good. Press releases, newsletters, logos, hosted luncheons, and picnics are just some of the methods used. Some kind of event, like a corporate challenge with suppliers, to raise awareness of your efforts, could be used. Golf tournaments, company festivals for customers and employees, a canoe race, or a 5-kilometer run are examples. The objective is the marketing trade-off in cause marketing—use logos, public relations, celebrity endorsements, television or media coverage freely. This is not exploitative, it is the value of the partnership. The small business needs to concentrate on the local marketplace in positioning with current customers or targeted companies. It needs to determine via its strategic planning process what it wants to accomplish with its program. It may be to secure customer loyalty, new business, greater dollars spent per customer, better merchandising, more inventory turn per square foot, higher unit price, more subscribers, more customers, or bigger customers. Each consideration should be evaluated as to the tactics to be developed. If the goal is to just do something good, that works too.

Businesses in the future will feel the effects of this massive trend shift. Some business practices will be abandoned; many new ones will develop. As a strategist who has been closely monitoring the long-term characteristics, I would like to shift focus slightly to the role of futurist. As futurist, I simply extended the trend line and used current philanthropic economic initiatives as a beginning to accomplish their goals.

So as not to appear totally naive or out of touch with reality, let me state clearly at the outset of this discussion that, unfortunately, I think there will always be a group defined as disadvantaged. The demographics of this group may shift, but they will always be economically depressed. There will always be some environmental or ecological need, and there will always be people in crisis.

That said, let me state clearly that things will greatly improve in our society, much due to the economic success of philanthropic economics. Future generations will continue along the line of the enlightened consumer. It is fair to state that we will not become more ignorant, and this will keep American business focused on social responsibility. More American business subscribing to these economic principles translates into more resources being allocated into socially relevant areas, and thereby helping more people, families, groups, cultures, and issues.

■ PHILANTHROPY—THE GROWTH INDUSTRY OF TOMORROW

More and more industries will be created in support of this strategy of social responsibility. Philanthropy will become a growth industry. Private foundations will become very popular for big business and not big business. The private, nonprofit family foundation will not only become an extension of the business strategy that was deployed through their companies, but will also become desirable after they sell their business. There is now and there will be real economic incentives for estate planning and family tax planning. Reasoning to conserve capital and maintain high-level economic control offer the use of new personal funds in the focus areas most important to the foundation creator.

This basic fact will benefit professionals who manage foundations, law firms, accounting practices, marketing, consultants, insurance companies, and investment companies. A special class of management and workers will be developed that is capable of working within the foundation arena. Fringe industries will be identified that provide services to the private foundation market. The growth of this industry will not simply depend on the "super rich" to make it work. The growth will come from the middle-class business owner who eventually sells the family business and ends up with $1 million or more. This group will become "the new philanthropists." This person may have been the local franchise owner of the Ben & Jerry's Ice Cream Shop or The Body Shop. The success and indoctrination they would have had received from their years with enlightened capitalists would surely help them become candidates for such a trend.

Extending the trend line is relatively safe. As philanthropy begins to deepen its roots, there is an opportunity for vertical groups to be developed around specific causes that independent foundations set as strategic alliances among themselves. This will lead to cluster centers, and some states and cities may vie for philanthropic centers, much as they compete for other industries. Some state is going to become the philanthropic capital of the country. There is real economic power in this philanthropic growth industry. This industry will flourish in the coming years. This will result in business preparing for the future transition.

■ CONCLUSION

The factors that contribute to the success of the companies and individuals highlighted in this book are varied and far-reaching. They share a vision of the future that is impacted by their thoughts, deeds, and actions. Whether they are designated as enlightened capitalists, socially responsible corporations, activists, volunteers, or cause marketers, they are doing more than serving their own interests, they are concerned about broader interests, such as children, the environment, education, how people treat one another, and global peace. They put themselves on the line each day with visions and programs.

There is a risk to this. When they start on this journey, there is no turning back. Their courage and commitment are to be applauded.

Today, when the business climate is, at the very least, slow, when it would be easy even for the most secure to rationalize avoiding this type of activism, they still move forward with their plans of betterment and positive change.

Not all the socially responsible companies out there made it into this book. It is unfortunate that the hundreds of companies that are fully engaged in the philosophy could not be included. Moreover, some talented and committed individuals from the media, sports, and entertainment fields were not included, as well as those who were excited to speak of their various causes, yet did not want publicity based on their celebrity status to shift the spotlight away from the issues.

When researching the various nonprofit organizations that benefit from the support of corporate America, I found, in general, a sense of working partnerships and not simply passive interests. In other words, I see it working. I see volunteers coming from all walks of life. I see their efforts being rewarded by the respect and gratitude that they are given in return.

As I go around the country talking to groups and businesses, I see real excitement, as if "This is what we've been waiting for" is written all over their faces. I meet entrepreneurs weekly that have ideas for a better world, on how to raise money or how to employ the disadvantaged, I really see it!

When you put this book down, after the last page, it will only say, NOT THE END.

If the truth be known, only a very small percentage of business is engaged in this philosophy. And this caring philosophy comes with its detractors—those who still believe that business should not get involved in political issues, those who are motivated by greed, and those charlatans disguised as do-gooders who only look to profit from it.

We will be criticized and minimized for this attitude, but each day in subtle ways the message will be brought home. Your teachers may be the children. During the start of Earth Week 1992, there was a prime-time special on CBS called "What About Me, I'm Only Three." This environmental special focus was hosted by Ann Margret and directed to the children. Top performers such as Loni Anderson, Dick Clark, Louis Gossett, Jr., Linda Gray, Valerie Harper, Mariette Hartley, Joe Penny, Ashley and Mary Kate Olsen, Lou Diamond Philips, Dennis Weaver, Alabama, John Ritter, and William Shatner pointed out how they could be more responsible to the planet.

This array of talent was assembled due to a lesson taught by 3-year-old Tyler Weed to his dad, television producer Gene Weed. The motivation for the theme "What

About Me, I'm Only Three" came from Gene as he observed the now second-nature recycling mentality that little Tyler has. During our interview, Gene went on to say that for folks like us, our age group, conservation is new and sometimes a tough new discipline to get in to. The young kids do it second nature. At age 3, they are more aware than we are. Gene examined the concept of getting more 3-year-olds involved, and the television special sprang to life. The sponsor, the Matrix Corporation, has long been an environmental supporter. I congratulate Tyler Weed for showing us just how effective you can be at age 3. I understand from Gene that Tyler already has a willing student in his little sister Chelsie.

This new responsible television programming is indicative of our time. No matter how or where you choose to get involved, both you and your business will benefit. This investment of time and resources will be the best type of investment. The first step is always awareness, and I hope this work will serve that purpose. My personal desire is that it will also motivate.

Good luck.

Index

A

Adolph Coors Company, 144,
172-83, 228
charitable giving, 172
employee wellness center,
173-74, 228
environmental initiative, 174,
182-83
higher education programs,
175-76
"Literacy. Pass It On"
program, 177-82
celebrity spokespeople,
179-80
Laubach Literacy Action,
180, 181
literacy hotline, 179
Literacy Volunteers of
America (LVA), 181
national literacy partners,
180-81
Opportunities
Industrialization Centers
of America, 181-82
overview, 178
public awareness
campaign, 178-79
SER-Jobs for Progress, 182
prevention programs, 174-75
product and social
responsibility, 174-82
responsibility advertising,
176-77
sponsorships, 177
volunteerism, 173
Advertisers, social concerns
and, 10-11
Advertising, 10, 66-68
evolution toward
values/sentiments, 67-68
NBA "Stay in School"
program, 68, 78-79
print advertisements, 67
AIDS, 59, 61, 66, 224, 229
as driving force, 52-53
movie industry and, 66
Akers, John, 147
Algal Turf Scrubber (ATS), 116
"All Babies Count" program, 59
Alley, Kirstie, 60
Alterra Ventures, 121
American Express, 26
Anheuser-Busch, 144
Apple Computer, 228
Aqua Futures, 121
AT&T, "reach out and touch
someone" commercials,
67-68
Athletes and Entertainers for
Kids, 61
Aveda Corporation, 3, 107
Valdez principles and, 107
Awakenings, 65-66
Awareness:

and elective/selective change, 7
methods of, 8-12

B

Baby boomer era:
driving forces, 37-53
AIDS, 52-53
decadence, 50-51
freedom, 37-38
microprocessor, 52
motivation/enlightenment, 38-39
rise of the Japanese, 47-50
television, 39-43
women's movement, 43-47
opposing forces, 53-56
Bartles and James wine coolers, television commercials, 68
Ben & Jerry's Homemade, Inc., 3, 11, 84-96, 109, 138, 141, 239, 241
Ben & Jerry Foundation, 84
corporate mandates, Leave No Child Behind program, 89-91
corporate philosophies, 96-97
environment program, 85-89
community outreach, 88-89
company waste stream, 86-87
energy conservation, 87-88
Green Teams, 85
products/packaging, 86
mission statement, 84-85
Native American community, purchase of products from, 93-94
rainforests, purchase of products from, 92-93
urban disadvantaged, partnership for, 91-92
Beyond the Trust Gap (Horton/Reid), 225
Big business social responsibility profiles, 143-98
Adolph Coors Company, 172-83

Coca-Coca Company, 187-90
Herman Miller, 192
IBM, 144-54
Johnson & Johnson, 155-59
Kellogg Company, 168-71
Levi Strauss & Co., 183-87
McDonald's, 190-92
Merck Pharmaceutical, 162-68
Nike, 159-62
Prudential Insurance Company, 171-72
recent CEP award winners, 193-96
Body Shop, Inc., The, 2, 96-102, 109, 241
awards, 101
base of operations, 98-99
company profile, 98-102
future of, 102
international sales, 102
principles, 100-101
products, 99-100
profits, 100
social concerns, 101-2
Born on the 4th of July, 66
Boyz n the Hood, 65
Broad, Martha, 93
Budweiser Bear, alcohol initiative commercial, 68
Business life cycles, social venturing and, 235-36
Business Manager's Thinking Model of Social Responsibility, 9
Business problems, 4

C

Cable television, 63, 64
Calvert Social Venture Partners (CSVP), 113-16
Chektec, 119
Duraplast, 120
Ecological Systems, Inc., 116-17
Environmentally Safe Products, Inc., 117
High Social Impact Investment Fund (HSII), 139

Katrina, Inc., 117-18
LiteTrends, Inc., 119
MEE, Inc., 120
Shaman Pharmaceuticals,
   Inc., 118
TireGator, 118-19
Cause alignment, 11, 204, 218-19
Cause-related marketing, 26
Celebrity champions, 58-63
CEOs, enlightened, 219-24
CEP, *See* Council on Economic
   Priorities (CEP)
Chektec, 119
Children's Defense fund, Leave
   No Child Behind
   program, 89-91
Children's Miracle Network
   (CMN), 60, 62, 208-16
Chouinard, Yvon, 3, 108
Church & Dwight Co., Inc., 193
Coalition for Environmentally
   Responsible Economies
   (CERES), 106
Coca-Cola Company:
   Coca-Cola Foundation, 187-90
   programs, 189-90
   Coca-Cola Scholars, 188
   Mean Joe Green commercial,
   67
   "We Mean Business"
   scholarships, 188
Cohen, Ben, 3, 83-84, 93, 141,
   142, 239
Colgate-Palmolive, 4
Collins, Phil, 61
Comic Relief (HBO), 64
Common bond, determining,
   208-10
Conservatree Paper Company,
   193
Consumers:
   concerns of, 10
   environmental issues and, 7-8
   motivators of, 5-7
   questions for, 8
Coors Brewing Company, *See*
   Adolph Coors Company
Coors, William K., 173
Corporate change, consulting
   for, 18-20
Corporate culture, 50, 222-23

strategic planning and, 238
Corporate social responsibility,
   23, 26
Costner, Kevin, 65
Council on Economic Priorities
   (CEP), 12-15, 67
   criteria for research/grading
   of corporations, 14
   recent award winners, 193-96
   "X" rating of, 67
Covenant Portfolio, 138
   Social Venture Network
   (SVN), 138-42
Creative thinking, 36
Cruise, Tom, 59
"Cry Out" environmental
   booklet, 59, 60

D

Dances With Wolves, 65
Danson, Ted and Casey, 60
Discovery Channel, enlightened
   programming, 64
Ditton, Andy, 172
Donnelly Corporation, 194
Do the Right Thing, 65
Dreyfuss, Richard, 59, 139-41
Drucker, Peter, 45
Dupont, television commercial,
   68
Duraplast, 120

E

Ecological Systems, Inc., 116-17
Employees, enlightened, 230
Enlightened capitalism, 81-110
   Aveda Corporation, 3, 107
   Ben & Jerry's Homemade,
   Inc., 3, 11, 84-96, 109,
   138, 141, 239, 241
   Body Shop, Inc., The, 2,
   96-102, 241
   CEOs, 219-24
   Esprit de Corp, 3, 102-3
   McKesson Corp., 103-5
   Matrix Essentials, Inc., 3,
   108-9

Patagonia, 3, 108
Salad King, 105-6
Stonyfield Farms, Inc., 3,
    106-7
working model of, 199-216
Enlightened CEOs, 219-24
Enlightened consumer, 5-8
Enlightened employees, 230
Enlightened managers, 225-30
Enlightenment, 38-39
    evolution toward, 53-56
Entrepreneur magazine, 22-23
Entrepreneurs, consulting for,
    20-23
Environmentally Safe Products,
    Inc., 117
Equalizer theory, 35-36
Esprit de Corp, 3, 102-3
Eco Desk, 103
Executive Odyssey, The
    (Harmon), 225
Exxon Corporation, Prince
    William Sound incident,
    232

F

Family Channel, enlightened
    programming, 64
Family value structure, decay
    of, 51
Federal Express, mission
    statement, 237
Feeling Better Health Daycare,
    121
Fitzpatrick, James, 22
Force field analysis, 31-36
    driving forces, 31, 35
    force 10 drivers, 33-36
    as great equalizers, 35-36
    force level indicator model, 34
    opposing forces, 31, 35
    value/weight of forces, 32-33
FTD Florist, global warming
    commercial, 68

G

General Mills, Inc., 193-94

"Give to the Earth
    Foundation," 107
Glassman, Bernie, 91-92
Glover, Danny, 179-80
Goldberg, Whoopie, 59
Good Intentions Aside (Nash), 225
Great Treesome program, 108
Greenfield, Jerry, 3, 83-84, 239
Green marketing, 7
Greyston Bakery, 91-92
Guffey, John G., 113-14

H

Hart, Lyndall, 31
Head motivator model, 8-9
"Healing Forest Conservancy"
    foundation, 118
Heart motivator model, 8-9
Henley, Don, 58-59
Herman Miller (furniture
    manufacturer), 192
Hershey Foods, 4
Hibbert, William V. "Jack,"
    182-83
Highland Energy Group, 121
H. J. Heinz Company, safe
    netting practices and, 12
Horizontal thinking, 36, 218
Hotenner, A. E., 105
Human immuno-deficiency
    virus (HIV), *See* AIDS

I

IBM, 36, 78, 144-54
    approach to social
        responsibility, 147
    business schools, role of,
        151-52
    "Distinguished Corporate
        Citizenship" study, 148-50
    initiatives:
        arts, 154
        disadvantaged, 153-54
        educational, 152
        employee involvement, 154
        environmental, 152
        health, 152

persons with disabilities, 152-53
Parkel speech, 144-47
partnership, need for, 150-51
reorganization of social policy activities, 180
Icons/images, 57-79
advertising, 66-68
NBA "Stay in School" program, 68, 78-79
print advertisements, 67
celebrities, 58-63
influence on the masses, 57-58
movie industry, 65-66
television, 63-65
Information source, 46
Investment banking, 111-42
Alterra Ventures, 121
Calvert Social Venture Partners (CSVP), 113-16
Covenant Portfolio, 138
Kinder, Lyndenberg, Domini & Co., 121-38
Sand County Venture Fund, 121
socially responsible investing (SRI), 112-13
community development investment, 112-13
guideline portfolio investing, 112
shareholder activism, 112
social venture capital, 113
stakeholders interviews, 137

J

Jackson, Bo, 60, 160
Japanese, 47-50
participative management/ quality circles, 49-50
JFK, 66
John Deere and Company, 29-30
Johnson & Johnson, 143, 155-59
initiatives:
environmental, 158
philanthropic, 158-59
"Life for Life" wellness program, 157
social responsibility:

approach to, 156
defined by, 155
importance to, 155-56
volunteerism, 156-57
special constituencies, 157-58
Worldwide Child Survival Program, 158-59
Johnson, Magic, 61
Johnson SC & Sons, 4
Jordan, Michael, 60
Joukowsky, Tom, 121

K

Katrina, Inc., 117-18
Keidenran, 148-49
Kellogg Company, 4, 168-71
awards, 170
corporate contributions, 169-70
Kellogg, W. K., 168
Kieschnick, Michael, 121
Kinder, Lyndenberg, Domini & Co., 121-38
basic data gathering step, 136
"Company Reviews," 122, 135, 137
Domini Social Index (DSI), 122, 134-35
literature reviews/company contracts, 136-37
research discipline, 135-37
services, 121-22, 134
Social Investment Database Service, 137-38
Kinder, Peter, 122
Knight, Philip, 159-60

L

Lager, Fred "Chico," 91, 92
Lanier, Bob, 62
Larson, Ralph S., 155
Lateral thinking, *See* Horizontal thinking
Leadership, definition of, 222
Leadership in Entrepreneurial Achievement and Philanthropy (LEAP) award program, 22

Lee, Spike, 61, 65
Left brain thinking, 36
Legitimate power, 46
Levi Strauss & Co., 183-87
  diversity of initiatives, 185-87
  historical commitment, 184
  Levi Strauss Foundation
    (LSF), 184
  mission statement, 183
  social investment, 184-85
Lewin, David, 150
Lisa Lisa, 180
LiteTrends, Inc., 119
Loggins, Kenny, 61
Logical thinking, 36
Long, Howie, 61
Lotus Development
  Corporation, 194-95
*Love & Profit: The Art of Caring
  Leadership* (Autry), 225

M

McCormick, Richard, 195
McDonald's, 190-92
  beef suppliers, monitoring of,
    191-92
  black history education,
    initiative for, 191
  McRecycle USA Program, 192
  Ronald McDonald's Houses,
    191
McGregor, Douglas, 44-45
McKesson Corp., 103-5
  awards, 104-5
  projects, 104
Management by objectives
  (MBO), 45
Management by results, 44
Manager, enlightened, 225-30
Managing from the Heart
  (Bracey), 225
Marlin, Alice Tepper, 12-15
Marshall, Leonard, 62
Marsh, Dave, 58
Matrix Essentials, Inc., 3, 108-9
  Great Treesome program
    and, 108
  System Biolage, 109
May, John, 113, 114

MEE (Motivational Educational
  Entertainment), Inc., 120
Merck Pharmaceutical, 143,
  162-68
  awards received by, 163-64
  Children's Inn, 167-68
  donations, 165, 167
  education initiative, 165-66
  global environmental policy,
    164-65
  internal communications
    campaign, 166-67
Miller, Arnold and Sydell, 3
Minger, Terry, 183
Mission statements, 234-38
  cause-alignment planning
    and, 236-37
Motivation, for the enlightened,
  38-39
Motivator models, 8-9
Movie industry, 65-66
  AIDS and, 66

N

National Conservatory, 7
National Foundation for the
  Improvement of
  Education (NFIE), 159-61
National Parks and
  Conservation Association
  (NPCA), 108-9
National Parks Foundation, 7
National Water Management,
  121
NBA "Stay in School"
  program, 68, 78-79
Nelson, Willie, 60
Nestle Company, 78
Network Earth (Turner
  Broadcasting), 64
New Jersey shore:
  Hands Across America event
    at, 27
  ocean dumping at, 24-26
New Jersey Shore Foundation,
  25
Newman, Paul, 59, 105-6
Nicholas, Francis "Bibby," 94
Nike, 159-62

Boys & Girls Clubs of
America, 161
community programs, 161-62
Ghostwriter project, 161
"Just Do It" grants program,
159-61
scholarships/internships, 161

O

Osborne, Jeffrey, 180
Osmond, Marie, 62
Ouchi, William, 45

P

Palmer, Arnold, 60
Parkel, James P., 144
Passive consumer, myth of, 1-2
Patagonia, 3, 108
PBS (Public Broadcasting
System), enlightened
programming, 64
Personal computer,
time-sensitive population
and, 52
Personal power, 46
Philanthropic economic
business strategy, 217-44
Philanthropic economics, *xvi*, 1,
4, 199-216
Philanthropy, 241-42
Platoon, 66
Polaroid Corporation, 4
Power:
forms of, 46
values and, 51
Priorities, setting, *xvi-xviii*
Privatization, 233
Procter & Gamble, 4
Pronatec, 121
Prudential Insurance Company,
171-72, 196
READY program, 172
Social Purpose Investment
Program, investments
through, 171
Pure Harvest, 121

Q

Quaker Oats, 4

R

Rainman, 65-66
Reactive planning, 220
Rechelbacher, Horst, 3, 107
Redford, Robert, 59
Reputation, social venturing
and, 231-34
Reward or punishment power,
46
Rhodes, Donna, 160
Roddick, Anita, 2, 96-98, 142,
239
Rodriguez, Chi Chi, 60
Ronald McDonald's Houses, 191
Rubin, Harriet, 225
Ruch, Richard, 192

S

Salad King, 105-6
Sand County Venture Fund, 121
Schering Plough, 25
Schneider, John, 62
Scott Newman Foundation, 59
Shaman Pharmaceuticals, Inc.,
118
Sierra Club, 7
Silby, D. Wayne, 113, 114
Singleton, John, 65
Slimfast, television commercial,
68
Smith, Fred, 237
Social activism, 2, 17-30
analyzing trends of, 31-56
getting started toward, 28
Social needs, 4
Social responsibility:
advertisers, 10-11
extremes in, 11-12
growth of, 54
Social Venture Network (SVN),
138-42
"Bridges" next-generation
program, 141

mission statement, 139
venture capital feature, 139
Social venturing, results of,
    231-41
business life cycles, 235-36
cause alignment:
    incorporating into
        business, 239-41
    planning, 236-38
    mission statements, 234-35
    reputation, 231-34
Specific knowledge power, 46
Starkist Tuna, safe netting
    practices and, 12
Stone, Oliver, 66
Stonyfield Farms, Inc., 3, 106-7
    "Adopt a Cow" program, 107
    company objectives, 106
    Valdez principles, signing of,
        106
Strategic alliance:
    building, 207-8
    small businesses and, 231
Strategic planning:
    corporate culture and, 238
    social issues as part of,
        218-19
Supermarkets General Holdings
    Corp., 196

T

Tang, Michael, 113
Target marketing, 204-6
Taylor, Elizabeth, 59
Technothink, 52
Television, 63-65
    cable, 63, 64
    double-standard of, 64-65
    socially conscious
        programming, 63-64
Theory of X and Y, 44-45
*Theory Z: How American
    Business can Meet the
    Japanese Challenge*
    (Ouchi), 45
TireGator, 118-19
Tom's of Maine, 196

U

Upper Deck Company, 78
USA Communications printer
    program, 202-16
    cause, identifying, 206-7
    cause-alignment test,
        applying, 204
    Children's Miracle Network
        (CMN), 208-16
    common bond, determining,
        208-10
    future role of, 214
    printing industry segments,
        203
    setting up, 212-13
    strategic alliance, building,
        207-8
    target marketing, 204-6
    value-added benefits,
        incorporating, 210-12
U S WEST, Inc., 195

V

Vagelos, P. Roy, 162
Value-added benefits,
    incorporating in
    strategic alliance, 210-12
Vertical thinking, 36, 217-18

W

Wal-Mart, 229-30
Weed, Gene, 243-44
"What About Me, I'm Only
    Three," 3, 243-44
Williams, Vanessa, 180
Winfield, Dave, 62
Women's movement, as driving
    force, 43-47
Woods, Sandra, 183
Woodward, Joanne, 59, 105
World Wildlife Fund, 7

Z

Zofcom, 121